THE
ROMAN
EXPERIENCE

Consulting Editor

MORTIMER CHAMBERS

University of California, Los Angeles

THE ROMAN EXPERIENCE

ALFRED A. KNOPF, INC.

NEW YORK

L. P. WILKINSON

King's College, Cambridge

THIS IS A BORZOI BOOK
PUBLISHED BY ALFRED A. KNOPF, INC.

First Edition
987654321
Copyright © 1974 by Alfred A. Knopf, Inc.

Library of Congress Cataloging in Publication Data

Wilkinson, L P
  The Roman experience.
  Bibliography: p.
  1. Rome—Civilization.   I. Title.
DG77.W69   913.37'03'2   74-7451
ISBN 0-394-31080-2

To Donald Lucas

Preface

      This book presupposes a skeleton knowledge of the facts of Roman history (a list of principal dates is given at the beginning). My object has been to clothe the skeleton with human flesh. If it needs strengthening first, recourse may be had to such an account as C. G. Starr's *The Ancient Romans* (1971), or to another of the short general surveys, some available in paperback, that are listed in the Bibliography at the end of the book.

My innumerable debts to secondary sources are perforce unacknowledged, but I should like to mention a few recent works that stand out in my mind as I look back over what I have read: A. J. Toynbee's monumental *Hannibal's Legacy,* M. Grant's *The World of Rome,* J. P. V. D. Balsdon's *Life and Leisure in Ancient Rome,* C. G. Starr's *Civilization and the Caesars,* J. A. Crook's *Law and Life of Rome,* and E. R. Dodds' *Pagan and Christian in an Age of Anxiety.* Sociological articles and an unpublished dissertation by my old pupil Keith Hopkins were of particular interest. But my debts to older, standard writers such as Friedländer, Dill, and Warde Fowler are also immense.

To Professor Mortimer Chambers I am indebted both for general advice as to approach and for many shrewd but friendly criticisms. I am also especially grateful to several friends who took great trouble for me. Mr. D. W. Lucas, besides being a scholar of exceptional competence and acumen, was the only one I felt I could dare to ask to read my messy manuscript. He made many valuable suggestions. So did Mr. G. T. Griffith, who read the whole typescript with a historian's special knowledge. To Mr. J. A. Crook I am particularly indebted for expert assistance with passages on Roman law. Dr. A. H. McDonald was very helpful on one particular topic, and on another Miss Elizabeth Rawson, to whom I am also extremely grateful for consenting to read the proofs. Of course none of these people is in any way responsible for faults that remain. Finally, I should like to pay tribute to the accurate typing of Mrs. Kay Serby of the University Typewriting Office at Cambridge.

L. P. WILKINSON
King's College
Cambridge

CONTENTS

Chronology

REPUBLIC

*(Indented items belong roughly
to the period indicated alongside.)*

EMPIRE

*(Indented items belong roughly
to the period indicated alongside.)*

THE
ROMAN
EXPERIENCE

Chapter One

SOME GENERAL REMARKS

There are many good books about what the Romans did, but there may still be room for one that focuses on how they felt. Though deeply conscious that filling this gap, insofar as there is one, would require not only insight but a lifetime of alert reading, I have tried to represent the Romans' experience more from within than has been customary. My interest is more in people than in actions and institutions—history with a human face. But this becomes problematic because evidence is so scarce. Until late republican times, for lack of firsthand documents, more is known about national character (which indeed mattered more then) than about personal outlook. And even after that time, though we can gather what the ex-consul Cicero felt from his letters, what the emperor Marcus Aurelius felt from his "meditations," it is hard to discover or imagine what the ordinary, inarticulate person felt.

The Romans of this title require definition in time. We shall be concerned with them as they were primarily during the three centuries that separate Scipio Aemilianus (185–129 B.C.) and Marcus Aurelius (A.D. 121–180). During this central period their experience forms a pattern. In it we see what may happen when a stable agricultural society of hard-working peasants is turned by circumstances into an affluent empire; when a stable polity depending on compromises accepted in the process of experience is disrupted by impatient reformism and selfish reaction; when weariness of violence and inefficiency induces a mood that acquiesces irrevocably under efficient autocracy and bureaucracy; and when autocracy, while quenching the spirit of those who should be leading citizens and adventurers in ideas, is itself bedeviled by problems of succession and of the psychology of absolute power.

There is a tendency to see the Romans, stiff with *gravitas* and respect for tradition, cocooned in formal and uncomfortable togas, as an immensely important but fundamentally dull people. Until now they have been studied and compared, much to their detriment, with the classical Greeks, generally considered one of the most brilliant races that ever lived. The Romans, in fact, were far more similar to the contemporary Hellenistic Greeks, whose faults they were too apt to copy. But a nation has some right to be judged by its best products, or at least not to be judged by its most notorious; and while grateful for the *gravitas* that gave us Lucretius, Vergil, and Tacitus, we should not forget the fun and liveliness of Catullus, Propertius, Ovid, Petronius, Cicero (as shown in his letters), and Horace. And besides Caesar and Augustus, there were many vivid personalities—Cato the Censor, the satirist Lucilius, the able and civilized voluptuary Maecenas, and the many-sided emperor Hadrian. We have only to read Plutarch's *Parallel Lives* to see how interesting the Romans were.

Negative Aspects

That there was in the Romans the streak of cruelty often associated with them is undeniable. It may not, however, have been indigenous. Gladiatorial contests, at any rate, were introduced by the Etruscans and not until 264 B.C., when three pairs of gladiators fought in the funeral games of one Marcus Brutus. Indeed they seem to have originated as a form of funereal sacrifice, not as a spectacle. But at the funeral of Flamininus in 174, thirty-seven pairs fought, and by then spectacle must have become the chief aim. In 65 B.C., under the pretext of honoring his father, who had died twenty years before, Julius Caesar had 320 pairs of gladiators do battle.

It is also true that in war, terror was recognized as an instrument of tactics. Polybius described how a town was taken by the Romans: at first every living thing they encountered was slaughtered, even dogs; then, at a given signal, they turned from slaughter to plunder. As the slave population grew, so did obsessive fears of general uprisings. When Spartacus, in 71 B.C., organized one and nearly succeeded, six thousand of the recaptured slaves were crucified along the highways as a warning to the rest. Deserters, too, could expect no mercy, even from justly admired commanders. When the younger Scipio took Carthage, he threw the deserters to the beasts; and after the Battle of Pydna in 168 B.C., Aemilius Paullus had the non-Roman deserters trampled by elephants. The communities in South Italy that went over to Hannibal were made a terrible example when the tide turned in Rome's favor. Many thousands were sold into slavery. Sulla put ten thousand Samnites to death to reassure the South Italians. Julius Caesar, an intellectual and in some ways a civilized and refined man, refused to let certain Spanish towns surrender so that his troops would have an excuse to pillage them. He sold whole populations into slavery; beheaded the entire Senate of the Veneti; massacred the helpless Usipetes and Tencteri; cut off the right hands of all men in Uxellodunum who were in arms; and kept the Gallic hero Vercingetorix in captivity for five years only to lead him in triumph to a miserable strangulation.[1]

---

[1] All the more credit to Pompey for settling many of the pirates he had subdued on the land, instead of crucifying them, and for breaking with custom in executing no prisoners after his great Triumph in 61 B.C.

But were the Romans so much more brutal than other people in that era of violence? Perhaps they were only more often in a position to be brutal. Those Campanians who went over to Hannibal had put all the Romans they could find into protective custody in the baths, then suffocated them by raising the heat. In one day in 88 B.C., Mithridates, king of Pontus, is said to have massacred eighty thousand South Italian traders and agents in Asia Minor. Moreover, the Roman scene was for four centuries astonishingly free from political murder. Other countries enjoyed no such immunity. Ptolemy of Egypt, on the death of his father in 222 B.C., murdered his brother Magas and his supporters. Hanno at Carthage plotted to massacre the whole Senate at his daughter's wedding. One Damasippus in 164 B.C. actually did massacre the whole Senate of Phacium. Attalus III of Pergamum murdered all his late father's council, along with their wives and children. Again, republican Rome showed remarkable respect for the lives of her own citizens. The right of appeal to the people in capital cases, including even treachery in wartime, was jealously guarded. In fact, if condemnation appeared imminent, the accused was generally allowed to escape into exile.

We must, however, look at things in perspective. Whole generations, indeed ages, of otherwise civilized people may have had moral blind spots. Many of us eat meat. How do we know that in a hundred years or so this practice may not seem as incredibly callous as accepting the slave system—and for reasons most eloquently expressed two thousand years ago by Ovid's Pythagoras in *Metamorphoses* (15. 116–126)?

Poor sheep, what harm do you, a placid tribe,
Born to serve man, whose nectar we imbibe
From udders full, who wool for clothing give,
Less useful if you die than if you live?
Oxen, what harm do you, beasts without guile,
Innocent, simple, born for honest toil?
Thoughtless, nor worth the bounty of the plough,
He who his partner of the fields, but now
Unyoked, can bear to slay, with axe to rive
That toil-worn neck that often did revive
His stubborn fields and make his harvests thrive!

Another aspect of Roman barbarity was the selling of conquered peoples into slavery. This was common Greek practice in the fourth century. To Aristotle, non-Greeks were slaves by nature. But the enslavement by his pupil Alexander in 335 of so famous a Greek people as the Thebans shocked the Hellenic world, and there is no known recurrence of such enslavement in Greece for more than a century. The Romans carried on the evil practice from the beginning of the First Punic War, selling twenty-five thousand Agrigentans in 262, and it became general again all over the Mediterranean world after 223. Hannibal, for instance,

sold twelve hundred Romans to the Achaeans, who did not wake up to the fact
that it would be politic to release them until eight years after the Battle of Zama.
King Philip V of Macedon also participated. The number of involved slaves was
appalling, and otherwise reputable people did not balk at it. Scipio sold Africans
freely; Cato, the Bergistani. The father of the Gracchi boasted on his votive
tablet of having killed or enslaved eighty thousand Sardinians in 177; and in
167, by order of the Senate, Aemilius Paullus sold 150,000 inhabitants of seventy towns in Epirus. It was generally accepted in antiquity that civilization
must include slavery.

Indifference to Truth

A less glaring but more insidious defect in the Romans was indifference to truth.
This displayed itself in various areas, among them religion. Polybius' famous
remarks on this subject are so significant as to deserve quotation here:

> What gives the Roman Commonwealth its distinctive quality is, in my opinion, its
> conception of the gods. I believe it is the very thing that among other peoples is a
> reproach, awe of the supernatural, that maintains the cohesion of the Roman state.
> These activities are clothed in the greatest solemnity, and introduced to an extreme
> degree into both public and private life, a fact which will surprise many. My own
> opinion is, that they have adopted this course with an eye to the common people. . . .
> I hold that it was not at random nor haphazard that the ancients introduced among
> the people notions about the gods and the terrors of hell, and I consider that moderns
> are rash and foolish in banishing such beliefs. (*History*, 6. 56)

This account is probably too rationalistic as to the origins of religious cults, but
not as to the Roman attitude toward them, at least after the Second Punic War,
though one may surmise that many people continued genuinely to harbor
vestigial superstitions. It will be shown later how Polybius' pragmatic attitude
gained currency in the last century of the republic; and it was still that of Seneca
in Nero's day.

The religious revival sponsored by Augustus was intended as a contribution
to moral and patriotic regeneration. One can understand the feeling that
prompted it. Even though morality was less closely bound to religion than it is
in Christianity, there was a fear of what might rush into the vacuum if traditional beliefs were generally abandoned, and there was also a sentimental at-
tachment to age-old ceremonies. After all, many unbelievers today would feel
uncomfortable if they did not get married in church and have their children
christened there, or if all churches were turned into museums or allowed to
decay. Livy's apology to his Augustan readers for retailing prodigies—that is,
miraculous signs and portents—is pertinent here:

> I am well aware that, as a result of the same disregard that leads men generally
> nowadays to believe that nothing at all is portended by the gods, no prodigies are

reported officially or included in histories. Yet as I write of antiquity my mind becomes somehow antique, and I feel a certain scruple which prevents me from considering unworthy to be related in my history what those very sagacious men thought to be a matter of public concern.

Equivocal about truth in metaphysics, the Romans were also not greatly interested in the facts of nature. Lacking the curiosity of the Greeks, which had outlived some of their other virtues to triumph at Alexandria, the Romans contributed little to the ascertainment of truth in mathematics or the natural sciences. Superstitious beliefs about illness long inhibited their adoption and development of Greek medical science. There were some who had scientific interests, such as the younger Seneca and the elder Pliny in the first century A.D.; but the *Natural History* of the latter is not a product of scientific research by the author but an encyclopedia covering some twenty thousand topics, each entry relying, often uncritically, on just a few sources.

Indifference to truth was also countenanced by an import, the insidious dangers of which Plato had foreseen—the art of rhetoric, which had been practiced in Greece for two or three centuries before it became popular in Rome. The art flourished in city-states, where political and legal decisions were made by comparatively small numbers of people assembled in centralized places. The Forum of Rome, with its platform for political speeches (the Rostra) and its nearby Senate House and law courts, was an ideal place for a good speaker to exercise power: not until the invention of radio was oratory to have such scope as in the Roman Republic. Politics there became largely a matter of prosecutions, and the duty of a forensic orator was to his client, not to truth. As a result of the importance of such oratory, higher education at Rome consisted in rhetoric—if you wanted to study philosophy you generally went to Athens—and what mattered in the schools of rhetoric was to present a case, any case, effectively. All this encouraged a practice equivalent to the "doublespeak" of George Orwell's *Nineteen Eighty-Four* and could lead only to "doublethink" as well. The millionaire Seneca with his five hundred citrus-wood tables was unabashed in his praises of simplicity.

One feature of Roman life that strikes a reader of Cicero's letters is a degree of social insincerity that goes beyond what we consider normal today, though it is found in other political societies. He will address a man with fulsome warmth in one letter and in the next letter tell someone else he thinks the man a monster. The letters of Augustus to Tiberius that Suetonius quotes display an affection belied by the hard facts of his treatment. Yet we must bear in mind that anyone who engaged in public life was constantly meeting his colleagues in the Forum, which measured about two hundred yards by seventy yards. You simply had to be on affable terms with most people, otherwise the embarrassments would be intolerable. There were, of course, occasional *inimicitiae,* formal breaches resulting from some injury or insult, but even these were often ended by a formal reconciliation engineered by a third party.[2]

Finally, Latin literature too had a peculiar relation to truth. It had originated as translation from the Greek; and even when it began to free itself, the process was only gradual. The maturest of Latin poets, Vergil, still positively preferred to start from or allude to predecessors; and the well-educated listener (poetry was composed primarily for recitation, and for an educated elite) would enjoy recognizing the allusion. Even "personal" poets like Horace and the elegists are less autobiographical than used to be supposed: their poems are based largely on tradition, though adapted to experience. Composers of bawdy verses were particularly insistent that their lives not be judged from their writings. Yet to pretend you were relating or expressing your own experience was part of the game. Rhetorical education, supervening on a literary tradition that hardly recognized the maxim "look in thy heart and write" (Catullus and his friends were exceptional), encouraged the view of a poem as a verbal artefact—the attitude, in fact, that has become known as classicism.

Contributions

All this may seem rather lowering; but there is much on the credit side. If the Romans were unoriginal, they were at least discriminating learners. They had the modesty to appreciate what was superior in the Greeks they had mastered physically, even in the contemporary Greeks of the decadence. None of the other important peoples who came in contact with Greece—Carthaginians, Egyptians, Parthians, Macedonians, Etruscans—have left any literature, save only the Jews. And as time went on the Romans, led by Cicero and others, came to perceive that the earlier, classical Greeks were far greater than the later *Graeculi,* or Greeklings, as they sometimes called them. Rome's reaction to Greece was a mixture of admiration and contempt. Thus Cicero remarked of the two leading orators of the early first century that although they were conversant with Greek culture, "one of them affected to despise the Greeks, the other not even to have heard of them." But in the better minds admiration won. "To the Greeks the Muses gave genius, to the Greeks resounding utterance, since they were greedy for nothing save praise." So said Horace in the *Ars Poetica,* thinking no doubt of the great age of Greece. He added by contrast a sketch of Roman boys in school learning commercial arithmetic (though in fact Roman schools were exact copies of Hellenistic ones). Meanwhile Rome absorbed the practical lessons she could learn, both in government and technology, with an alacrity equaled only by the Japanese in modern times. It was the Senate itself that

---

[2] We do hear that Brutus did not speak to Pompey for more than twenty years, relenting only when Caesar crossed the Rubicon and his enemies closed their ranks. But he had an exceptional reason: Pompey was responsible for his father's murder.

ordered the third-century agricultural treatise of Mago the Carthaginian to be translated into Latin.

Art

Take art again: the Romans are important only in two branches. By appreciating the potentialities of brick and concrete, of the arch and dome, they demanded of architecture a grandeur consonant with the greatness of their national spirit and achievements. And from familiarity with the realism of Etruscan terra cottas and of the death masks that hung in noble houses—but following also a Hellenistic trend—they developed a portrait sculpture that reflected the interest in individual human beings characteristic of the late republic and the empire. But they were also avid collectors of art—from Syracuse, for instance, as early as 211 B.C. Polybius deplored this because it corrupted the simplicity of life that had been one of Rome's great virtues and because the sight of lost treasures was a standing provocation to their original owners. The Romans' artistic possessions were indeed plundered as often as bought; and they always had a conscience about the bronzes carried off at the sack of Corinth in 146 B.C. Although, of course, such art objects could be mere status symbols, we have no right to assume that genuine appreciation was not involved. Aemilius Paullus was awestruck by Phidias' statue of Zeus at Olympia. The canard making Lucius Mummius a laughingstock for allegedly threatening shipping agents that any works of art from Corinth damaged in transit would have to be replaced by replicas just as good does at least indicate that many people knew the distinction. The art of copying works became highly developed in the first century B.C., sometimes with modifications that, even if the craftsmen were Greeks, produced something recognizable as a Roman style. There was also a development of devices for suggesting spatial depths in relief sculpture and painting, though so many of the artists seem to have been Greeks that we can speak with confidence only of indirect Roman influence through the taste of patrons. It is interesting that the man who pressed for works of art hidden away in private houses to be made available to the public should have been a man of action, the great Augustan soldier-administrator Marcus Agrippa.

Politics

Politically the Romans were, until the breakdown at the end of the second century B.C., outstanding for a quality they called *consilium:* something more than common sense—let us call it good sense. Whereas sharp-witted people often suffer from perpetual faction because each individual is too conceited to allow even the possibility that his reasoning may be awry and too smart to be willing to subordinate his immediate personal advantage to the long-term common good, the Romans' capacity for compromise and self-restraint amounted to collective genius. The Roman constitution was as full of illogicalities as the British, and likewise a product of evolution and custom rather than of designed and written formulation. Romans were fully conscious of its rationale. The elder Cato is quoted by Cicero as saying:

> Our constitution is superior to those of other states because every one of them has been established by a single author of their laws and institutions. . . . Ours is based on the genius not of one man but of many; it was established not in one generation but in a period of centuries and ages. For there never lived a man possessed of so great genius that nothing could escape him; nor could the combined powers of all men living at one time possibly make all necessary provisions for the future without the aid of actual experience and the test of time.

For a long time this constitution worked, such was the virtue of consensus; and it bred a respect for law and order that was to be one of Rome's chief gifts to the Mediterranean world and ultimately to still more distant lands.

Law

No less empirical, and no more monolithic, was Roman law. In the thousand years that ran from the Decemvirs' Twelve Tables of 450 B.C. to Justinian's Corpus there was no complete codification. The Tables, the germ of jurisprudence learned by heart at school down to the days of Cicero's boyhood, were never formally abrogated, and a hard core of them remained in force. But the Civil Law derived from them was, like Roman religion, too much wedded to the exact words of certain set forms.[3] It therefore tended to be corrected or supplemented by the Praetor's Law, which was adaptable to the increasing complication of society. The City Praetor was an annually appointed law officer who, on his appointment, issued an *edict,* a revised version of his predecessor's, in which he gave notice how he proposed to deal with various types of cases. He might himself be knowledgeable in law, for the Roman ruling class was intensely law-conscious, as the currency of legal terms in their literature, philosophy, and even stage jokes testifies. But in modifying and supplementing the edict, as also in formulating for the judge the issue to be decided in each particular case, he paid attention to that peculiar element in the Roman citizen body, the jurists (*iurisprudentes, iurisconsulti*), who either advised him as members of his council or gave answers (*responsa*) to specific inquiries. Jurists were amateur experts in law, aristocrats whose only qualification was acquired repute. They worked by precedents and experience, not by any theory. It was their common opinion, embodied in successive court decisions, that ultimately determined what was law, and to them was due the development of legal science, impregnated with ideas of *bona fides* and fair dealing, which was one of Rome's chief contributions to civilization.

---

[3] Thus we hear of a man who sued for destruction of his vines losing because the only clause in the Twelve Tables he could adduce specified "trees."

Humanity

As yet these contributions may seem to provide no more than a framework for true civilization. But within it the best Roman minds of the late republic, notably Cicero, developed and came to recognize by name a really civilized concept, *humanitas.* This was a combination of the Greek *paideia,* for which the nearest English equivalent is "culture," and kindly consideration—respect for others born of self-respect. It was complementary to the sterner quality of *virtus* (manliness) and came eventually to transcend barriers of race and rank.

Along with *humanitas* went a regard for women that contrasted with Greek narrowness and accorded them a quite new position. Young girls were educated together with boys, and we hear of many highly educated women—indeed, bluestockings were a butt of the satirists. The matron, or *materfamilias,* was held in great respect. Women went out into society. An independent woman could also acquire great wealth and consequent influence (this was a result particularly of the great casualties in the Second Punic War), though she had no official place in the state. Lucullus had to have recourse to Cethegus' mistress to get the command against Mithridates; and a letter of Cicero's gives us a vivid glimpse of an informal council of state at Antium (Anzio) three months after Caesar's murder in which leading parts were played by Brutus' mother, half-sister, and wife. In legend some women figured as paragons, and from about 100 B.C. they could be honored with a funeral laudation; the reverence in which the six Vestal Virgins were held is a reminder of their place in religion.

With respect to the family, pride was all-important. In a noble house a child grew up with the death masks and inscribed citations of his ancestors on the walls around him. Family fame was "the spur that the clear spirit did raise." We hear of a certain Metellus weeping at the recital of the deeds of his forebears. He was quick to protest to Cicero when he felt that another Metellus had been slighted: the *dignitas* of the family was involved. Leading men were also obsessed by their individual *dignitas,* their sense of what was due them for their services to the state, something not unlike the Oriental concept of "face," which must be saved even at great cost. It was avowedly to vindicate his own *dignitas* that Caesar crossed the Rubicon. The highest recognition of a man's *dignitas* was the award of a Triumph, in which, impersonating Jupiter himself, he was drawn in a chariot, his children with him, to the Capitol.

Literature

Another peculiar possession of the Romans the merits of which they came to appreciate and consciously to exploit was the Latin language. It has nothing like the flexibility of Greek. It is exasperating in its syntactical deficiencies, which in hindsight seem like willful self-denials. Its genius largely rejected the enrichment that compound words had given to Greek, and a Roman caution inhibited the development of adventurous metaphor. But Latin—the "lapidary" language of inscriptions on many more materials than stone—is capable as few other languages are of the economy that allows neatness and elegance and of the sonorous grandeur that suited the dignity of the national character at its best. The former quality, the terseness that permits and prompts epigram, was discovered comparatively late. Though clearly appreciated by Cicero, it was first systematically exploited in extant literature by his younger contemporary Sallust, and was to find its perfect scope in verse in the Odes of Horace and in prose in the audacious style of Tacitus.

The sonorous grandeur was already manifest in the poems of Ennius around 200 B.C., in his adaptations of Greek tragedy, and in his epic *Annals* of Rome's beginnings and history. The dignity of the Greek trimeter and the majesty of the Greek hexameter, which he imported, gave it scope. It was to find its fullest expression in the prose of Cicero and the verse of Vergil. The nobility of the language went with that quality which Shakespeare's Cleopatra called "the high Roman fashion," a pride and grandeur expressed in dramatic gestures, in the ceremony of public life and the ceremonious courtesy of private. To it belonged the rotundity and largeness of conception that produced the Pantheon, the Colosseum, and the Pont du Gard.

Turning Points in Roman Culture

It rarely happens that history is so obliging as to provide a date that can be taken as a significant turning point with such plausibility as the year 146 B.C. In that year Scipio Aemilianus finally destroyed Carthage and so removed from Rome all political threat and commercial rivalry in the western Mediterranean. In that year the last of the leagues that could conceivably limit Rome's authority in Greece was crushed when Lucius Mummius destroyed its leading city, Corinth, while the once powerful kingdom of Macedon became the first Roman province in Greece. Wealth and slaves poured into the capital; and with the removal of danger (the Germanic pressure had not yet begun) citizens relaxed and looked around for enjoyment. About the same year political persecution at Alexandria scattered the scholars of its famous academy, the Museum, over the Greco-Roman world, and at least some settled at Rome.

Granted, the process had begun earlier. Some dated it from 187, when Manlius Vulso's army returned from Asia laden with costly furniture and excited by new ideas of table luxury. Spain now sent abundant silver and gold. And such was the wealth that poured into Rome in 167 after the defeat of the Macedonian king Perseus by Aemilius Paullus that direct taxation of Roman citizens in Italy became unnecessary for a century. Whatever factors we may discern in the change that came over second-century Rome, the Romans themselves were clear that it was basically one of morals.

It was a peculiarity of the Romans that they allowed private morality to be a matter of public concern. Once the censors acquired, late in the fourth century, the responsibility for ejecting senators who seemed to them to be unsuitable because of either their private or their public conduct, they interested themselves more and more in questions of morality, especially in the second century, when the old way of life was dissolving. The Senate itself passed numerous laws aimed at controlling expenditure on luxuries in minute detail; Julius Caesar as dictator undertook a *cura morum* (care of morals) in the same spirit; and Augustus, as soon as he became princeps, (head of government) attempted to introduce legislation on morality. Among other things (and though he was himself a keen gambler), he reenacted laws against games of chance, first introduced in 103; evidently Romans were prepared to interfere even with conduct not directly antisocial.

The change, however, was also recognized to have been social and intellectual. New ideas had created a furor of discussion when in 155 a delegation of three Greek philosophers from Athens gave lectures during their stay. What makes Rome vital for us is largely what she made of Greece, though critics like Sallust were to look back with admiration to the early republic and deplore what happened after 146 (for they, too, agreeing with some Greek observers, dated the great change from that year). Upper-class citizens of Rome, as distinct from Roman citizens in Italian municipalities, became more individualistic and sophisticated, less public-spirited and disciplined, less admirable perhaps, and possibly less contented, but more interesting as people.

Another date that stands out as a significant turning point is 31 B.C. When Caesar (Augustus) defeated Antony and Cleopatra in the naval Battle of Actium, a century of civil strife came to an end. At the cost to the ruling class of political freedom, the Roman world acquired tranquility and a positive attitude toward empire. The dying republic and the dawning principate produced the two geniuses who were to be, centuries later, the educators of Western Europe, Cicero and Vergil. The empire provided the structure of law and government that enabled Europe beyond the Alps to emerge from barbarism. It was Roman civilization, mental and material, that made possible the spread of Christianity. But the change in 31 B.C. was, even more than that in the previous century, one that affected primarily the upper classes. The Senate lost its role of policy-making, while the *Equites,* or knights (see note, p. 77), gained a new one of administration. The Forum ceased to be the center of public life, or at least of power. Literature, too, was profoundly affected, after the glow of the Augustan dawn had faded. But we must keep reminding ourselves that Roman history as we know it is largely that of the ideas, acts, and fortunes of the upper or educated classes: the life and character of ordinary citizens are only casually and obliquely revealed. For the latter part of the year 31 meant the end of the civil war that had disrupted their lives, but probably not otherwise the beginning of something new. The chances and hazards of social mobility might increase, but the great majority would be unaffected by them. Throughout the ages the mentality of those whose prime care is subsistence has not varied greatly.

Chapter Two

EMERGENT CHARACTERISTICS (TO 146 B.C.)

What the Romans were like down to the third century B.C. can only be deduced from their institutions—political, social, and religious—from the way they reacted in well-attested crises, and from the legends they preserved. No literary documents from this time are extant. Probably there were none. They were an agricultural people by origin, proudly telling how Cincinnatus, after rescuing the state in a crisis by a sixteen-day dictatorship, went back to his plough. Such people are unlikely to lead very variegated lives or to record idiosyncrasies such as might interest us:

Man comes, and tills the soil, and lies beneath.

Until the third century no one even had a memorial tombstone. Cumulative pride in the family and in the community were the rewards of life. And even down to the beginning of the second century the Romans are of interest to us for what they were collectively, indeed for the degree to which they succeeded in repressing individuality. Disposed to the principle of counter-checks, they elected consuls to serve and command for one year only, and in pairs.

In the early republic, Rome had developed national characteristics that led to her amassing an empire. It is this development that we must look at first, beginning with what permeated everything, her religion.

Religion

William Warde Fowler, whose Gifford Lectures give one of the most sympathetic and discerning accounts of Roman religion, defined *religio* as "a feeling of happy dependence on a higher Power, and a desire to conform to His will in all the relations of human life." One cannot help sensing that here a Christian is reflecting backward his own conceptions (note the reverential capitals): the fear of anything is to him the beginning of wisdom. The Roman preoccupation with *numina,* vague deities that had to be propitiated,[1] reminds one rather of the rituals developed by obsessive neurotics. To some extent, however, the ordinary man was relieved by the elaboration of the state cults. Regulated by *pontifices* (pontiffs—religious experts), citizens who were generally not professional priests, originally all patricians, these cults undertook the burden of maintaining the "peace of the gods" by the observance of "divine law," providing a kind of national spiritual insurance throughout the comforting regularity of the calendar.

Some *numina* were personified abstractions. That these were felt to have real independent existence and power is shown by a curious story of Marcellus. In 222, during the Gallic War, he vowed a temple to Honor and Virtus. Fourteen years later its dedication was still being blocked by the pontiffs because you could not sacrifice one victim to two deities; and supposing the temple were struck by lightning, how would you know which of the two should be propitiated?

Any reader of Livy will be aware of the importance attached to prodigies under the republic. These ranged from bees swarming in the Forum through the birth or discovery of children of indeterminate sex[2] to the consul's cow saying "Rome, beware!" or an infant shouting "Io triumphe!" in its mother's womb. When the consuls entered on office at the beginning of the campaigning season on the first of March, so much of their time was spent on expiating prodigies that military operations were prejudiced; but it was not until 153 that this was obviated by the transfer of the beginning of the year to what it has remained ever since for Christendom, January 1. Early in 193 so many earthquakes were reported that the Senate could not be summoned because the consuls were occupied full-time with expiations. Finally the consuls proclaimed, on the Senate's advice, that on any day when an earthquake had been reported and rites ordained, no one should send in another report of an earthquake. In 176 the Senate was terrified by a report from one of the consuls that when the entrails of a sacrificed ox were boiled, the liver melted away. Worse still, the other consul, after sacrificing three oxen, had not found one whose liver was perfect. (He was told to go on sacrificing till he did find one of good omen.) We hear of a priest being deposed for presenting the entrails of the victim in the wrong way, or because his special cap fell off during sacrifice, or because a shrew squeaked at the moment of silence.

But the awe of the supernatural had also its practical advantages. These were particularly apparent in the sanctity protecting oaths. Whenever the Romans formed a camp, the tribunes administered to all, slaves included, an oath that

[1] As Sir Frank Adcock used to say, "If the Romans had had bicycles, they would have had a goddess Punctura."

[2] It was to expiate the birth of an androgynous child of exceptional size in 208 that Livius Andronicus was commissioned to compose the first known Latin lyric poem, a hymn in honor of Juno Regina, goddess of women, to be sung by a choir of thrice nine girls dancing through the city.

they would steal nothing and would hand in anything they found. Again, oaths were administered to ensure that booty was fairly distributed—obviously a most important matter since, as Polybius realistically observed, it is in most cases for the sake of gain that men are prepared to endure hardship and risk their lives: otherwise there would have been constant jockeying for assignments that provided direct access to booty. Contractors for olive picking swore an oath that they had not formed a secret ring to raise the price, and their employees swore that they had stolen no olives. A seller of wine could be compelled to swear that he had measured the amount correctly. In one form of lawsuit before a praetor, theoretically at least, either party might invite the other to swear an oath that his case was just; if the latter swore, he won forthwith. Polybius also ascribed to the sanctity of oaths in Rome something vital that he found too rare among the Greeks, the scrupulous handling of public money (though by his time the distinction may have been only one of degree). Cicero reckoned this to be one of the chief justifications of religion, and in earlier times it was effective.

But another, more general, effect was attributed to religion. It was not, in those days, the "opiate of the people," in the sense that it did not dull their resentment of this life by assuring them of the chance of happiness in another, though the festivals (*ludi*), introduced particularly in the anxious times of the Punic Wars, were religious entertainments that would be a distraction. It was, however, what kept people in their place, inasmuch as it persuaded them that the maintenance of divine favor toward the community depended on the observance of rituals that only members of the ruling class could perform. The magistrate's *imperium,* his power of command, itself embraced religious functions. All the ordinary man could do was see that he did not infringe the peace of the gods by some inopportune word or deed. Thus, since holy days were polluted if a priest *saw* a man working, a crier went ahead of a procession, and a worker was supposed to lay down his tools as it passed. It was a grim boost for orthodoxy when the progressive consul Gaius Flaminius, having neglected his state religious duties and hastened to his army for fear his aristocratic enemies would deprive him of his command, was punished by defeat and death at Trasimene. How different was Quintus Fabius, the cautious *Cunctator,* or delayer, who even in a military crisis left his army to go to Rome and perform the due sacrifices.

Roman state religion had no element of passion nor any idea that an individual could be possessed by a divinity. It was essentially a matter of placating unknown powers. Aulus Gellius, looking back, expressed surprise that the Romans had not recognized any spirit of earthquakes, seeing that they were most punctilious and wary in observances. Under the strain of Hannibal's presence in Italy there was a failure of nerve—at any rate, among the common people. The old religion seemed to be inadequate. Accordingly there was decreed a wholesale *lectisternium,* a feast laid out publicly for the gods, who reclined in pairs on couches. After the disastrous Battle of Cannae in 216, human sacrifice, almost unknown otherwise in Rome, took place. Polybius remarked that in times of danger the Romans were much given to propitiating both gods and men and thought no rites unbecoming or beneath their dignity. When Hannibal appeared before the walls in 211, the women swept the floors of the temples with their hair. Finally, in 205, the black stone of Pessinus in Asia Minor, fetish of the exotic Cybele, the Great Mother, was brought to Rome with great solemnity. Perhaps this was done to satisfy popular superstition, but her worship was immediately entrusted to the safe custody of patricians. From 191 her stone was lodged in the exclusive quarter of the Palatine and kept well out of sight except at her annual games and procession, with its house-to-house collection; and she was gradually purged of her more outlandish accompaniments. No Roman was allowed to participate in her orgiastic rites until a hundred years later; nor was the Board of Ten, whose duty it was to consult and interpret the Sibylline Books (see p. 50), ever again so rash as to prescribe the importation of a foreign deity. When in 213, with eighty thousand men killed either at Trasimene or Cannae or in Spain or Gaul and the remainder largely absent with the armies, the women got out of hand, the response of the praetor had been to order that all written formulas of private prophecy, prayer, or sacrifice should be brought to him, and that no one should sacrifice in public with any strange or foreign rite.

In 186 occurred the great scandal of the Bacchic outbreak, with rumors of nightly meetings of mixed sexes and also of homosexual practices. For some time endemic in Magna Graecia and Etruria, the orgies had now flared up and spread to the young people of a Rome whose population had become much more heterogeneous. The Senate treated it as secret conspiracy, so serious that they felt obliged for once to interfere with the internal affairs of the Italian allies also. Yet strangely enough there appears in the sternly repressive decree (extant in the form of the consul's summary) a clause that would never have occurred to that reckless persecutor of bacchants, Euripides' Pentheus:

If anyone considers such a rite to be of venerable tradition [*Sollemne*] and necessary, and feels that he cannot abandon it without offense, he shall report it to the praetor, and the praetor shall consult the Senate. If, with a quorum of not less than a hundred present, the Senate give him permission, he may perform that rite, so long as not more than five persons are present, there is no common fund, and no matter of ceremonies or priest.

No one was likely to seek such permission; but nothing could show better than this ostensible safety valve the caution of the Roman ruling class regarding religion, its desire to regulate everything and to guard against any possibility of misjudgment, and also the element of reasonableness and tolerance in the national character.

Had the normal Roman religion any moral content? At one level astonishingly little. Many are surprised that the debt-ridden, sexually and politically unscrupulous young Julius Caesar should have been made Supreme Pontiff (*Pontifex Maximus*). But that was nothing to what had happened in 209. Since the Flamen Dialis, priest of Jupiter, had to observe a number of strict taboos (he was not, for instance, allowed to leave his house for a single night), the family of one Gaius Valerius Flaccus obtained the post for him because his behavior had been scandalous. (It worked: he was completely reformed.) Here is a conception of priesthood as the performance of magic, in no way dependent on the character of the performer. What this legalistic-minded people felt to be essential was exact adherence to liturgy and formula. In 176 the Latin Festival had to be repeated because at one sacrifice a magistrate in a small town near Rome had omitted to pray for the *Populus Romanus Quiritium:* no wonder one of the consuls had died meanwhile of a fall. We hear of an occasion when a sacrifice had to be repeated thirty times until the liturgy was perfect.

What religion did impose was a sense that everything must be done decently and in order. The Senate could be convened only after sacrifice. It could pass resolutions only in a temple, so that shrines had to be attached to existing halls likely to be used for its meetings. If war was to be begun, it must be solemnly declared by religious functionaries, the fetials (*fetiales*). And here an element of morality was indeed involved, since in theory to make war unjustly was impious —the proverbial tribute of hypocrisy to morality. Every war had to be in defense of Rome or her allies. (By the same token, no modern state has a Ministry of Offense.) Originally, too, all booty belonged to the gods, though in course of time it was diverted to the Treasury. It became common form—we find it in Cicero, Sallust, Horace, and Livy—to claim that Rome became great because she was religious.

The word *pietas* sums up Roman religious feeling. It can generally be rendered more fairly by warmer words such as "devotion" and "loyalty" than by "duty" or "obligation," and embraced attitudes to both gods and men. It was *pietas,* the recognition of the supremacy of moral values, that prompted the chivalry characteristic of the Romans in the time of Pyrrhus: even down to the second century B.C., older senators retained an idea that ambushes and night attacks were "Punic trickery" and "Greek cleverness." *Pietas* operated most strongly within the family (the word *familia* included the whole household, with slaves and cattle). Throughout all Rome's vicissitudes the religion of family life persisted. Ultimately it was based on the farm unit of house, plot, spring, and burial ground. There were the Lares, spirits of the land (or ancestors(?)); the Penates, spirits of the larder; and Vesta, whose altar was the hearth. And there was the *Genius* (in women, the *Juno*), something like a guardian angel, of the acknowledged head of the family, the *paterfamilias.* The spirits (*manes*) of the family ancestors had to be propitiated. There was also a feeling that children were somehow sacred, centuries before Juvenal wrote *maxima debetur puero reverentia* (the greatest reverence is owed to a child). In token of this they wore a garment with sacred associations, the *toga praetexta.*

Closely connected with *pietas* was *fides*, good faith, the quality that held the Roman state together, and thus one of the first to be officially deified. In Vergil's vision of the return of the Golden Age, justice will be maintained by "white-haired Faith," along with Vesta and the brothers Romulus and Remus. (The ancient mind tended to deify abstractions.) We can observe how these two qualities were associated in the opening of Catullus' impassioned prayer to be freed from his entanglement with Lesbia (76):

If a man can take any pleasure in recalling the favors he has once done, when he feels that he is *pius*, and has not violated sacred *fides*, nor in any compact abused the holiness of the gods to deceive men. . . .

Fides, as a sense of moral obligation, specifically bound patron and client together, and over a large sector it was this relationship that gave meaning to men's lives. Its violation was affirmed by the Twelve Tables to damn a patron and was bracketed by Vergil with father-beating as a qualification for blackest hell. Leading citizens had not only an inherited, legally attached, following (*clientela*) of freed slaves and their descendants, but a large number of voluntary dependents—immigrants and so forth. These "clients" they defended in the law courts and helped with gifts and favors, in return for attendance, services, and support in elections. A nobleman's fortunes must have furnished his clients with a focus of enthusiasm such as is provided today by a local sporting club. He could acquire and pass on to his heirs clients from far afield by commanding an army, liberating a city, acting as a commissioner or arbitrator, or in the highest degree by becoming what the elder Scipio was to Spain, or Marcellus to Sicily, or Flamininus to the cities of Greece. (Ultimately, however, it was Italians with voting rights at Rome who were the most valuable clients.) The conception of clientship was so deep-rooted in Roman mentality that it dominated her foreign policy, especially in the Greek east, until after the time of Sulla (78 B.C.). The Senate preferred to influence client states bound to Rome by the moral ties of *fides* rather than govern provinces under a *Lex Provinciae*. Kings and chiefs relied on their *amici* at Rome for power and security, so public clientship was abetted by private. Later, when clientship ceased to be the Senate's foreign policy, it was the individual followings of Caesar and Pompey that emerged as forces dominating the Roman world.

The concept of *fides* was thus important as regards allies. At Carthage, says Polybius, nothing that resulted in profit was disgraceful, even open bribery in elections (implying that in the Rome he knew, this was not so). At Rome it was positively not done to receive direct payment even for services such as pleading in court. The Aetolian Greeks were agreeably astonished when Titus Flamininus, sent to deal with the situation across the Adriatic after the defeat of Hannibal's Carthage, proved not to be corruptible by King Philip of Macedon. We possess part of a paean sung in his honor by girls of Chalcis:

And we reverence the good faith of the Romans which we have solemnly vowed to cherish. Sing, girls, of great Zeus and Rome, and with them of Titus and the faith of the Romans. Hail, Paean Apollo! Hail, Titus our savior!

Polybius again confirms that this reputation was true of the earlier part of the second century, though not of the latter. It must be confessed however that good faith was not always extended to enemies. Titus Didius triumphed in 93 for having annihilated a whole tribe of Spaniards, men, women, and children, after enticing them into a stockade under the pretext of allotting them land. And whether at the Caudine Forks in the fourth century or at Numantia in the second, the Senate was capable of saving its defeated forces by wriggling out of an agreement.

Social Relationships

By and large the Roman Senate, after the struggle between patricians and plebeians had been settled in 367, was obviously a friendly body—past all conception, as some Carthaginian envoys reported. There being no hotels, senators put their private houses at each other's disposal for stopping on journeys. Private messengers collected and carried mail for friends. Above all, there was an elaborate nexus of credit among those of equal status, ultimately secured on the value of land. A sense of *officium* (obligation) operated, and a feeling that it was bad for your class if anyone went bankrupt. Nor had divorce yet disrupted family and interfamily life as it did in the late republic (the first divorce at Rome took place in 235). From the age of twelve, in early times, sons could attend debates in the Senate with their fathers, trusted to keep what they heard confidential. Political marriages were of course frequent. Women married younger than men, and often remarried after their husbands' death. Hence there was a network not only of cousins but of half brothers. Adoptions also were frequent. Of the two sons of Aemilius Paullus by a wife he divorced, the elder was adopted by a grandson of Quintus Fabius Cunctator, the younger by a son of Fabius' chief political and military rival Scipio Africanus, while his daughter married the son of Scipio's opponent Cato. (Scipio's daughter, after his death, married another political opponent of his, the father of the Gracchi.) It is only in the second century that bitter political animosities come to the fore, and even then there seems to have been a large middle group between the supporters of Scipio and Cato, respectively. Some scholars have sought, by studying the behaviors of individuals, to discern the operation of established and cohesive groups of noble families. There was certainly a good deal of "ganging up" by noble families, but personal feelings may often have outweighed political considerations, even if, in a world of arranged marriages, Romeo-and-Juliet affairs were out of the question. Gelzer is probably nearer the mark when he says, "It would be contrary to the character of a Roman senator for him to be tied to a group."

An astonishing feature of Roman family life, of whose uniqueness the Romans were themselves aware, was the legal position of the paterfamilias, your oldest surviving male ascendant, in whose power you remained even if you were consul. In republican times he even had power of life and death over you, however infrequently exercised. You could not marry without his consent, and he could compel you to divorce your spouse. You could own no property; even if you acquired it yourself, dowry included, it accrued to him. If you had to borrow for your daughter's dowry, he did it for you. His wife alone was immune, and that only as remaining in the power of *her* oldest male ascendant, and only if she had not married under the old, gradually obsolescent form by which she passed "into the hand" of her husband.

This being so, it was perhaps fortunate that the average life was short. It was a young man's world: the word *senex* (old man) was applied to anyone over forty; and an old slogan went "Sexagenarians off the bridge!" Before Sulla, quaestors were quite often in their twenties. At Rome in republican times two of them were responsible for disbursing authorized payments from the Treasury. In the provinces, where they were aides to governors, their duties could be judicial as well as financial, and they might command troops. Praetors, primarily responsible for supervising justice, were often in their thirties; and not a few reached the consulship at what became the lowest statutory age, forty-two. Scipio Africanus received a proconsular command at twenty-six; Flamininus was still in his twenties when he was exceptionally made counsul and commander against King Philip; Scipio Aemilianus had become an outstanding leader years before he was made consul, by special dispensation, at thirty-eight. Gaius Gracchus was only twenty-one when he became one of the three commissioners appointed to the considerable responsibility of carrying out his brother's agrarian law. Pompey was twenty-five when Sulla bestowed on him the name "Magnus," and he assumed the consulship arbitrarily at thirty-six. The future Augustus was one of the three rulers of the world at twenty-one, his general, Agrippa, the same age; and Horace, whose father had been a slave, commanded a legion when scarcely twenty-two. Augustus made the age of eligibility twenty-five for quaestors, thirty-three for consuls.

Virtus: Courage and Patriotism

Virtus (manliness) beyond the ordinary was another characteristic of the Romans. The first appearance of a Roman in extant literature is in the third-century Alexandrian poet Callimachus: in a papyrus giving fragments of a summary of his famous poem the *Aitia,* a Roman who has been wounded while leaping upon the leader of a horde attacking the walls of his city is bidden by his mother to be proud of his ensuing limp. Polybius thought that Roman discipline depended on the severity of punishments—death by stoning for a breach of the rules for sentry duty (since the safety of the whole camp depended on sentries), the bastinado (a cudgel) for throwing away one's arms and for such odd offenses as boasting with a view to obtaining a decoration, or homosexual practices. We hear of soldiers who had not fought well being compelled to take their food and drink standing for the rest of the war. Cowardice in a whole unit was punished by the execution of one man in every ten—decimation. Punishment apart, the normal pack of a Roman soldier was itself a severity, since it weighed over forty pounds, and his arms and armor as much again.

Another ruthless but effective form of severity was refusal to ransom prisoners of war. Even after Cannae, when Rome was desperate for manpower, in preference, and at greater expense, eight thousand sturdy slave volunteers were armed, and some boys younger than seventeen were called up. The story of Regulus in the First Punic War was famous, a paradigm to Cicero as it was to Horace: having come to Rome from captivity at Carthage on parole, he spoke passionately and successfully against making peace and went back to the certainty of a cruel death. Other such paradoxical stories of self-sacrifice for the state figured prominently in the legends the Romans cherished: of Decius Mus, who solemnly "devoted" himself and the enemy to the gods of the underworld and charged to his death; or of Lucius Brutus, who was alleged to have executed his own sons.

But courage was also instilled by the prospect of rewards. Some of these were tangible. There were rewards presented on the field, after a citation—a spear or a cup for conspicuous bravery in hand-to-hand fighting, a golden crown for being the first man up the wall when a city was assaulted, a wreath for saving the life of a Roman citizen. The decorations were displayed in the winner's home and carried or worn by him in religious processions, in which he had a special place reserved for him. But besides these tangible inducements there were intangible ones of honor. At the funeral of a Roman of distinguished family, proclaimed throughout the city by a crier, masks of all his ancestors who had held high office were worn by impersonators who rode in separate chariots and sat on ivory thrones on the Rostra for the occasion. The dead man himself was impersonated by a kinsman of similar stature wearing the most honorable robes to which he had been entitled; and an adult son or near kinsman recited from the Rostra the achievements of each ancestor, ending with an encomium of the deceased. We may well believe Polybius when he tells us that the thought of these occasions was a great incitement to patriotic self-sacrifice.

To individual courage the Romans added collective courage, the doggedness, also observed by Polybius, that never knows when it is beaten. This was strikingly shown, for instance, when they had to take to the sea, an untried element for them, in order to come to grips with Carthage. In 253 B.C., out of 364 ships, they lost 284 in a storm off Sicily. Undaunted, within three months they built another 220, with the aid of which they took Palermo. They gave this spirit official recognition when, after Cannae, the Senate thanked the consul Varro (whom politically they regarded as a renegade and whose rashness had been responsible for the disaster, but who had rallied the survivors) for not having despaired of the republic. The difference lay in having a citizen and allied army instead of relying, like the Carthaginians and some of the eastern kingdoms, on mercenaries. The Roman army, more than most, fought for political and moral traditions besides the fruits of victory.

Times of crisis were often opportunities for Romans to display their faith in Rome. In the acute shortage of arms after Cannae old spoils were taken down from the temple walls and the manufacture of arms was speeded up. Free contingents of allies were hastily organized. To obviate the spread of alarm and despondency crowds were forbidden to gather at the gates. Attempts by the enemy to parley were disregarded. While Hannibal in 211 was camping before the walls, the site of his camp was put up for auction and realized a normal market price; and reinforcements were sent off to the Spanish theater of war, recognized as vital in the long run.

Two years after this crisis another arose through exhaustion of the Treasury. In response, contractors for repair of temples and so forth undertook to operate free or on credit; the owners of the slaves enrolled in the forces who had been freed as a reward for winning the Battle of Beneventum forwent compensation until after the war; the trust funds of wards and widows were lent to the state; and many Equites and centurions in the armies waived their pay. An obligatory loan was imposed on the richer classes, with a graded surtax to pay for rowers. By 210 the situation was worse; but the threat of an uprising at home melted away when first the senators and then the Equites gave all the gold, silver, and bronze they had, except a symbolic ring apiece for members of their family, to the Treasury.

Treatment of Allies and Conquered Peoples

In the sphere of external politics the Romans collectively displayed an ingenuity and good sense amounting to genius. Having rejected in 340 the proposal of their Latin neighbors for a federation, they set about binding central and southern Italy together, despite the difficulties created by differences of language, under their hegemony. This they achieved by two major means: first, by the Latin device of planting "colonies," groups of Roman families who volunteered to settle in strategic, often coastal, sites on conquered land—Antium (Anzio) in 338 was the first; and second, by incorporating as municipalities within the Roman state certain ancient Latin towns. The people in both classes of towns thus acquired dual citizenship, local and Roman, a concept that was to become of the greatest importance. Non-Latin Italian communities were attached to Rome by separate alliances that inhibited them from combining against her and gave them, as an incentive to cooperate, the chance for promotion to the rights of Latins. These devices provided the Roman commonwealth with both a solid structure and a capacity for expansion. To the Greeks, non-Greeks—barbarians—were natural slaves and even Greeks of other cities were foreigners. The Romans had much less racial prejudice. They had an astonishing readiness to give citizenship even to freed slaves.

In confiscating land from conquered Italian peoples for their own use the Romans must have caused considerable distress to those expropriated. But the evidence we have suggests that a good deal of the land, perhaps two-thirds, was left untouched. They were also unique in exacting no tribute from their allies, whereas Carthage taxed hers to pay for her mercenary armies. Indeed, with occasional exceptions, the Romans behaved with moderation. They posted no garrisons in allied towns except Tarentum, a key outpost. What the allies had to contribute was an agreed quota of soldiers and ships on demand, amounting all together to rather more than half the total forces, while proportionally Rome contributed nearly twice as many men. And they had to accept her judgment as to when war was necessary. As a mark of trust and courtesy a proportion of allied soldiers was selected to serve special duty near the commander's person. And all allied troops received free the grain that Roman soldiers had to purchase out of their pay.

In return the allies, while retaining control of their internal affairs, gained a deterrent, or at least a defense, from aggression much more effective than anything they could have mustered themselves, as well as an equal share in any booty. They could rely on Rome for protection from the wild tribesmen of the hills, from the Gauls in the north, and from one another (the Greek plague of intercity warfare was endemic) in the south. In carrying out her part of the bargain she would go to great lengths. Thus in 271 three hundred Romans who had treacherously occupied the allied town of Rhegium (Reggio) were brought to the capital, scourged in the Forum, and beheaded. In some cases the ties between other cities and Rome were strengthened by marriage; this was especially so in the case of Campanian Equites. As in Greece, the nobility and gentry reached out to their like across state frontiers. Distinguished citizens of allied communities were also adopted, during the age of Rome's expansion, into her aristocracy. In her capacity for assimilating those she conquered Rome was, except for the period between the Hannibalic and Social Wars, remarkable.

And so, when it seemed that Hannibal would win the Second Punic War, the majority of the allies in central Italy did not desert to him. His gesture of releasing without ransom all his Latin (and presumably other non-Roman) prisoners after Trasimene had little effect. And even after Cannae, when he repeated the gesture, there were many instances of loyalty. Predictably, there were exceptions: Capua, the flourishing commercial city of Campania, Rome's rival in wealth, went over, as well as the untamed hillmen—Samnites, Lucanians, and Bruttians; and Greek cities with strong democratic parties were liable to revolt, since the prominence of the Senate gave Rome an oligarchic image. But many cities, Neapolis (Naples) and Rhegium for instance, remained loyal. Petilia even resisted to her own destruction, although the Romans had felt bound in fairness to give her leave to follow her own interest since they were in no position to send her help.

It is a significant fact that the two great trumpeters of Rome's peculiar virtues in this period, Ennius and Polybius, should neither of them have been Romans.

Ennius, born and bred in the extreme south of Italy, heir to the Greek language and culture but able to speak Oscan as well as Latin, composed a Latin epic on her origins and history that not only revealed the potentialities of what was to be the medium of Vergil but educated generations of Romans in patriotism. Polybius, one of eight thousand Greek hostages, won the friendship of Paullus' son, Scipio Aemilianus, and wrote his history with the precise object of showing what it was about Roman political institutions that enabled her, in the space of less than fifty-three years, to conquer almost the whole inhabited (he should have said Mediterranean) world. As a contemporary witness who tried to tell the truth in history, he is of exceptional value.[3] For all his initial admiration of Rome he did not hesitate on occasion to criticize her; and from his privileged position he did all he could to secure the release of his less fortunate fellow hostages from their callously and unnecessarily prolonged detention.

Another interesting testimony comes from the First Book of Maccabees, Chapter 8, where we learn that Judas Maccabaeus, hard pressed by the Seleucid Greeks of Syria, sent two envoys to Rome in 161, having heard not only of her military power but of the welcome she gave to those who became her allies: any who joined her could be sure of her firm friendship. He particularly admired the Senate, familiar as he was with the dynastic intrigues in the kingdoms that emerged from the breakup of Alexander's empire, and the way in which the senators all obeyed whoever was consul without envy or jealousy. The chief responsibilities were shared. There were no professional politicians, governors, judges, lawyers, or priests. Even generals were amateurs.

Government by Consensus

As for politics at Rome, the unwritten constitution operated by that remarkable nexus called *Senatus Populusque Romanus* depended on a consensus. The long struggle between patricians and plebeians had been dismal, but at least it had been bloodless, which is more than could be said of the struggles between oligarchs and democrats in the more "civilized" city-states of Greece, or between the factions at Carthage. The plebeians had used the weapon of secession, equivalent to a general strike, and the patricians had ultimately given in.[4] To Pyrrhus' envoy in the early third century the Senate seemed "an assembly of kings." There were popular reformers active between the First and Second Punic Wars, but the people's favorites, Flaminius and Varro, proved responsible for the disasters of Trasimene and Cannae. The result was reaction. The Senate's

---

[3] Of forty books covering the years 220–144 B.C., the first six survive intact; the rest only in excerpts. His attitude toward the Romans became less favorable as he went on.

[4] The patricians were descendants of original aristocrats and senators of Rome. But after the plebeians' war for the right to qualify for the Senate and the chief magistracies there emerged equally aristocratic plebeian families. Any family that previously had a consul was now called "noble."

steadfast and conciliatory conduct, and its spectacular successes in the fifty years that followed, induced the people to leave the conduct of foreign and financial affairs to such evident experts. Looking back on this period, not only Cicero but even Sallust, who distrusted the Senate, saw it as one of harmony and good government. On the chief occasion when the people did demur, over the declaration of war against Macedon almost immediately after the defeat of Carthage at Zama, though thoroughly war-weary, they allowed themselves to be overpersuaded. All in all, up to this time, they showed the qualities of "perception of the common good, sagacious deference towards the right leader, steadfast spirit in prosperous and evil days, and above all, capacity for sacrificing the individual for the general welfare and the comfort of the present for the advantage of the future" that earned the reverent admiration of the nineteenth-century German historian Theodor Mommsen.

But everything depended on noninsistence on constitutional rights. In theory (that is, time-honored principle) the magistrates, annually elected, who alone could summon the Senate and control its agenda, were absolute rulers for that period. In practice they consulted as much as they could this experienced body from which they came and to which they might have to give an account of their stewardship. In theory the people alone could make laws, though their scope was limited to voting yes or no to a proposal put to them by a magistrate. In practice decrees of the Senate had great executive force in many spheres. In theory the people chose the magistrates. In practice they generally elected nobles from families conspicuous for public service and were greatly influenced by the obligations of clientship and their patrons' wishes (admittedly also, as wealth increased, by bribery). In theory the tribunes were the watchdogs of the people, and they never quite forgot their origin: any one of the ten could veto the act of a magistrate or a proposal for legislation, or himself propose legislation to the people. In practice, unless they were revolutionaries, they consulted the Senate, of which they became in the second century ex officio members, and put the resultant motion to the people. Cicero saw the tribunate as a sort of safety valve, a comparatively responsible element in what might otherwise have been an uninformed and rudderless Assembly. Polybius, preoccupied with logical Greek theories of constitutions, failed to make clear what the Alexandrian Eratosthenes had perceived some sixty years before him, that the Roman state depended not on forms, but on compromise and consensus.

As to law, the Twelve Tables of 450 marked a stage in the long but bloodless struggle of the plebeians to achieve equality with the patricians. As a codification (perhaps with some amendments) of miscellaneous customs their significance was political rather than jurisprudential: the law was in the future to be common knowledge, not a secret preserve of patrician pontiffs. The Tables were (to judge from the surviving fragments, perhaps one-third of the whole) overwhelmingly concerned with private law, but they also contained public law and even rules for municipal hygiene. Some of the features stand out as exceptional.

Thus it is unusual for a people at such an early stage of development to be able so completely to disentangle law from religion; or, for instance, to recognize the validity of individuals' wills. The importance of the patron-client nexus in Roman society is startlingly highlighted by the provision that any patron who, in violation of *fides,* cheated a client should be liable to the death penalty.

The most characteristic features of Roman law in the republic were thoroughly and natively Roman. *Patria potestas,* the lifelong authority of the eldest male ancestor over the lives and property of his family, is one striking feature. Another is the very early development of the disposition of property by wills. Property could be left in any desired way; and as to automatic descent of property on intestacy, the Romans had no preference for first-born sons, or even for sons over daughters. Free marriage and free divorce are characteristic and oddly liberal-looking. In property there is early care for, and elaboration of, all the rules for neighborliness—the rights of way and water and the duties of one property owner to another. With respect to contracts, by striking contrast with Greece, one notes the sanctity of the verbal contract, the simple oral statement ("Do you promise?" "I promise.") as opposed to the written, and also the rise in the middle republic of the marvelously adaptable consensual contract (contract by consent, however expressed, of the parties involved) for sale and hire and partnership. Damage to property, regulated initially by a laconic early statute, was brilliantly developed by legal interpretations proposed by the jurists and accepted by the praetors who ran the courts. And in the sphere of personal assault, physical or verbal, the same kind of development took place: a flexible and sophisticated law conjured by interpretation out of primitive origins.

Perhaps the greatest progress from rigidity and formality to flexibility is to be seen in the Roman law of procedure—how a man went about obtaining judgment against his neighbor. The progress was especially due to two facts: first, that in all Roman civil law the judge for a case was a layman, a member of the public, chosen with consent of the parties for that case (or a small jury of such laymen); and second, that the praetors were magistrates with *imperium,* that tremendous power to act which the Romans placed in the hands of the men they chose to run their institutions. Thus the praetors in charge of the courts were able, at every stage, to place alongside the stern formalities of the primitive law alternative procedures and extra rights and remedies, filling gaps, smoothing harshnesses, providing for exceptions and equitable considerations. And both they and the judges of individual cases, being laymen, relied on the advice and interpretative subtlety of those aristocrats learned in the law who made such skill and advice their principal interest in life (for not even these jurisprudents were professionals). The formulary system of the late republic, by which the parties to litigation were brought to agree before the praetor upon a statement of the case to be tried by the chosen judge—subtle, adaptable, practical—was indeed a characteristic Roman masterpiece.

Emergence of Individual Personalities

We have mentioned that our interest in the Romans down to the middle of the second century B.C. is for what they were collectively, for what they achieved by subordinating the individual. Evidence of this subordination may be found in the number of cases in which one man after another in a family bore the same three names.[5] What mattered was the family, the clan (*gens*), and the city. Annual tenure of the offices of state, and sharing of the highest, the censorship and consulship, put a brake on the development of a personality cult; and as a further precaution there was a prescription, which lapsed but was renewed after the Hannibalic War, of a ten-year interval before a man could be reelected consul. A high ideal of collective amateurism took priority over one of specialized but dangerous efficiency. Nevertheless, personalities did emerge, and partly as a corrective and partly to convey something of the flavor of upper-class life at least, sketches of three of them—Appius Claudius the Blind, Publius Cornelius Scipio Africanus the Elder, and Marcus Porcius Cato the Censor—are given here.

Appius Claudius

Appius Claudius is the first Roman to emerge as anything like a personality, though our picture of him is blurred because the first Roman historians wrote so long after his time. Later annalists, whose tradition is preserved by Livy, and Livy himself, tended to recreate the unknown past in terms of the present they knew, and family pride further distorted the record. We have little really reliable literary evidence for the period down to 220, the year that Polybius chose for the beginning of his history. The scraps of tradition about Appius' political activity are so disconnected that they allowed one great historian of the nineteenth century to imagine him as the last bastion of patricianism against the new plebeian nobility, another as a demagogue and would-be tyrant, a premature Caesar. If there is any truth in those scraps, he may have wanted to enlarge the Senate of landowners by introducing a small number of citizens from other classes, perhaps even freedmen, known in the Forum as men of substance, and to increase the influence of urban citizens as a whole in electing to magistracies and in voting on everyday legislation. But here all is uncertain. Something of a portrait does, however, emerge from information less liable to have been distorted by political bias.

Appius was born about 350 into the ancient patrician clan of the Claudians. He must have proved a success as a soldier in the Samnite War that broke out in 327, for he was three times elected a military tribune. Recalled to the consulship in 296 at the crisis of the Third Samnite War, he did valuable service, and

[5] All Roman citizens had a clan name (*nomen*), e.g. Cornelius, fem. Cornelia. Men also had a preceding name (*praenomen*), e.g. Publius, and often a following one (*cognomen*), e.g. Scipio. Some even had a fourth, e.g. Gaius Julius Caesar Strabo.

afterward dedicated a temple in the Campus Martius to the war goddess Bellona. As curule aedile, an office he held twice, he would have administrative, economic, and architectural duties in the city. This experience prepared him for the great works of his censorship in 312. Two censors were appointed every four years (later, five) to serve for eighteen months. Their original function, holding a census to determine the liability of citizens for duties and taxes, had been enlarged to include the letting out of contracts for public works; and more recently, it would seem, the periodical review of the membership of the Senate had been transferred from the consuls to the censors. In fact, the censorship was to become more powerful and prestigious than the consulship itself. It was in this capacity that Appius attempted any political reforms with which he should be credited. But his censorship was in any case memorable for two great public works sufficient to immortalize his name. He persuaded the Senate to build the first of Rome's great aqueducts, called after him the Aqua Appia, bringing water to the populous district that had been his care as aedile, and to construct the great south road, the Via Appia, running initially as far as Capua and serving incidentally as a strategic road for the war against the Samnite hillmen.

This many-sided man is also the first name in Roman literature, as the author of a collection of maxims (including the famous *Faber est suae quisque fortunae,* "Each man is the forger of his own fortune"). He instituted a reform of Roman writing to make it more representative of the spoken word. And no doubt it was under his influence that his secretary Gnaeus Flavius, son of one of his freedmen, published a handbook that gave citizens a knowledge of the civil law and its formulas of procedure, hitherto a preserve of the pontiffs.

Cicero, in his dialogue *On Old Age,* gives us two glimpses of him:

Though both blind and old, he managed his four sturdy sons, his five daughters, a great household, and those great clienteles; for he did not sluggishly give in to old age, but kept his mind taut as a bow. He maintained over his household not merely authority but absolute command. His slaves feared him, his children revered him, and in his house the ancestral ways and discipline flourished.

And then, near the end, his finest hour:

When opinion in the Senate was veering toward peace and an alliance with Pyrrhus, he did not hesitate to say, as Ennius expressed it in verse:

Your minds that ever yet were straight and strong,
Why do they now swerve madly from the path?

and so forth—you are familiar with the poem, and in any case the speech itself is extant.

The authority of the ex-consul persuaded the Senate; otherwise the course of world history might well have been very different.

Publius Cornelius Scipio Africanus

Publius Cornelius Scipio was a charismatic figure who proved also to be a soldier of genius. The Second Punic War gave him his opportunity. When his father and uncle, after considerable successes, had been defeated and killed in Spain, a vital theater as a potential source of supplies and reinforcements to Hannibal, who was now operating in Italy, Scipio was unanimously and enthusiastically chosen by the people in 210, though only twenty-six, to go out and take over the command from an ex-praetor. He had held no high office but was simply a proconsul, *privatus cum imperio* (a citizen given supreme authority). He had come to the fore after the rout at Cannae when, a military tribune aged twenty, he had been chosen with a colleague to take command of four thousand survivors and by courageous intervention had shamed and fortified some young nobles who were thinking of abandoning Italy.

Having arrived in Spain, he won the seasoned soldiers by his charm and tact. After a winter of preparations he showed his military flair by disregarding three Carthaginian armies encamped along the frontiers and swooping down on their base, New Carthage (Cartagena). He captured the city ultimately by a surprise attack through a lagoon and thereby acquired a base and a coast road while depriving the enemy of silver mines they needed for paying their mercenaries. He then proceeded to train his troops in the execution of a new kind of tactic and the use of a new weapon, the Spanish cut-and-thrust sword. Traditionally the troops had been drawn up in three ranks, in quincunx formation $\therefore$ with gaps between groups (*manipuli*) for skirmishers to advance and retire. They could not wheel or turn, and there was no scope for initiative or flank attack, no effective use of cavalry. At Cannae Hannibal had won by an enveloping movement. Scipio learned the lesson. At Baecula in 208 he won by ordering troops from the second and third ranks to move around to the wings and deliver flank attacks. Once the battle had begun there was to be no attempt at unity of command: the maniple was the unit. Two years later, at Ilipa (near Seville), he developed these tactics, himself leading one of the wings. His victory not only ended the war in Spain but ensured that his innovations had permanent effect in Roman warfare.

It was in Spain also that he showed those qualities of chivalry that were to make him a hero of legend. The romanticization of Alexander was already a flourishing industry, and Scipio was ultimately seen as a second Alexander. We cannot tell, for instance, what truth there is in the story of his restoring to her father intact a beautiful Spanish girl who had been brought to him as a special prize: but the continence of Scipio became an immortal theme, as in Handel's opera named after him. It is clear, at any rate, that he treated people with generosity and imagination, allowing two important Spanish chiefs, for instance, to share the Roman camp. It was indeed, like Caesar's famous clemency in later times, a case of enlightened policy. The Carthaginians had been arrogant tyrants in Spain, unlike the Romans in Italy. To win over the Spaniards was an obvious aim (the fact that by contrast he sold African prisoners into slavery is significant). In Spain he acquired, as it were, a whole-sale foreign clientele.

Polybius emphasizes his good sense in not exposing himself unnecessarily to danger in battle. Yet his courage is shown by his romantic secret visit to the African king Syphax, whom he helped to detach from the Carthaginians. There he found himself dining at the same table as his enemy Hasdrubal, son of Gisgo, and exercised his charm on both host and fellow guest. The other Numidian king with whom he had dealings, his future ally Massinissa, was impressed at their first meeting by his natural majesty, his long hair and soldierly appearance (which was not studied elegance), and his youthful bloom.

Scipio was also the first Roman general to enjoy so long and close a relation-ship with his army (the importance of which was shown when he fell ill and a serious mutiny broke out on the rumor that he was dead), and possibly the first to be saluted by his troops as *Imperator*. It was by this title that he asked Spanish chiefs to call him, instead of that of king, so invidious at Rome, which they offered him. He probably had to be careful about the Senate. Though he was a noble, he could not have forgotten that it was to the people that he owed his command, unprecedented for one who had held none of the higher offices; and the Senate must have feared that he would appeal to the people over their head. The fear would not have been allayed by the recollection that as aedile in 213 (elected though under the legal age) he had made the innovation of a free distribution of oil during the Roman Games. In particular he had to reckon with opposition from Quintus Fabius Maximus and his supporters. Fabius had re-stored the situation by his delaying tactics after Cannae, but ten years later Hannibal was still in Italy. Here was a rival commander, absurdly young, who had inherited from his father and uncle a strategy of daring attack.

On returning to Rome he gave an account of his stewardship to the Senate in Appius' Temple of Bellona outside the walls. He was deemed, as being only *privatus cum imperio,* to be ineligible for a Triumph. Accepting this piece of legalism, he entered the city on foot and deposited in the Treasury over fourteen thousand pounds of silver, against which he was allowed to draw in order to provide the games he had vowed in the crisis of the mutiny he had successfully dealt with. He also sacrificed a hecatomb to Jupiter on the Capitol. But what mattered was that he was elected consul for 205, with Sicily for his province and the right to invade Africa if the interests of the state required it. This represented a victory for his strategy over that of the Fabians, who had acqui-esced only after he had gone so far as to threaten a constitutional showdown by appealing to the People over the head of the Senate. The cautious, war-weary outlook of the Fabians envisaged no more than the restoration of Italy and its agriculture, and the ultimate defeat on her soil of Hannibal, who was in a hopeless position after the defeat of his brother Hasdrubal at the Metaurus, in northern Italy. Scipio had shown evidence of a wider vision when he stayed in Spain after Hasdrubal had eluded his victorious grasp at Baecula and crossed the Alps. The Carthaginian empire there must be fully liquidated. Now he wished to go over to Carthage herself (knowing that Hannibal would have to leave Italy to defend her), with the object, not indeed of annihilating her, but of ending for good her domination of the western Mediterranean. In Sicily he trained his army, which through the skeptical parsimony of his opponents in the Senate consisted largely of volunteers, with the ironical addition of the legions of Cannae survivors, long humiliated by degrading conditions of service in the island. He also set about charming the Sicilians, since he was well aware of the importance of a friendly base for overseas operations. And here we come across another important side of his nature: he was apparently a genuine phil-hellene quite apart from policy; and a large part of the island's population was Greek.[6] At the Greek city of Syracuse he reputedly walked about the gymnasium in Greek cloak and slippers, consorting with rhetoricians and athletes. This was too much for the toga-clad senators. Commissioners sent to investigate another alleged scandal were also charged with investigating Scipio's personal behavior. He countered their investigation not by evasion but by putting on a military display for them of such dazzling brilliance and efficiency that even those who had been suspicious of the African venture returned to Rome as ardent converts to it. The expedition sailed in the spring of 204.

It sailed in a hurry, and for an interesting reason. King Syphax, having engaged to support Scipio if he landed, had succumbed to a charm even greater than his, that of Sophonisba, daughter of Hasdrubal, son of Gisgo, who brought off the coup of a diplomatic marriage. He therefore honorably sent envoys to Sicily to tell Scipio the deal was off. Afraid that morale would deteriorate if this information got out, the Numidian envoys' presence being patent, Scipio told his army that they had come from Syphax to tell him that the time for invasion was ripe.

This episode is significant for the consideration of the vexed question of the "Scipionic myth," the halo of divine guidance that shone round his head. The idea seems to have arisen from his having told his troops before the assault on New Carthage that his plan of attack had been suggested to him by Neptune (in a dream, according to Polybius, of which he told them the evening before). What gave credibility to this was the fact that the attack was made possible only because the lagoon temporarily became shallower. But really this was a regular phenomenon of which he had been apprised by local fishermen. As for the rest of the myth, it was believed that Scipio used to go up onto the Capitol in the small hours of the morning before undertaking any great enterprise to commune alone with Jupiter in the inner sanctuary of his temple; and further, that the watchdogs did not bark at him (which was thought miraculous, but could be due simply to familiarity). Certainly the idea that he was especially connected with Jupiter Capitolinus was fostered. He built a triumphal arch nearby, and his own image was at some time placed in the temple instead of in the hall of his

[6] One visible sign of his philhellinism was his legendary introduction to Rome of the practice of shaving every day, as fashionable Greeks had done following Alexander.

house. He must have been well aware of traditions about Alexander and his mysterious communing with Zeus Ammon at the oasis shrine in Egypt. According to Livy, he acted and spoke in public as if guided by dreams and divine inspiration. It is only consistent to accept the idea that he could have lied to his troops about the dream at New Carthage, as Polybius and Livy believed, if he lied to them about Syphax's envoys. A Roman would consider himself justified by the interests of the state.

By the middle of the second century the myth was widespread. It had borrowed from Alexander and others the story of a mysterious snake that had visited his mother's bed before his conception. Ennius seems to have fostered in a poem the idea of his becoming a demigod after death, like the Greek heroes and like Romulus in his own epic *Annals*, which survives only in fragments. When Cicero wished to end his *De Re Publica* with a mystical revelation of an afterlife among the stars for those who had deserved well of their country, the elder Scipio was the natural medium.

But to return to events. The campaign in Africa, made possible by the prolongation of his command "for the duration," was conducted by Scipio with the same brilliance as that in Spain. The victory on the Great Plains, again won by envelopment tactics, brought Hannibal back from Italy at last, and Zama, in 201 enabled Scipio to dictate terms that scotched the war party there and left Carthage dependent and tributary though not beggared. At last he celebrated a Triumph, with great splendor, and a year later the games he had vowed in Africa. His victories were portrayed in frescoes, he took the name Africanus (the first Roman to derive one from a conquered land), and he saw his veterans settled by senatorial commissioners on domain land in South Italy. Yet he did not greatly enrich himself. Nor did he show any signs of disloyalty to the constitution or of using his influence with the people to undermine the Senate and obtain monarchical powers for himself. And when the Senate shortly afterward persuaded the people to resume war against Philip of Macedon, Scipio, though still only thirty-five, did not, it would seem, covet the command, since his veterans were prepared to serve under the still younger man to whom it fell, Titus Flamininus.

Insofar as we can discern his policy, it was one of direct rule in the western provinces (Sicily, Sardinia with Corsica, Spain), and for the rest, both in the West and in the Hellenistic East with its established mixtures of monarchies, leagues, and independent cities, of extending Rome's protectorate through diplomacy backed by military prestige. By contrast, some senators favored a "Little Italy" policy—security with no imperial commitments. It was he who founded the first Roman community outside Italy—Italica, in Spain.

Although he did not receive the command in the war against Philip, he was far from being out in the cold. In 199 he was leader of the Senate (*princeps senatus*), a great compliment for one of his years, even granted his prestige as a conqueror, and also censor, no less a compliment since the field for the patrician place was both large and distinguished. A group formed around him and his clan, the Cornelii, that soon secured more than its share of the magistracies. Yet he may well have wanted no more than to wrap himself, like Pompey on his return from pacifying the east, in his own *dignitas,* perhaps to enjoy cultural pursuits, were it not that he felt obliged to support his friends. The fact that as censor he removed no one from the roll of the Senate, despite the way in which the Fabii, Servilii, and Claudii had ganged up against him, showed that he had no vindictiveness in his nature. Indeed he was to be accused of undue softness to Carthage and Hannibal, and later to King Antiochus of Syria.

In 194 Scipio was eligible for the consulship again, having respected the rule that ten years should elapse after a previous tenure, and he won a sweeping victory at the polls. By now Philip had been tamed, but a new danger had appeared from farther east, since Hannibal, exiled from Carthage, had been received by Antiochus. News of this conjunction may have influenced the electorate. Scipio's consulship proved uneventful save for an innovation, perhaps intended as a sop, that seems out of character and that he is said subsequently to have regretted—the allocation of special seats to senators at the national festivals. But his holding office then was to have the curious effect that when he really was needed, as a general, he was, owing to the ten-year law, eligible to be employed only as a voluntary aide to his inferior brother Lucius. Meanwhile the consul was obliged to witness the spectacular three-day Triumph of Flamininus, all Roman forces having been withdrawn, against his own better judgment, from Greece. But 191 was to see the high-water mark of the Scipionic fortunes, when friends of his returned to Greece to drive out the invading Antiochus; and next year his brother Lucius became consul with his friend Laelius as his colleague. At the head of the first Roman army to cross into Asia, the Scipios gave diplomacy a chance; but the terms were too stiff for Antiochus, who had to be crushed at Magnesia in 189.

The sequel was melancholy. No suggestion was made that Lucius' term of office should be prolonged, and the brothers returned to Rome to find their friends under attack. They had become too grand, with their titles of Africanus and Asiaticus, for an oligarchy of equals. Though Lucius (after some opposition) was allowed a Triumph, Publius was soon accused of a comparatively minor irregularity concerning the application of an indemnity extracted from Antiochus. Reminding the senators that fifty times that sum had been deposited by the brothers in the Treasury, Scipio tore up the account books in their faces and even laid hands on a sacrosanct tribune when he was about to arrest Lucius. This conduct renewed their fear that the popular hero would appeal to the people over their heads. With similar arrogance he told a quaestor who balked at opening the Treasury on a forbidden day that it was thanks to himself that the Treasury had any locks at all. Finally he was himself brought to trial, in 184, on charges of improper negotiations with Antiochus six years previously, including the spontaneous release by Antiochus of Scipio's captured son. The Senate disapproved in any case of personally initiated negotiations. It was also arguable that the terms eventually granted had shown undue partiality to the king; and Scipio had dealt as a friend and equal with both Philip and Antiochus. He won a Pyrrhic victory on this occasion by appealing once more to his deserts as savior of the state: if not for him no one would be there to speak at all. Yet the charges remained unanswered, and he withdrew, an embittered man, to his modest villa at Liternum, near Naples. There he died soon after, and there by his own wish he was buried; and from the Rostra no funeral eulogy was pronounced of the conqueror of Spain, Africa, and Asia Minor. The ultimate supremacy of the anonymous senatorial majority had been vindicated.

Yet few Romans were accorded greater ultimate glory. Dante represented St. Peter as acknowledging that the Eternal City owed its eternity to Zama. Through Cicero's "Dream of Scipio," with Macrobius' commentary, he became for Renaissance humanists an instrument of Providence, *praeparator evangelii;* and he was the hero of Petrarch's Latin epic *Africa.*

Marcus Porcius Cato

The chief instigator of the attacks on Scipio was Marcus Porcius Cato, who could hardly have been less like him (save that, as Toynbee remarks, both were natural actors), a man of genius "who, whatever he was doing, seemed to have been born for that." Born in 234 in the Latin town of Tusculum (above Frascati), he was brought up working with his own hands on a Sabine farm (presumably also family property), and he made a local reputation by going around on foot to neighboring towns in the winter intervals between campaigns to defend people free of charge by his remarkable eloquence. He, like Scipio, got his chance partly through the Second Punic War, in which he distinguished himself, and partly through the patronage of a neighboring noble, a member of the great Valerian clan, whom he was able in turn, when he had reached the top by his own merits, to secure as colleague in the consulship and censorship and to elevate to the dignity of *princeps senatus.* He was persuaded by this Lucius Valerius Flaccus to seek a political career at Rome. With his reddish hair and piercing gray blue eyes and his eloquence sharpened with biting wit, this plebeian "new man"[7] must have been a striking figure among the candidates.

We know a good deal about Cato because we have, besides Livy's account, the summary of a life by Cornelius Nepos as well as a life by Plutarch no doubt indebted to it. His living voice is heard in fragments of eighty speeches—seventy more were known to Cicero—and his extant book *On Agriculture.* He left also apothegms, a book of aphorisms on morality, and letters to his son. His advice on writing was given in four Latin words, *rem tene, verba sequentur,* which may be faithfully if diffusely rendered, "stick to the meaning, and the words will take care of themselves." Such an extremist is a magnet for spurious anecdotes, but much of the evidence is reliable.

---

[7] A "new man" was one who, by being elected consul, entered the small circle of "noble" families who almost monopolized that office, thus ennobling his own family forever.

He served in the army from the age of seventeen and saw himself as a soldier and a son and grandson of good soldiers. Strong, healthy, and temperate in his habits, he carried his own armor on the march, an orderly coming behind with his utensils. He normally drank water, taking a little wine only when he needed a restorative. In battle his shouts and behavior were deliberately fearsome. All his life puritanism was to be an obsession with him. He owned nothing that was unnecessary: needless luxury was unpatriotic, in peace as well as war. He consciously made himself a paragon of righteousness and abstemiousness, an impregnable bastion against the current of luxury and immorality as well as a champion of plebeians against aristocratic arrogance. Setting himself up as the traditional simple Roman, hostile to corrupting Greek influences, he boasted that he never wore clothes or kept slaves worth more than a small sum or drank better wine than his galley slaves, even as a campaigning consul. Indeed he boasted altogether too much for our taste, or for Plutarch's. The impression was increased by the fact that he was put into the position of making a speech on his own virtues to the host of citizens when the merits of his censorship were challenged. But he was so successful in keeping his conduct impeccable that he survived nearly fifty prosecutions unscathed.

In Quintus Fabius, five times consul and *princeps senatus* in 209, of whom his patron Valerius Flaccus was an adherent, Cato found an embodiment, though a patrician one, of what a Roman and a general should be. But when, after distinguishing himself in the decisive Battle of the Metaurus, he was elected quaestor for 204, the lot determined that he should serve under Scipio in Sicily. There are difficulties of dating about the story that it was Cato who was behind the reports that led to the inquiry by the Senate's commissioners into Scipio's behavior at Syracuse; but we may well believe that the normal godsonlike relationship of quaestor to commander did not develop in this case, especially as they were almost the same age. Incompatibility was to lead to enmity.

As praetor in Sardinia in 198, still on foot and still with only one attendant to carry his impedimenta (in this case a robe and a chalice for sacrificing), Cato went around from city to city. Firm in executing the orders of the Senate and in the seat of justice, he was yet popular because he did not burden his province with the expense of providing for a large and extravagant retinue. In 195 he was elected consul, a remarkable tribute to his character (especially as mentioned before, he was a "new man") and thus became a noble. Obtaining Spain as his province, he conducted a successful, if somewhat ruthless, campaign, in which he boasted that he had captured more cities than he had spent days in the country and taken no booty for himself beyond what he had eaten and drunk. On the strength of this victory he was awarded a Triumph. Even after his consulship he continued to do active service; and it was he who at Thermopylae, by his own account, reminded his commander, Acilius Glabrio, of how the Greek position had been turned for Xerxes three hundred years before by way of a little-known mountain path. Setting out himself to find this path, he succeeded, assisted by a mountaineering expert, after the prisoner purporting to guide them had lost his way in the dark, with the result that Antiochus was defeated and had to evacuate Greece.

It is in his private life that the virtues and limitations of the man appear most clearly. No business was too pressing to prevent his being there when his wife bathed their infant son. (She herself suckled the boy, and also the sons of their household slaves, in the touching belief that this would make them more attached to him.) Maintaining that nothing so precious as education should be left to a slave, he taught his son to read, wrote out for him in large letters a history of Rome, initiated him into law, and trained him in athletic and military exercises, in boxing, and in swimming through the Tiber's roughest places in all weather. (The boy proved delicate, like Scipio's son, though he showed bravery at the Battle of Pydna, and died when he had attained the praetorship after marrying a most eligible bride, daughter of Aemilius Paullus and sister of Scipio Aemilianus.)

When his wife, who was of higher lineage than he but of little wealth, died, he consoled himself quietly with a slave concubine (for he was not a prude in sexual matters, as is shown by the well-known tale, referred to by Horace, of his applauding a young man for going to a brothel rather than becoming involved in adultery—provided he did not make it too much of a habit). The story goes that, perceiving his son's disapproval, he went downtown and without ado married the daughter of one of his former assistant secretaries. Be that as it may, he certainly married again; and his second wife was the great-grandmother of the equally famous Cato of Utica.

When he was young he thought it unseemly to complain to slaves about deficiencies in the food and drink served to him. But later, when he entertained, he punished any shortcoming with a flogging as soon as the meal was over. For he believed in the importance of hospitality and was an agreeable host in the country to his neighbors, old and young, a well-informed conversationalist who barred only discussion of people he thought unworthy.

His attitude to his slaves was characteristic. He bought young prisoners of war whom he could train in his ways, not elegant or handsome ones, but good sleepers, if possible, since he thought these proved most amenable and hardworking. When not asleep they were expected to be busy. Their whole life had to center on the *familia,* for they were never to enter anyone else's house unless sent by master or mistress; and they were instructed, if anyone inquired what Cato was doing, to answer "I don't know." But within the *familia,* since he believed that emotional entanglements were corrupting to slaves, he arranged a prostitution system and himself fixed the tariffs. If any of them wanted to make money for themselves by purchasing and training boys as slaves, he lent them the necessary sum and kept the boys until they were ready, often then buying them for his own *familia* for the highest price bid at the sale. Where a slave was guilty of an offense for which death might be the penalty, he held the trial before his whole household. But when the slaves seemed to be living in particular harmony together, he suspected them of hatching conspiracy. And there is no mitigation for the ruthless injunction in his book on agriculture, "sell worn-out oxen ... an old slave, an unhealthy slave, anything superfluous." Plutarch was outraged, not only by this equating of men to animals, but by such lack of feeling for his animals, shown also by his boasting that, to save the state the cost of transport, he had left behind in Spain the horse that had carried him through his campaign.

The work *De Agri Cultura* is most revealing. It is really a general handbook. For instance, it contains many recipes, including the famous one, "If you want to drink a lot and eat freely at a dinner party, eat some raw cabbage soused in vinegar before and after." There are sidelights on religion. On taking over a new farm you must not forget to salute the *Lar familiaris;* and on thinning a grove you must sacrifice a pig to the god or goddess, whichever it might be, to whom it is sacred. What work can be done on holy days is characteristically prescribed in terms of a reply to a bailiff's (farm foreman) excuses. The bailiff may consult no fortuneteller, prophet, diviner, or astrologer, and perform no rites except those at the crossroads and the hearth. The female housekeeper must not meddle in religion at all without orders; and no woman may take part in, or even witness, the rites of Mars Silvanus, though even a slave male may. Religion shades into magic: there is a curious rite to be performed over a dislocated joint; and you must yourself be standing, and fasting, when you gather, macerate, and administer the ingredients of a medicine for a sick ox.

The parsimoniousness of other injunctions (e.g., "give a sick slave less food") bears on another, rather surprising, side of Cato. He was a dedicated businessman, perhaps because (like that other rustic moralist, Hesiod, whom he recalls) he was aware of the extent to which respect depends on wealth, but also because he found agriculture too precarious for a living—you could be "ruined by Jupiter" (i.e., the weather). He bought up not only natural pasturage and forests, but land with hot springs, fuller's earth, or bitumen, and even lent money on the security of ships (which was not quite respectable for a senator), though only to those who could muster fifty adventurers with a ship each. Nor did his lofty views about educating your own children prevent him from hiring out an accomplished Greek slave he possessed to educate the children of his friends.

In fact the introduction to the *De Agri Cultura,* with its conventional pieties about the sure livelihood, sterling merits, and freedom from disaffection of the peasant farmer, is the merest eyewash. The author is writing for men such as he was himself, agricultural capitalists with farms worked by slave gangs. What he has in view is the optimum size for marketing—a vineyard of about 65 acres and an olive farm of about 160.

His hatred of any form of luxury received public expression when it was proposed, after the removal of the danger from Hannibal and Philip, that a measure introduced at the height of the Punic War forbidding a woman to possess more than half an ounce of gold, or wear an embroidered garment, or ride in a carriage in the city, should now be repealed. Cato as consul inveighed against the proposal, but the women demonstrated and won the day. He was in any case a believer that women's place was in the home, he denounced their increasing influence in public life and supported a bill that forbade anyone to make a woman his heir. "We rule the world, but our women rule us," he is reported to have complained. A law of the same year, 205, had forbidden the erection of statues to women in public places. (We hear that there was one of Scipio's daughter Cornelia, mother of the Gracchi; and among women noted for display of luxury in clothes and utensils at women's festivals was Scipio's wife, Aemilia.)

Cato had to wait another eleven years to achieve his ambition, years in which anxiety increased about military indiscipline and influxes of oriental luxury. Then, in the aftermath of the Bacchanal scandal, with an avowed policy of cleaning up society, and contrary to the wishes of the nobles, he was elected to his famous censorship of 184. Every censorship ended with a ritual purification of the people (*lustrum*): this was to be a moral one. As censor he had authority simply to issue edicts. Cato put what amounted to a 3 percent tax on ornaments, women's finery, and certain vehicles. Statues and other art objects were taxed.[8] His heaviest tax was on recently bought slaves worth more than 10,000 *asses* (double the normal price) who were under the age of twenty. This was directed mainly at those who had been affected by the Greek habit of keeping elegant pages and catamites (male concubines); a good-looking slave could fetch more than a farm, he complained.

In reviewing the membership of the Senate he expelled several members and did not confine himself to juniors, as was usual. One was a former consul, Lucius Flamininus, brother of Titus the conqueror of Philip, whose crime was to have beheaded a condemned prisoner at a feast to gratify his Carthaginian catamite, who had complained that in order to be at his side he had had to miss his first gladiatorial show. When challenged by Cato to clear himself he was convicted by his silence. A possible future consul was expelled for kissing his wife in broad daylight in front of his daughter. One Nasica, a Scipio, was punished for an unseasonable joke about his wife.

When he reviewed the Equites, he expelled with ignominy an enemy of his on the pretext that he had neglected some religious rite of his *gens,* jeering at him also as being disqualified by fatness for cavalry service. He also refrained from prolonging the right of Lucius Scipio to a public horse, a calculated insult. The "new man" was castigating all deviations of the nobles from the strict path of rectitude, some of which had become common form. Ancestors were irrelevant: what mattered was how you yourself behaved.

This lack of respect for status he carried into the other sphere of a censor's responsibility, public works. Private individuals were made to pull down build-

---

[8] He especially disliked statues and was scandalized to learn that they were raised in the provinces even to women, even to two Greek cooks. One can only imagine his reaction when Lucius Scipio put up a statue of himself in Greek costume on the Capitol. By 158 the private erection of statues was to become such a nuisance that it had to be restricted to those voted by the Senate and People.

ings that encroached on public land. By contrast he built, against senatorial opposition, a covered place alongside the Forum for the transaction of public business. Called after him the Basilica Porcia, it was perhaps the first example of a Greek-type building erected in Rome, although it was in the old Tuscan style, not the new Hellenistic. Private individuals were also stopped from diverting public water to their houses and gardens. Fountains were paved, drainage improved, and sewers constructed to serve poorer quarters that had had none. In the teeth of senatorial opposition, led by Titus Flamininus, Cato strove to have contracts for works allotted to the lowest bidder, and for tax farming to the highest. If senators and businessmen fumed, the people at least were pleased. They voted the erection of one statue he is not recorded to have deplored, of himself, in the Temple of Health, though he is said to have boasted previously that his only image was one carried around in the hearts of the citizens.

In the history he wrote late in life, called *Origins,* perhaps the first history written in Latin and an important source book for later writers, he put the Romans in their place by describing the origins of Italian cities as well as the capital, emphasizing that this one or that was far older than Rome. He devoted two books to the discipline and way of life of Italian peoples, attributing what was good in Roman mores to his Sabines, and inserted an encomium of Italy that was to find successors in Varro and Vergil. In describing the Second Punic War he named no general, so as to discourage a personality cult and give due credit by implication to the rank and file, and emphasized this by mentioning only two names, those of an obscure tribune of the soldiers who had done particularly meritorious service, and Surus, bravest elephant of the Carthaginian army. By contrast, Scipio had allowed his own head to replace Hannibal's on the coins of captured New Carthage, and Flamininus had gone so far as to have coins struck in Greece with his name as well as his head on one side and Victory on the other. (To the Romans, heads on coins suggested kings; and it was 150 years before that of another Roman was seen on one.) Cato also objected to Roman generals taking poets in their suite to celebrate their victories, after the manner of Alexander, as Marcus Fulvius Nobilior had taken Ennius.

But although his censorship was salutary in exposing present practices to the light of earlier integrity, Cato was reactionary in politics, castigating symptoms without getting down to root causes. He achieved nothing permanent except a legend. The natural tendency of a "new man" who has arrived is either to succumb to the aristocratic embrace or to take revenge. Cato seems to have been vindictive, to have enjoyed prosecuting and exercising his cutting eloquence, and he was still prosecuting at the age of ninety. His feud with Scipio and his friends, no doubt sharpened by their philhellenism, was unfortunate, for they were among the more enlightened people of his day. Without actually securing convictions, he succeeded in smearing them. He was right in advocating a fair chance for "new men," but he exacerbated politics without achieving, or even aiming at, reform. Acilius Glabrio, for whom he claimed to have won the victory of Thermopylae, was a "new man." Cato accused him, when they were rival candidates for the censorship, of holding back part of the spoils, but withdrew the charges with suspicious readiness once he was himself elected. In his last years his animosity was directed against Carthage, though he had favored leniency to Macedon and peace with Rhodes. Having observed with alarm, while serving on a commission there, her revived prosperity, he thereafter ended every speech, whatever the subject, with "and my proposal is that Carthage be annihilated"; whereupon Nasica, a Scipio, took to ending his with "Carthage must be spared," giving an eminently Catonian reason—that Rome needed an external threat to keep her from becoming flabby.

Most unfortunate of all was his excessive reaction against the influence of everything Greek—medicine, philosophy, rhetoric, poetry, fine arts. To some extent he was acting a part, that of the honest, ignorant countryman, concealing his wider interests. In his history he allowed that the earliest settlers in Italy were Greeks, his own Sabines descended from a Spartan called Sabus, Tibur (Tivoli) founded by the Arcadian Catillus. The old name Quirinus, identified with Romulus, he derived from the Greek work *kyrios.* Perhaps he had no choice here if he was not going to invent against all tradition. But he seems also to have spoken Greek from the first and had a thorough knowledge of Greek literature; moreover, to be a prolific writer, as he was, in itself betrayed Greek influence. The first three books of the *Origins* were examples of a contemporary Greek genre, *ktiseis,* "foundations." He knew Herodotus' account of Thermopylae and Aristotle's theory of the ideal mixed constitution. It was he who brought the half-Greek Ennius to Rome with his forces returning from Sardinia, whether advisedly or not. (He may later have come to regret having introduced this hellenizer of Roman literature, the translator of the subversive book of Euhemerus, who asserted that the gods were men deified by men, the close associate and eulogizer of the Scipios.)

Socrates he dismissed as a prattler and revolutionary, justly put to death for questioning the faith and laws of his city. But it was really the contemporary Greeks to whom he took exception. When Scipio, at Polybius' instigation, approached him about the return of the Achaean hostages cruelly and unnecessarily detained in Italy for so long, three hundred out of an original thousand, he only replied, "As if we had nothing better to do than to sit here all day and dispute whether some wretched old Greeks should be carried to their graves by Roman or Achaean undertakers." Professing to believe that Greek physicians could not be trusted to give reliable service to non-Greek patients, he wrote his own handbook for his household. The last straw was the visit to Rome in 155 of the embassy of three Greek philosophers (see p. 13). The young went wild, especially about Carneades, who made a speech commending absolute justice on one day, and on the next argued that absolute justice would require Rome to give up all she had conquered: since she would clearly be very unwise to do so, it was evident that justice could be incompatible with wisdom. This was too much for Cato. When the three put their case in the Senate, he proposed that it should waste no time over the matter, since these Greeks were so persuasive that they would obviously get whatever they wanted: let them go home and leave young Romans to listen to their laws and magistrates as hitherto. His fears of rhetoric were not groundless, but when he prophesied to his son that Rome would lose her empire when she became infected with Greek literature, he deserved the scorn that Plutarch could not forbear to express. Simply putting the clock back was no solution.

He survived until 149, and if legend is true, mellowed. In Cicero's dialogue *On Old Age* he appears as the hero, and as a friend of Scipio Africanus the younger, the destroyer of Carthage, who, though both nephew by marriage and grandson by adoption of his enemy Africanus the elder, was also brother of his daughter-in-law, Tertia Aemilia—which only shows how misleading it may be to construct hypotheses on the assumption that Romans behaved in accordance with consistent feuds and alliances. The aged plebeian "new man" had become the friend and connection by marriage of the young patrician noble.

The images of both Scipio and Cato were no doubt doctored by mythologizing annalists, and the conflict between them may have been antedated and overdramatized. But between them their lives and personalities give us a glimpse of the individuality that could coexist with the rigid senatorial orthodoxies of their day; and they symbolize the conflict in the soul of Rome in this transitional period between devotion to the old way of life and the spell of the Greek mentality, to which we may now turn.

Chapter Three

THE IMPACT
OF GREECE

The cultural history of Rome became progressively the history of her transfiguration through contact with Greek ideas. Legend apart, she was early a debtor to Greece through her Etruscan masters. Through them came the Greek alphabet, vines and olives, bronzes and ceramics, and crafts of war. Rome was like any other Etruscan-ruled city and resembled a Greek polis with her acropolis (the Capitol), her agora (the Comitia), and her boule (the Senate). Heraclides Ponticus, writing of Rome's temporary capture by the Gauls in 390, referred to her as a Greek city. Six years before that event Camillus, on capturing Etruscan Veii, had dedicated a bowl to Apollo at Delphi.

Religion

Indeed Greek influence was particularly felt in the sphere of religion. The old Roman religion of spirits (*numina*) was largely impersonal. Even the sex of some deities remained uncertain. But other gods were early imported. Minerva, from Etruscan Falerii, formed a triad on the Capitol with Jupiter and Juno. Some newcomers, absorbed as Rome's influence spread, were admitted even into the *pomerium,* the sacred heart of the city—Hercules, for instance, and the twins Castor and Pollux, who came from Tusculum. The gods were still largely functional, names with little personality attached. But Hercules, connected with trade, was certainly the Greek Herakles, and the twin gods were the Greek Kastor and Polydeukes. The more the Romans came to know about the Greeks, the more they sought to identify their gods with Greek gods. Thus Jupiter the sky god could clearly be equated with Zeus; Minerva the handicraft goddess, with Athena. The Greek Olympians were far from impersonal: they were a family with all the passions and experiences of humans. So first by word of mouth, and later through literature and art, the Romans acquired what they had lacked before, a rich mythology. Yet the old *numina* had been impressive for their very impalpability, and gods with human form and all too human biographies, though at first easier to deal with, were eventually to prove less credible.

Another Greek import destined to be of great influence was the Sibylline Books, which reputedly came from the old Greek colony of Cumae, north of Neapolis. In fact all importations of Greek deities were initiated by these Books—Demeter, Dionysus, and Persephone (under the names of Ceres, Liber, and Libera) as early as the beginning of the fifth century—though the Senate kept a tight control of their prerogatives. The Books were kept secret in the Temple of Jupiter by a permanent Board of Ten, who consulted them by order of the Senate in times of crisis. It was they who, during a plague in 399, prescribed the first *lectisternium*. Gods in human form desiring food and drink were a Greek conception; and their feasting supplied the element of melodrama that the crisis seemed to call for. It also provided an occasion when the whole population could assist instead of having a priestly aristocrat do mumbo jumbo on its behalf. All distinction between indigenous and imported gods was finally obliterated at the great *lectisternium* of 217: the Sibylline Books had superseded the old *ius divinum*. In the next year, after Cannae, Fabius Pictor, who wrote a history of Rome in Greek, headed an embassy to Delphi to inquire what the Romans should do to defeat Hannibal. When Roman armies first crossed into Greece in the second century, their commanders made offerings at Greek shrines, giving an example to their troops, and thus senatorial control was loosened.

Growing Greek Consciousness of Rome

The Greeks in turn began to take notice of Rome toward the end of the fourth century, their awareness stimulated by the Sicilian historian Timaeus. Alexander the Molossian, an adventurer and an uncle of Alexander the Great, entered into relations with her. Demetrius Poliorcetes, King of Macedon, appealed to her in 290 to keep down the pirates of Antium. In 326 she captured Neapolis (Naples) and began to be looked to as protector of the weak oligarchic cities of South Italy (called Magna Graecia) against marauders from the mountains, more effective and acceptable than the various champions summoned by them from Greece. In 275 she outfaced the last of these, her rival, King Pyrrhus of Epirus. Now that she had united the whole peninsula southwards from where the Apennines cross it, she derived Greek influence directly from Magna Graecia rather than indirectly from Etruria. She had effectively made Italy a part of the Greek world; and later she signalized this by coming into line with Greek numismatic practice and striking a silver coin modeled on the Athenian drachma.

An immediate result of Pyrrhus' resounding nonvictory was that King Ptolemy Philadelphus of Egypt sent a mission, which was reciprocated, to make a pact of friendship with Rome. One of his poets, Lycophron, in his *Alexandra*, a long oracular utterance put into the mouth of Cassandra, prophesied in riddling terms the coming greatness of Rome. Soon Massilia (Marseilles), an old Greek colony, was invoking her aid against encroachments by Carthage on her commercial sphere of interest in the direction of Spain. Increasing trade abroad led to the appointment, in 241, of a "praetor for foreign affairs," to deal with disputes between Romans and foreigners on a basis of equity. When in 229 she was able to report to Corinth that she had, as invited, put down the pirates that plagued the Greek seaboard of the Adriatic, her citizens were formally admitted to the Isthmian games, which was almost tantamount to being made honorary Greeks. And indeed, though officially the Romans were "barbarians" (Plautus retains this term for them in the mouths of Greeks in his plays), they had long been regarded as akin. Polybius never applies the word to them when speaking for himself. King Philip of Macedon remarked in 200 that no one who saw a Roman camp could think of its makers as barbarians. His younger son, Demetrius, having lived at Rome as a hostage from 196 to 191, came to regard it almost as his home.

The Greek world had been preoccupied with the East, even as far as India, when the Second Punic War woke it up to what was happening at its back door. Already in 229 Rome had established a protectorate over the east coast of the Adriatic. All Greece, even the islands off Asia Minor, so Polybius tells us, now turned its eyes westward, aware that its future would be in the hands of the victor. When Philip of Macedon was discovered in 214 to have been intriguing with Hannibal, the Romans espoused the cause of the Greek cities that were his subjects or his enemies. Fortunately for these cities, there had arisen during the war a wave of philhellenism at Rome, led, as we have seen, by Scipio himself. It attracted men endowed like him with a broader humanity, anxious to earn the good opinion of the Greeks. They wanted to be hellenized, though on their own terms. It is possible that Fabius Pictor wrote his history of Rome in Greek in order to present her case to them.

Official Policy Toward Greece

After the defeat of Carthage the Senate embarked on a new policy for the East. It had tried one of peace with Philip and failed. It now gave him an ultimatum, to stop waging war against Greeks on pain of incurring Rome's enmity, and after war ensued, demanded in 198 that he should evacuate the whole of Greece. The victory of Cynoscephalae in the next year put the Senate in a position to enforce its demand. The instrument of its policy was Titus Flamininus, who had been elected consul before the age of thirty. There is no real evidence that he was culturally a philhellene, but he was well qualified for his assignment. He introduced a new flexibility into Roman diplomacy. Plutarch describes him as generous, averse to violence, never nursing grudges, persuasive, and good at saying forceful things with humor. He had had experience with Greeks when in command of the garrison at Tarentum during the Hannibalic War. He knew their language and, what is more, was prepared to speak it to them.

After Cynoscephalae the Greeks may well have assumed that they had merely exchanged one master for another, Philip for Rome. "Freedom" for them had long ago come to mean little more than local autonomy, something not incompatible with being garrisoned and paying tribute. At the Isthmian games of 196 Flamininus' herald came forward to announce Rome's intentions. Freedom was to be restored to the Greek communities, without garrison or tribute, and with the retention of their traditional laws. The Greeks could not believe their ears and asked the herald to repeat his proclamation. They then went wild with joy. Flamininus was asked to preside at the Nemean games and did so gracefully. He dedicated at Delphi his own shield, six others, and a gold wreath, with proper Greek epigrams in pairs of elegiac couplets attached. And he became the first, and for long the only, Roman to whom a cult was established, one destined to survive for three centuries or more.

The Senate's policy appears to have been as follows. Averse to annexation as ever, it would extend to the Greek communities a protectorate analogous to that of patron and client with which it was familiar in its social life. The only limitation on Greek freedom would be a moral one, the obligation of gratitude, *pietas* in return for *fides*. With this policy, prompted no doubt more by regard for Rome's interests than for those of the Greeks, Flamininus identified himself, though he was prepared to infringe *fides* on occasion for the sake of expediency and he was not above double-dealing that may even have been self-interested. When the commissioners sent out to implement Rome's decision, nervous about the intentions of Antiochus of Syria, wished to retain control of the three fortress towns that Philip named "the fetters of Greece," Flamininus managed to dissuade them from an act that would have frozen the warm new Greek trust in Rome's good faith. And his policy prevailed when all her forces were withdrawn from Greece in 194. Meanwhile he endeavored to bring home to the Greeks the ill effects of their factions and persuaded some communities to recall their exiles. His protestation of his own good will and Rome's was eloquently expressed in a letter to a Greek city that has come down to us because the recipients had it engraved on marble. Crowns of gold presented to him by the cities of Greece, to the number of 114, were carried in the procession on the last day of his Triumph. By making Roman control psychologically acceptable to many Greeks he profoundly affected future relations between the two peoples.

If philhellenism at this period was to a large extent a matter of policy, it was a policy that Rome actively pursued. Already at the Olympic games of 208 a Roman envoy had invited all refugees from Greek Sicily to return to their homes, where their property would be restored; and Scipio honored this undertaking for the Syracusans in 205 at the cost of evicting some of Rome's Italian allies. After Cynoscephalae envoys were sent to Antiochus requesting him to free the Greek communities under his sway, and when he tried to take advantage of Philip's defeat and secure pickings, he was told bluntly, "No Greek shall ever again be subject to foreign rule," though later Rome found it convenient to forget this. The policy paid. Greek cities in Asia Minor began to dedicate temples to a new goddess, Roma; and states that had a grievance against Antio-chus, even leading ones like Rhodes and Egypt, began to take their complaints to the Senate. Among them was Athens, for which the Romans had a particular regard because of her great past, her continuing cultural leadership, and her independence of Macedon. Some said that a minor grievance of hers provided the Senate with its pretext for reopening the Macedonian War in 200; and it was out of deference to her that the Romans softened their terms to the recalcitrant Aetolian League in 190.

The honeymoon period of relations between Rome and the Greeks, associated with the activity of Flamininus, lasted for only a few years. The Greeks did not understand what was expected of clients: it had to be spelled out to the Aetolian League. In 184, faced with more recalcitrance from the Achaean League, Rome gave what amounted to orders. The Senate, besieged by plaintive embassies, became aware of the constant hostilities within and between Greek communi-ties, where the alternating upsurge and repression of those demanding redistri-bution of land and cancellation of debts caused chronic bloodshed. Rome also resented the ingratitude that great powers that are generous often experience. She began to be devious herself in dealing with them, generally favoring oli-garchs, as ever, against democrats. After the defeat of Antiochus she never recognized any state as an equal. Besides, even philhellenes could not help discovering, now that they were at close quarters, that these Hellenistic Greeks, however bright and talented, were not the same as those of the classical age, whom they had come to admire through reading their literature. As Cato put it: "The words of Greeks are born on their lips, those of Romans in their hearts."

On the Greek side a change of feeling set in after the defeat of Antiochus had brought security. Polybius noted that a minor reverse suffered by the Romans in 171 caused widespread satisfaction. He attributed this to the human ten-dency, evident at the games, to favor the weaker; but actually the Greeks, besides being treated in a somewhat highhanded manner, may have felt they would prefer to live between balanced powers, to either of which they could appeal, rather than under the protectorate of one. Nevertheless the Romans always treated Greeks more indulgently than they did Macedonians or Africans or Spaniards. There was a "special relationship." From this time, however, "divide to rule" seems to have become a positive policy in their dealings with them, as it had been with their Italian allies.

After Pydna Aemilius Paullus had the courage to earn the disapproval of his troops by insisting on discipline. Restraining himself equally (by Roman stan-dards), he took no personal booty except the twenty-thousand-volume library of the Macedonian palace (the palace where Aristotle had taught Alexan-der), which he destined for his sons—the first great library to become available at Rome. Following his victory he toured Greece, with his son the younger Scipio as his aide, restoring peoples to liberty again and visiting places of historic and cultural interest. All were astonished at his affability and his concern for their affairs, even their pastimes. At Amphipolis he held an elaborate festival graced by performers from all over Greece, to which even Asiatic Greeks were invited. On the other hand he carried out enormous deportations from Epirus, the excuse for which is obscure, with crafty efficiency. Plutarch credits him with repugnance; but no Roman commander refused to carry out even the most ruthless decisions of the Senate, not even otherwise upright characters such as Aemilius and his son, or Tiberius, the father of the Gracchi. The danger now past, Rome cared less about appearances: she behaved as what she was, the dominator of the world.

Though Greek envoys had, until Sulla's time, to address the Senate through an interpreter, decisions affecting them were drafted in their language also; and by now many Romans of the ruling class understood it, whereas Carthaginians, at least up to Hannibal's day, were discouraged from learning it and advised to use a public interpreter service. There were schools of Greek declamation at Rome as early as 161. Aemilius spoke consolatory words to the defeated and captive Perseus in Greek. "The fondest father in Rome," he had procured expert Greek slaves to train his sons in various skills. One of them, Scipio, also had lessons from Metrodorus, whom the Athenians considered their best philosopher. This, and not Cato's, was to be the future pattern of aristocratic Roman education. Tiberius Gracchus engaged Greek teachers for his two sons, the future radical reformers. He himself was familiar with various Greek dialects and published a speech he had made to the Rhodians in their language. (It was left to Cato to make a point of addressing the Athenians in Latin though he knew their language quite well.) But the language must have been widely familiar in other classes also at Rome. There was an influx after the Pyrrhic and Punic Wars not only of skilled Greek slaves, many to be freed, but of free Greek artisans and professional men. At this stage, before the arrival of thousands of barbarians, the common people of Rome must have contained a fair proportion of men much more cultivated than the original plebeians, perhaps than some senators.

Until the middle years of the third century the Hellenization of Rome had progressed gradually and perhaps imperceptibly. It now gathered pace. In the words of Mommsen (*History of Rome*), "The Romans began to feel the lack of a richer intellectual life, and to be startled, as it were, by their own utter lack of mental culture." In the twenty-three years of the First Punic War many Romans saw service in Magna Graecia, including the cultural centers of Sicily. It is significant that the first Roman Festival after victory was won, in 240, included as a supplement to the circus races the novelty of Greek plays, a tragedy and a comedy, in Latin versions composed by Livius Andronicus, a teacher of Greek origin who had been freed from slavery by his master. If it is true, as one tradition asserts, that he was brought to Rome as a small boy among the thirty thousand captive slaves from Tarentum in 272, then he must have acquired at Rome not only his mastery of Latin but his Greek culture, in a milieu of Greek slaves and immigrants. These plays, and his translation of the *Odyssey* into the old Italian measure called Saturnian, really inaugurated written Latin literature. (The previous poetry implied by the existence of this measure may have been largely oral.) They also inaugurated translation as a European art transcending mere word-for-word rendering. The astonishingly rapid development of Latin literature was due to his pioneering enterprise. He had to select or coin a poetic diction, match Greek words with Latin, and recognize and develop the peculiar potentialities of the language. His *Odyssey* was read in schools for at least two centuries—by Horace, for instance. We have the titles of eight or nine of his tragedies. They suggest that he went back beyond the Hellenistic tragedians to the great ones of the fifth century. If so, this was in itself a signal service. Though Cicero, who knew his plays, pronounced them not worth a second reading, in historical perspective he is a major figure.

Hard on his heels came a greater genius, Naevius—the only one of the early poets to be born a Roman citizen—outspoken, full of "Campanian pride" and the new Romano-Italian patriotism. He is best known for his epic in Saturnians on the First Punic War, into which he inserted the story of Aeneas' coming to Rome from Troy by way of Dido's Carthage. Representing Rome as founded by the will of the gods, this South Italian presaged Ennius, and ultimately Vergil, in recognizing the Romans as a people with a mission. But he also wrote plays, not only versions of Greek ones to rival those of Livius, whom he surpassed especially in comedy, but original ones on Roman subjects. It would appear that he was the first and last Roman dramatist to introduce personal remarks, in this recalling rather the Old Comedy of Aristophanes than the New of Menander, which nevertheless must have provided his basis. Anyway, his outspokenness provoked the powerful family of the Metelli, and he ended his days in exile. "It is dangerous," said Ennius, "for a plebeian to mutter aloud"; even under the republic this was so.

It was at the time when philhellenism was at its prime at Rome that Ennius began his literary career. He revolutionized Latin poetry by replacing the Saturnian with the Greek hexameter. He could hardly have ventured or accomplished this if his audience had not been to some extent attuned to the rhythms of Greek poetry. Ennius' contemporary Plautus further familiarized the Romans with Greek meters and with the ever-popular New Comedy of fourth-century Athens. Plays were connected with religious festivals, of which several new ones had been established during the Second Punic War. The world of New Comedy was a gay one in which, for instance, young men, abetted by sympathetic slaves, deceived their fathers in their pursuit of glamorous courtesans, whom they could not however legally marry until, in the denouement, the girl turned out to be freeborn after all. Plautus introduced odd references to Roman institutions that amused, as anachronisms do, by their incongruity, and a great deal of Roman spirit. But the audience thoroughly understood that this was a Greek world, a world of temporary escape from the moral restraints of normal life. He could not, however, make a courtesan an idealized human being like Habrotonon in Menander's *Arbitrators*: that would have been too much for the matrons of Rome in his day. And occasional hints suggest that he has a mild contempt for this Greek way of life and expects to carry his audience with him. *Pergraecari* was the word—"to be ever so Greek."

This was in the time of Scipio Africanus. In the next generation, in the time of Aemilius Paullus, there appeared in the circle of his son Scipio, then barely twenty years of age, an African slave who acquired on manumission the name Terentius. The six plays of Terence, though not slavish imitations, are conscious efforts to reproduce far more nearly the spirit, style, and appurtenances of Greek New Comedy. The Hellenization of Rome had in fact proceeded so far that instead of having Greek comedies adapted for the Roman stage simply because there were no others available, as by Plautus, the object had become to put on something as Greek as possible. Plautus was out to make his audience laugh. Terence was more interested in presenting them with problems of complex situations and drawing subtle characterizations. And by now it was no longer shocking to depict a magnanimous courtesan, such as Thaïs in the *Eunuch,* who knows what love is and really loves Phaedria.

The free of all classes and ages, and both sexes, were admitted gratis to the performances, though women had to sit at the back, presumably so as not to distract and tempt the men. The early Roman plays suggest some reflections on this audience. It seems to have filled the wooden stands erected for the festivals. Greek words were retained in the titles, used here and there in the text, and adapted for punning and coinage. We must suppose that a fair proportion of those present were familiar also with Greek meters and Greek mythology. As mass audiences go they cannot have been so very crass. They responded generously to Plautus' high-minded *Captives* and to the contest in self-sacrifice between Orestes and Pylades. Plautus could count on burlesque of styles being appreciated. More surprising is the intellectual effort expected by Terence's plays. It is true that there was less competition in entertainment than there is today, and true also that at the first production of his *Mother-in-law* the audience melted away to see boxers and a tightrope walker; at the second, to see gladiators. But the fact that they generally sat through these tragedies and comedies (we gather that, predictably, they preferred comedy) says much for their taste and intelligence, even though Plautus felt obliged to cater to the simpler ones with slapstick humor, as Shakespeare catered to his "groundlings."

The conscious foreignness of Plautine and Terentian comedy was emphasized by the costume, the Greek cloak, which gave it its name, *palliata.* But in the time of Terence there arose a new variety, the *togata,* set in Italian towns, with ordinary characters such as dry cleaners and weavers wearing the Italian toga. This had a directly opposite appeal, to people's love of genre, of seeing their own familiar world portrayed. There was more here about marriage (and incidental cuckoldry), less about smart courtesans. And, significantly, no slave was here allowed to be shown outwitting his master. This was to be real life. Side by side with it there persisted native Italian farces with stock characters, the so-called Atellane drama, something like the *commedia dell'arte.*

The other native production, much older, was satire, characteristically Italian in being a hodgepodge, varied in meter and subject, enlivened by fable and so forth. It became literary, nondramatic, though dialogue remained a frequent ingredient. We know little of what it was like at the early stage. To what extent, when it became literary, it received Greek influences is a moot point. How it acquired the quality we call satirical will be explained in Chapter Four.

The status of poets at this period was odd. Unlike prose, poetry was no occupation for a gentleman but for freedmen and other such humble people. The highly successful comic poet Caecilius was an Insubrian from Cisalpine Gaul, the first known Celt in literature. The profession was rather degraded in general esteem. Livius however founded a guild of writers and actors, which continued to honor him. Its headquarters was the Temple of Minerva on the Aventine. Ennius lived in the same humble quarter, modestly, with one servant. Like Livius, whose pupils he may have taken over, he read and expounded Greek poems as well as his own. He showed, however, that a poet could achieve social esteem, for he was taken on campaign by Marcus Fulvius Nobilior, whose exploits he celebrated and whose son procured for him Roman citizenship. He also wrote a poem eulogizing Africanus, and his bust was later placed with those of Publius and Lucius in the tomb of the Scipios. In his *Annals* he had no inhibition from introducing himself; and the epitaph he wrote for himself was defiantly proud: "Let no one honor me with tears or weep at my funeral. For why? I fly living on the lips of men."

Visual Arts

The visual arts also began to penetrate the consciousness of Romans in the third century. The first occasion was the Triumph in 272 of Lucius Papirius Cursor, captor of Tarentum, when statues and pictures were among the treasures displayed. Two thousand statues were carried off from the Etruscan city of Volsinii in 265. When Marcellus took Syracuse in 211 he flooded Rome with works of art looted from temples as well as secular buildings. By contrast, Fabius, when he retook Tarentum two years later, pointedly brought back one statue only, the Hercules of Lysippus, as a religious trophy; for already a group was forming in reaction against the craze for Greek things. But the tide could not be turned when the Romans became involved in the Greek mainland in the next century. Marcus Fulvius, returning after his successful campaign against the Aetolians in 187, founded a temple of Hercules and the Muses, adorning it with statues including a famous group of the Nine. The loot at his Triumph included 785 bronze and 250 marble statues. For the games that he celebrated for ten days many Greek performers were imported, and athletes as well as wild beasts were for the first time seen at a spectacle in Rome. All the royal treasure of Macedon graced the Triumph of Aemilius Paullus in 167. Rome was beginning to realize that leisure (*otium*) could be consciously cultivated as well as business (*negotium*).

In architecture the colonnade, that feature of leisurely Hellenistic life, was first introduced to Rome for the Emporium constructed between 193 and 174 in the wharf quarter. We have already seen Cato erecting the first of several enclosing buildings that rose around the Forum bearing the Greek name Basilica. It was not until 146 that marble was first used for building at Rome. Concrete, with all its potential for the grandiose, made its appearance about 120. We have no means of tracing by what stages the domestic architecture, a blend of Hellenistic and Italian such as we find in the House of the Faun at Pompeii, took hold of the capital, providing a setting for private *otium*. Servius Sulpicius Galba in the second century had a pavilion with a pyramidal roof in his grounds, separate from his atrium network, for purposes of secluded study. Many of the architects were imported Greeks. But one Roman at least became distinguished internationally, Cossutius, invited by Antiochus IV of Syria to redesign the temple of Zeus Olympios at Athens, whose completion he had undertaken to finance.

Little attempt, however, was made to develop a Roman visual art analogous to Roman poetry, though the tragic poet Pacuvius was also a painter. Nor must we suppose that the citizens, either senators or commoners, acquired quickly or uniformly a true appreciation of Greek art. When in 167 Lucius Anicius produced at his triumph four of the best oboe players in Greece, neither he nor the audience had any idea what to expect, and a scene of the wildest farce ensued. In 115 reactionary censors banned all musical instruments except the Italian oboe. But at least a respect for art spread. Mummius, who took nothing for himself from the sack of Corinth in 146,[1] marked his censorship four years later by presenting captured works of art to communities of the Roman commonwealth as far afield as Italica in Spain and Parma in the Po Valley. Corinthian bronzes became showpieces of many Roman houses.

Philosophy

But it was in the realm of ideas that Greece made most impact on Rome. The old religion did nothing for the emotional individual. If he was of the common people, he had recourse to quacks of various kinds, or more effectively to the Bacchanal rites, which were so widespread that in the "heel" of Italy, Apulia, in the year after the senatorial prohibition, seven thousand addicts were arrested at one time. Plautus seems to assume that his audience will be prejudiced against Bacchanals, but their topical interest is evinced by the titles of many Roman tragedies down to the *Stasiastae* (*Rebels*) of Accius, subtitled *The Triumph of Bacchus*. The more educated however probably had recourse to Pythagoreanism. Pythagoras was the great sage of Magna Graecia, a name to reckon with three hundred years after his death. Legend had it, anachronistically, that he had instructed Numa, the king to whom the Roman religious calendar was attributed. When, at a crisis in the Samnite Wars, the Delphic Oracle told the

[1] Some of his soldiers are said to have been seen playing checkers on famous pictures, but that could have happened in most armies at any time.

Romans to erect a statue to "the wisest of the Greeks," the Senate put its money on Pythagoras.

The chief Pythagorean doctrine was that of the reincarnations of the soul (which was separable from the incarcerating body), each new existence being determined, as to place in the chain of being, by ascetic disciplines here and purgations elsewhere. Ennius, in the introduction to his *Annals,* claimed to be a reincarnation of Homer, and he expounded the doctrine in his *Epicharmus.* In 181 there was a strange affair. A minor official dug up on land of his at Rome two coffins. One, which was empty, bore the name of Numa. The other contained books written on suspiciously new-looking material purporting to be by Numa and dealing with the Pythagorean philosophy. They eventually came into the hands of the praetor, who pronounced them subversive of religion. He allowed the discoverer to appeal to the tribunes, who passed the buck to the Senate; and the Senate authorized the praetor to burn them publicly. One can only suppose that their offense was "putting ideas into people's heads." But it is interesting that someone should have been prepared to go to such lengths to proselytize.

In one of his plays Ennius had made a character assert that philosophy should be taken in small doses. A few years later two philosophers were expelled from Rome. They were Epicureans, and one can well imagine what people like Cato would think of their hedonistic inactivity. In 161 the Senate authorized the praetor to expel philosophers and rhetoricians. The inclusion of the latter suggests that the offense was not propounding any specific doctrine but causing people to waste time. But it was certainly for what they taught as well that Cato wished to get rid of the three philosophic ambassadors in 154. The influence of the skeptical New Academy seemed particularly pernicious: Carneades threw doubt on religion.

The fact was that from contact with Greece the Romans were rapidly passing through a development in thought that had taken her three centuries. This was particularly so as regards belief in the old gods. For educated people in the Hellenistic world, such as Polybius, this belief had been superseded by philosophy, mainly rationalistic. Such rationalism did not preclude some form of belief in the existence of one god; and many vaguely believed in a power they called Tyche, in Latin Fortuna, which was something more than a personification of mere chance. We begin to hear stories of skepticism. Claudius Pulcher at Drepanum in 249 threw the sacred chickens into the sea with the words "If they won't eat, let them drink" (their not eating was a bad omen). Marcellus nullified what would have been bad omens if he had observed them by the simple device of drawing the curtains of his litter. Even Fabius Cunctator is said to have declared as augur that what was done for the safety of the state was done with the best auspices, and vice versa. One symptom was a growing difficulty in getting citizens to take on priesthoods that involved irksome restrictions. Ennius contributed by retailing the work of the Alexandrian Euhemerus, who maintained that the gods were mortals deified by man for their services, and perhaps also by his predilection for the tragedies of Euripides. And Plautus' *Amphitryon* was hardly conducive to reverent belief.

Rationalism had, or at least should have had, a striking success at the Battle of Pydna. The story is variously related, but it appears that Aemilius Paullus, on the morning of the battle, authorized Sulpicius Gallus, a tribune of the soldiers who had a keen interest in astronomy, to explain why an eclipse of the moon that had occurred on the previous night was a natural occurrence and not a prodigy. Not but what Aemilius had himself indulged the credulity of his troops, who had hopefully clashed bronze and held torches to heaven to aid the laboring moon, by sacrificing eleven heifers to her as soon as she emerged from the shadow. As M. L. Clarke has put it: "The Romans tended to live in two worlds, the Greek world of rational, intellectual speculation and the Roman world of sentiment and tradition, and the two were never completely harmonised."

Law

It is much debated, and by most scholars doubted, whether Greek influences had much effect on that most obviously Roman achievement, the law, though some have been found as early as the Twelve Tables. Abstract speculation about the nature of law was not to Roman taste, and the actual institutions of the Greek states were despised by them. They did, however, come by Cicero's time to accept the Stoic view of human law as reflecting the law of nature, emanation of the divine providence that produces order in place of "chaos and dark night"; and Greek logic and rhetorical theory were of some assistance when, in the late republic, it began to be thought necessary to systematize the structure of legal thought.

Of course Rome shared with Greece one never-mitigated harshness of law— the principle that slaves were chattels. But the Romans also accepted the Stoic view that slavery was contrary to nature, which meant that there were no valid justifications for the institution: it was just there. But as will be seen later, the need to use the slave in many social and economic roles obliged the law to treat him to a surprising degree as a person as well as a thing.

In 241 B.C. it was found necessary to appoint a second annual praetor (*peregrinus*) to share the responsibility for the judicial system with the existing one (*urbanus*) by taking over the increasing number of suits in which non-Romans were parties. Foreigners were not bound by the formalities of the *ius civile,* the law for citizens, and the new praetor therefore had greater freedom, in running his court, to grant or refuse actions. In fact, it may be that what went on in his court helped to lead to the Aebutian Law, by which the original praetor's court was also released from old formalities. The Romans naturally found that although some of their national rules of law did not correspond with what foreigners did, many of them worked well enough: for example, a promise was a promise, and the Roman courts were prepared to accept a suit on a promise (though the old Latin formal promise remained for citizens only). The rules that were recognized as belonging to everybody and were accepted in the Roman courts were called *ius gentium,* the law of the nations.

Under the influence of Stoic philosophy *ius gentium* was equated with the vague but uplifting notion of *ius naturale*; but apart from such talk it is not easy to see many practical consequences of Greek influence on Roman law, except that the categories of Greek philosophical and rhetorical discussion probably helped to sharpen and refine juristic interpretation of the rules of law as they applied to individual cases and sets of circumstances.

Luxury and Moral Degeneration

The subjugation of the independent Greek city-states by Alexander had weakened them as a focus for loyalty and endeavor. In the cosmopolitan Hellenistic world the individual was thrown back on himself. It was just when the Romans were themselves becoming more individualistic that they became involved with this people, supple, subtle, sophisticated—a dangerous contact for country cousins suddenly enriched. While historians, looking back, dated the corruption of the traditional Roman way of life, *mos maiorum,* from this or that event in the second century, all were agreed that the prime cause was the influx of wealth from the East. It has been estimated that in the thirteen years following Zama indemnities amounting to 27,000 talents[2] poured into the Roman treasury. The first importation of luxury goods was with Manlius Vulso's army, which after the fall of Antiochus had attacked and plundered the Galatians. But it got to a stage where each succeeding consul was liable to want his war so as to enrich himself and his staff. Even the commoners took their chance; not that they got very much—what each could carry himself and a gratuity graded by rank. Five thousand of Africanus' veterans volunteered when they heard he was going with his brother against Antiochus. The abolition of direct taxation after Pydna made the advantages of conquest apparent to all.

This age saw the rise to power of the *publicani,* rich contractors and financiers who had developed on a large scale, using captive slave labor, the old Greek system of family industries. Some had already, in the crisis of the Hannibalic War, stipulated that, in return for their loans, they should be exempted from service for the duration and should have their cargoes guaranteed against loss by storm or enemy action. Even so, there were some who resorted to fraud, and the Senate did not always feel strong enough to press charges against them. They were handsomely repaid as soon as conditions allowed. Now their influence began to be felt in public policy. The Senate was wary of them. After Pydna it closed down the gold and silver mines of Macedon partly, as Livy tells us, because they could not be exploited without the publicani (senators had

[2] One talent was roughly equivalent to a craftsman's earnings for twenty years.

been debarred from large-scale commercial or industrial activity by the Claudian Law of 218); and where the publicani were, there was an end of legality and freedom for the allies. Yet ten years later the ban was lifted. The publicani added to their wealth by enabling the state to exploit the extensive lands it had acquired, by supplying the armies, by tax farming from, and loans at exorbitant interest to, conquered peoples, and by reinvesting the profits in Italy and the West, largely no doubt in land.

The luxury of the newly rich took many forms, notably eating and drinking. The Greek drinking party was introduced, with its master of ceremonies and elaborate ritual of toasts. Ennius himself adapted a Greek work on delicatessen. One of Cato's complaints was that a pot of Black Sea caviar found buyers for the price of a yoke of oxen. Until 171 there had been not so much as a public bakery at Rome. Cooking had been done by the women of each house, and only for a special dinner party was a professional called in. Childless Romans—and some with children—now bequeathed sums to stand their friends huge banquets. The change came with a rush. Roman life had once been too austere, and the early misfortunes of the Hannibalic War brought it home to the Senate that morale required more entertainment. It was in the grim December after Trasimene that the old agricultural festival of the Saturnalia became the licensed jollification ancestral to our Christmas. After that festivals multiplied. At the Floralia, instituted in 173, perhaps on the model of that of Aphrodite of the Flowers in Greece, the chief attraction was obscene dances by prostitutes ending in a strip tease. The aediles responsible for organizing the games vied in extravagance, which became a form of political bribery. It may be a sign of a degenerating populace that the writing of plays (as distinct from reviving old ones) died out, and that the "legitimate stage" was overtaken in popularity by the mime, which reflected the life of the capital.

One must beware of exaggerating: only crime makes headlines. No doubt there were still reputable people in all classes. At home this was a period distinguished for harmony and good government. The Senate did attempt to stem the flood of extravagance. It forbade the new fashion of importing wild animals for shows, though the measure was repealed in 170, no doubt under popular pressure. It passed sumptuary laws. One, of the year 182, limited the size of parties, another, of 161, expenditure on parties. One object may have been to preserve the cohesion of the exclusive top class by preventing the richer members from humiliating the less rich. But such laws are notoriously difficult to enforce, and the frequency of their enactment betrays their ineffectiveness. Whereas in the first half of the third century a patrician had been expelled from the Senate for owning more than ten pounds of silver plate, the upright Scipio Aemilianus owned thirty-two, Gaius Gracchus was a connoisseur willing to pay fifteen times the value of the metal, and Livius Drusus had ten thousand pounds. As late as 125 the censors fined a man for having too expensive a house; but before long the orator Lucius Crassus, Cicero's mentor, was to own one valued at three million sesterces.

The puritans did however score one success. They persuaded the Senate in 154 to demolish before it was completed what would have been the first permanent theater in Rome, which had been promoted by the censors themselves, so that the city was without one for another century.[3] Further, the common people were for many years after that compelled to stand if they wanted to see a play. When Cato died in 149, the senators made a gesture to the antique spirit by having his bust placed in the Senate House.

Military and Official Degeneration

It must not be supposed that the Senate was indifferent to misconduct by senators holding commands abroad. Wrongdoers were often brought to book by private members acting for allies or provincials, notably by Cato. But sometimes prosecutions were not pressed. We have seen how Africanus protected his brother by *force majeure.* A significant case was that of Popilius Laenas in 173–172. He had wantonly provoked, in order to defeat, the Statielli, a Ligurian people. After a long struggle in the Senate he got away with making only minor restitution, perhaps because the lands he had seized had already been allocated to Roman citizens. The further a commander got from the city boundary, the more absolute became his *imperium.* "All power tends to corrupt . . . ," and we must remember that these men were accustomed at home to arbitrary power over their troops of slaves. Campaigns were initiated for the sake of booty, as by Vulso after Magnesia; or for the sake of winning a Triumph, however little the fighting, so that the Senate felt obliged to impose a qualification of at least five thousand killed in a single engagement. Things reached a climax in 150, when Sulpicius Galba massacred or enslaved seven thousand Lusitanians who had trusted his word. The nonagenarian Cato initiated a prosecution, but in the words of Mommsen (*History of Rome*), "The weeping children of the general and the gold he brought home with him demonstrated to the Roman people his innocence."

This was too much for the tribunes. Though senators by class, they rose against senatorial wickedness and incompetence; and 149, the year of Cato's death, was marked by the establishment of a standing court for the trial of such offenders. Unfortunately it had the weakness that the jurors were senators, any of whom might in future find himself before the court; and the dreadful tale of incompetence covered by bad faith in Spain continued until Scipio reorganized the province in 133. Thus when in 137 Mancinus made a capitulation on terms, the Senate refused to ratify these, and salved its conscience by making him an apparent scapegoat. He had to stand all day before the enemy's walls in his shirt with his hands behind his back—and he perpetuated the memory of the event by erecting a statue of himself in this guise on his return to Rome.

---

[3] Finally, in 55 B.C. Pompey was able to build the first permanent theater at Rome, but only by contriving that its semicircle of seats should also be steps up to a temple.

There may even have been an element of collusion, for he was subsequently elected praetor.

The corruption of the generals was matched by that of their armies. Upperclass young men began trying to avoid military service. In 151 officers were not forthcoming for the unpopular Spanish campaign. Scipio Aemilianus, who had been bound for Macedon, felt obliged to set an example by volunteering. When the consuls exercised their right of selection, certain tribunes, to protect their protégés, exercised their right of arrest and arrested the consuls. This at last induced a gleam of common sense: the draft was in future settled by ballot. Discipline also began to be lax in the rank and file. An ominous foretaste of this had been chicanery over the division of booty and favoritism with regard to leave in Vulso's army. Scipio, taking over from Piso before Carthage, found that soldiers were going out looting on their own, and a flourishing bazaar had grown up around the camp. At Numantia in Spain twelve years later he found not only a bazaar but two thousand prostitutes—not surprisingly, considering how long the men were kept away from home.

Scipio the Younger and Attempts at Reform

Polybius, in a memorable passage, tells how he first made friends with the young Scipio, barely eighteen, over discussion following a loan of books; and how, when other hostages were distributed to Italian towns, the brothers Fabius and Scipio persuaded the praetor to let him stay in Rome. One day, suddenly, as they were walking alone, Scipio asked Polybius why he always seemed to talk only to Fabius. Was it that, like the Romans, he thought Scipio indolent because he did not take part in lawsuits? What was he to do? His family said that what their house needed was not an orator but an enthusiastic leader. Polybius hastened to reassure him. It was only because Fabius was the elder. He said he would gladly undertake to educate him for a life of action worthy of his ancestors: there were many other Greeks who could instruct him and his brother in the literature they were so keen on. Scipio seized his hands, and pressing them with emotion cried that he could hardly wait for the day when Polybius should leave everything else, live with him, and devote himself wholly to making him worthy of his house and his ancestors. From that time Scipio was his constant companion: they were like son and father.

Scipio's first achievement was to earn in five years the reputation of being better behaved than any of his contemporaries. He then earned another for generosity to his relatives; and Polybius assures us that, despite all the wealth of Carthage and Spain, he remained a man of comparatively moderate means. As for a reputation for courage, he earned that in the royal hunting reserves of Macedon after Pydna, and on his return hunted with Polybius in the Campagna while the other young men were paying court to the great or prosecuting in the law courts. By such conduct, without injuring anyone, and by a route entirely different from the normal, he reached the highest position in the state. In 148 he achieved the consulship, at the age of thirty-seven—like his adoptive grandfather, by popular demand and before the legal age. And like his father Aemilius after Pydna, he carried out with unquestioning obedience the brutal orders of the Senate, at Carthage in 146 and at Numantia in 133. Indeed he cut off the hands of four hundred leading young men of a local Spanish town who were in favor of helping the Numantines.

Though he represented the growing number who were absorbing the good things that Greece had to offer, its literature and philosophy, he felt drawn to the aged Cato, and his severe censorship of 142 deliberately recalled Cato's of 184. He had no hesitation in blaming on Greece the contemporary vices of his generation at Rome. Fragments of his speeches recalling his people to the *mos maiorum* are extant. He denounced luxury, foppery, and the homosexual practices that were another thing Romans had picked up from Greeks, and had no inhibitions about naming individuals. Incredulous about what he heard of upper-class boys and girls going, with harp and lyre, to schools of singing and dancing, "which our ancestors considered a disgrace to free-born people," he visited one. There he saw three hundred young people engaged in these activities. One of them, the son of a candidate for high office, was executing with the castanets "a dance that would have disgraced a slave." He even degraded an Eques (knight) who, during the war on Carthage, had had a large cake made in the shape of that city and invited his friends to demolish it. In fact, for all his virtues, he seems to have been something of a prig.

On the positive side, he was interested in the more reputable products of Greek individualism, the Hellenistic philosophies. When the three philosophers came to Rome in 155, he eagerly went to hear them. But while the other young people were entranced by Carneades, he and his bosom friend Laelius were more attracted by the Stoic Diogenes of Babylon. As a result Diogenes' pupil Panaetius of Rhodes came to live for two years (143–141) in his house, after which he was his sole companion on a mission to the East and several times came over from Athens to stay with him. This association had momentous consequences. But the friends of Scipio and their influence belong to the next chapter. Attempting to reconcile the ideals of Cato and the first Africanus, he is a pivotal figure in the transition from the old Rome to the new.

In 145 Polybius, who had been at Scipio's side when Carthage fell, at last returned home. He ends his history with an expression of gratitude for concessions Rome made at his instigation in recognition of his good will and prays that this relationship may remain for his lifetime. Despite her treatment of his fellow hostages, he was devoted to her. He disapproved of radical governments and, like some modern imperialists, he could not understand how any people could prefer to be misgoverned by unscrupulous leaders of their own rather than enjoy greater security and welfare under the protection of a foreign power (as the Macedonians, deprived by Rome of Perseus, fought desperately on behalf of a cruel rebel leader who pretended to be his son). And yet he let slip a melancholy remark: "The destruction of Carthage is considered to be one of the greatest calamities. But perished Carthage has no memories: Greece lives on to remember her past happiness." Greek opinion, according to him, was divided. Some said Rome was only sensible to destroy her rival; some produced legalistic excuses for her; but some said she had no excuse and was going the way of Athens and Sparta.

In a sense the struggle between the representatives of the old Italian and the Greco-Asian ways of life was to be reenacted at the Battle of Actium. The former seemed to have triumphed there; but more than a century later Juvenal was to exclaim testily, "Romans, I cannot bear the city gone Greek." Yet it was primarily her willingness to respond to Hellenism that made Rome normative, largely for good, in Western civilization. Along with what was both sound and decadent in contemporary Greece she absorbed through literature something of the spirit of the great classical age of the fifth and fourth centuries. Vergil symbolically represented a civilized Greek, the Arcadian Evander, as already settled and courteously receiving Aeneas in the heart of the future city, on the Palatine. In historical reality, as Horace put it, "captive Greece captivated her barbarous conqueror."

Chapter Four

THE AGE OF REVOLUTION

The century-long revolutionary period of Rome, the period of violent struggle that ended only with the dominance of Augustus, is agreed to have begun in 133, when Tiberius Gracchus broke the standing constitutional consensus in deposing a tribune who obstructed his reforms, and for this became the victim of the first recorded political murder at Rome for four hundred years. But the cultural revolution had begun, as we have seen, with the accelerating influence of Greece over a century, and the economic revolution had also begun a century earlier. Since the economic one largely caused the political one, we will take it first.

Economic Revolution

The Italy that Rome united in the third century consisted of rich, arable lowlands farmed by peasants and uplands whose poverty drove the hillmen down to raid them. It became obvious, especially in Sicily, that much of the terrain was economically suited for ranching by capitalists, whose large flocks and herds could be driven to the upland pastures for the hot months, July to September—in fact, for an artificial form of the "transhumance" system already practiced in the East. The Punic Wars provided the capitalists with their chance; and the law against senators engaging in commerce induced them to invest their new wealth in land. Until now peasants, even if called up for military duty, had served only for summer campaigns comparatively near their homes. But in the Second Punic War two legions served in Spain from 218 to 211, their reinforced survivors for another five years. Those formed from the disgraced remnants of Cannae were kept in Sicily and Africa from 216 to 201. Moreover, the number of legions was increased tenfold. Old men, women, and boys had to carry on the family farms as best they could. Some farms were also ruined, with slow-growing trees cut down by the ravages of Hannibal and the scorched-earth policy of Fabius, who also concentrated people for safety in towns, into which crops had to be garnered by the beginning of summer (June 1). Large numbers of peasants drifted to Rome, stayed there to help with the arms industry, and developed a taste for city life that kept them there after the war. Why go back to drudgery on a remote and ruined plot? So capitalists could buy up small farms cheaply. Some land was also leased out by the state, and for this the rich could offer higher rent than the poor; some was simply occupied by squatting, a long-standing practice.

This process continued for fifty years after the Punic Wars, facilitated by Macedonian, Ligurian, Gallic, and Spanish campaigns. Peasants served for up to thirty years in the forgotten legions of further Spain, forgotten on purpose because it was less invidious and hazardous to do so than to try to raise new levies at home to replace them. Petitions for their repatriation, backed by successive commanders, went disregarded. Ironically, the victories of these peasant soldiers served to flood Italy with the slaves needed to run the large plantations and ranches of the capitalists that squeezed their own small farms out of business. The First Punic War had brought in seventy-five thousand of them, and it is estimated that between 200 and 150 an additional quarter of a million were transported to Italy. Capitalists could also afford to wait for the slow growth of trees, whereas some peasants had to borrow to tide them over bad years, thus falling into the hands of landed creditors. Some were bought out, some simply evicted. Meanwhile, the arms industry was converted to the manufacture of farm machinery, and the capitalists bought what they needed.

Another factor was that in the redistribution of lands after the Second Punic War priority was given to those who had made big loans in the crisis: only afterward came the turn of the commoners. And nothing of the conquered domain land of the Roman people, mainly in the far south, remained for allotments after 177. Most of central Italy was by now in the hands of the capitalists. Hence the aggressive activities of Popilius Laenas in 173–172 (see p. 63). (Already colonies had been planted in the Po Valley, at Placentia (Piacenza) and Cremona in 218.) For political reasons no land was assigned outside Italy: the ruling nation was to be kept distinct from the provinces and protectorates. One index of the dwindling of the peasantry was the difficulty experienced now in recruiting legions (there being a property qualification for service): whereas in the Second Punic War twenty-three were raised, by 180 it was hard to get nine. In 171 old centurions had to be recalled, including one from a Sabine farm who had served in twenty-two campaigns. It was the need for more peasant soldiers that primarily motivated the ensuing land bills.

Although Italy must always have been composed of small, self-supporting regions, since inland transport was difficult despite some great trunk roads so that the growing of cereals and vegetables remained the prime necessity, there was now a change of emphasis. Capitalists came to realize that whereas subsistence farming was precarious, cash-crop plantation farming of vines and olives to supply the growing cities of Italy could be more worthwhile. The loans for the Hannibalic War had been repaid largely from the territory around Rome, from which the capital could be supplied easily and at great profit. Again the peasant farmer was squeezed out, either to stay around abjectly as a seasonal hired laborer of the new master, or else, if he were more enterprising, to apply for a new farm in some distant region. Small farming thus tended to be confined to certain parts of the peninsula—mountainous country that was yet unsuitable for ranching, the Greek south coast, Campania, and the Po Valley (more wooded then, and the great place for raising pigs). For the rest, there was a considerable improvement in the general economy. The production of livestock became far more scientific; and large areas took on the appearance of a great fruit garden. This was the Italy whose beautifully cultivated lands were to evoke praise from Lucretius and Vergil, Varro and Dionysius of Halicarnassus.

But many of the dispossessed peasants drifted to Rome. There they presumably hoped to find industrial employment. Again, however, the constant influx of slaves, many of them highly skilled, would make it harder and harder to get work in the new bakeries and similar concerns, where slave and freeman worked side by side, perhaps even for the same wages.

Attempts at Land Reform

It became obvious to thinking people that new land must be found for the landless out of the great estates of Italy, which included a lot of public land that had been simply occupied by large-scale farmers. But one trouble was that some of these tracts had been in the hands of the same family for generations and had been greatly improved by it, or had been sold to other people as if they were owned outright. A more serious trouble was the self-interest of the landowners as represented by the Senate. Only one man conceivably had the prestige and popular support to break through this, Scipio Aemilianus. He knew it ought to be done, and his great friend Laelius brought forward a motion in 140. But when it became clear that the proposal could be implemented only by a long and bitter struggle, they shrank from the task.

Scipio's youthful brother-in-law and adoptive cousin Tiberius Gracchus did not shrink from it. Educated by Greeks, and a frequent companion of independent-minded Greek philosophers, he saw clearly what ought to be done and proposed a quite moderate bill that had the support of some notable senators. But he got the People to endorse two illegalities when passing it: deposing a tribune who objected and getting his own tribunate prolonged beyond one year. Soon after, on the charge of aiming to be king, he was murdered, together with three hundred of his supporters, by a senatorial gang. Even his reputable sponsors had been aghast at the rashness of his tactics; and Scipio, returning from Spain, would only say judiciously that if indeed he was aiming to be king he had deserved his death. Later writers such as Cicero and Juvenal thought of him as a rebel against the constitution, the man who inaugurated a century of bloodshed. To us he may appear rather as the only man who had the patriotic courage to try to break down a fatal wall of selfishness, however naive his trust in the casually assembled city rabble that went by the name of Concilium Plebis, and whatever political advantage he may have been seeking.

The Senate made no attempt to get Tiberius' measure reversed, though individuals evaded, by using straw men, his restriction of holdings of public land to three hundred acres a man. But the mysterious death of Scipio in 129 was alleged to be murder for his putting a brake on it. Be that as it may, in six years seventy-six thousand allotments were made—mostly to landless peasants, for the city proletariat was less interested. The success of the scheme is reflected in the register of citizens, which rose from 319,000 in 132 to 395,000 in 125. Probably no more could be done within the terms of reference, rather under 10 percent of the public land having been distributed; hence the new proposals made by Tiberius' young brother, Gaius, as tribune in 123. Gaius proposed including the leased parts of the public land in that available for allotment, and founding colonies (one at least abroad—Junonia, near the site of Carthage). He even planned to exploit conquered territory beyond the Alps for colonization, an idea not previously entertained. Meanwhile, Gaius would relieve the urban poor by selling corn at subsidized and stabilized prices to those prepared to line up for it. But he also suggested far-reaching political changes, which brought him into collision with the Senate. Eventually he was pushed by hot-headed supporters into provocative postures, and he too was killed by the backlash.

For the next hundred years land bills were on the agenda. Lengthening terms of military service were another factor frustrating attempts at reform. Originally the Roman army had been a militia recruited from those who had a stake in the country and could afford to equip themselves. But Tiberius Gracchus pointed out the irony of generals' exhortations to troops about to go into battle, to fight for family sepulchres, shrines, and altars, which in many cases they no longer had. The poor had ceased to be eager to serve their country or to bring up children. And now Marius' army reform again changed the situation. He regularized what had been already creeping in—enrollment of landless proletarians in the infantry, not merely in the baggage train as before—and instituted a professional and more egalitarian infantry of volunteers from any free class, trained in skills developed in the gladiatorial schools and serving for long terms. The army thus provided an outlet for the proletariat of both the capital and the Italian communities.

The new soldiers recruited under Marius' reform looked to their generals to supply them with allotments as well as booty bonuses by way of pension. Sulla, whose proscriptions (outlawry) and expropriations provided him with vast acres of land to spare, either sold it at high prices to millionaires like Crassus or squandered it on his favorites or used it to reward his veterans. He had to settle 120,000 people throughout Italy to fill the gaps made by the Social and Civil Wars. The land bills of the first century, notably those for the armies of Pompey and Caesar, were directed at settling veterans and less than previously at relieving unemployment in the capital. Hence the magnitude of the urban problem that still faced Caesar and the emperors after him.

But by 111 the public land in Italy had all been allotted, apart from Campania, the rich domain that Rome let out to her citizens: any future assignations must come from confiscations or purchases. Julius Caesar was far more constructive than Sulla. He tried energetically to revive peasant farming, though always with complete respect for existing property rights. For the land he purchased he gave priority, apart from veterans, to twenty thousand poor fathers of at least three children. In 45 he also made it a law that one-third of herdsmen on ranches must be freemen (partly perhaps as insurance against slave uprisings, and to create a reservoir of hardy recruits for the legions).

The Augustan regime also encouraged the restoration of the small farmer, but as a moral ideal rather than an economic practicality. It at least inspired an immortal monument, the *Georgics* of Vergil, ostensibly a didactic poem on the care of field crops, trees, large livestock, and bees, but effectually a descriptive poem—the first in all literature to be mainly such—of the landscape of the newly united Italy and of the life of the small farmer as hard but salutary and rewarding. Its idealistic character is shown by the astonishing absence of any reference to slavery (even on his Sabine farm home Vergil's friend Horace had eight slaves). There were however certain areas where owners and tenants of small farms still flourished—the Po Valley, Campania, the Greek South; nor must we forget that between Sullan times and the Battle of Actium veterans had been settled on the land to a number estimated at half a million, while Augustus settled many more in Italy and the provinces, purchasing the necessary land and paying gratuities out of his own vast resources. But beyond this he did little for agriculture.

Meanwhile the city proletariat had become more remote from its agricultural origins and consequently less interested in farming; hence the Gracchan restriction on the selling of land allotments had almost immediately to be abandoned. There remained the remedy of colonization. To begin with, though Gaius Gracchus' plans were buried, Narbo (Narbonne), founded in Gaul in 115, was allowed to develop. The strong senatorial objection to planting colonies on foreign soil had clearly become unrealistic. Julius Caesar as dictator exported eighty thousand colonists and planned many new foundations abroad, mostly in Spain and Narbonese Gaul but also elsewhere, to the detriment of provincials who had sided against him. Significantly, these colonies were to be commercial rather than agricultural. No doubt he hoped thus to offset his removal of 170,000 from the list of 320,000 city proletarians who in 58 had become entitled to corn not merely subsidized but free. But he was struck down before he could put his measures fully into effect.

Juvenal's catch phrase "bread and circuses" has been used with smug disapproval by moralists to denigrate both the providers and the recipients. But unemployment benefits and football, the modern equivalents, are not usually considered scandalous. Much is also made of the fact that holidays in the Roman year amounted to as many as a hundred days. But our weekends and legal holidays amount to over a hundred days, to which must be added two or more weeks' annual vacation. The numbers of the poor urban population were swollen by manumissions of slaves, which for the period 81–49 B.C. alone have been estimated at half a million, while their scanty earnings were shrunk by inflation due to vast influxes of gold and silver from the provinces. Some people were even reduced to selling themselves as gladiators, under the grim legal contract "to let himself be chained, scourged, branded, or killed without opposition if the rules of the institution so require." Violent fluctuations in trade terms led to widespread insolvency and consequent clamors, in 88, 63, and 48, for cancellation of debts. Caesar did at least alleviate the unemployment problem by vast building schemes—a new Senate House, a theater, a forum, the first public library, and a temple of Mars, not to mention schemes for draining the Pontine Marshes and the Fucine Lake.

Political Revolution

Rome's Relations with the Italian Allies

The other burning question of this period was that of the Italian allies. This problem, which should not have been unsolvable, was created by jealous fears of all classes at Rome—Senators and Equites for their privileges, urban plebs for their corn and seats at entertainments, peasants for their allotments of land. After the disaster of Cannae Spurius Carvilius had suggested to the depleted Senate that its members be recruited from each Latin community selected by senators. The proposal was indignantly rejected. It was inevitable that the differences of status between Rome and the allied communities be expressed in social behavior. In 173 Lucius Postumius, angry that he had not been made much of by the people of Praeneste (Palestrina) when he had visited it as a private citizen, demanded when consul that the mayor should come out to meet him and that he should be provided with free lodging and transport animals. The Praenestines acquiesced. Thus even old Latin cities were coming to be treated as inferiors. In the same year Quintus Fulvius Flaccus disgraced his censorship by stripping the famous temple of Juno Lacinia in the "toe" of Italy of its marble tiles for a temple he was building at Rome. (The Senate made him send them back, but no builder could be found competent to replace them.) In the next generation Gaius Gracchus cited the following instances. When a consul visited Teanum Sidicinum, southeast of Rome, his wife requested the use of the men's baths, had all the men turned out, and then complained that she had had to wait and that the baths were not clean; whereupon the chief citizen was stripped and scourged in the Forum. Hearing of this, the people of nearby Cales prudently passed a bylaw that no one was to use the baths when a senior Roman official was in town. A Venusian herdsman jokingly asked some litter bearers if it was a corpse they were carrying. The passenger, a young Roman official, had him scourged to death by the bearers.

Further troubles arose from the inability or reluctance of the Italian communities to provide their quota of troops. In 209, during the Hannibalic War, twelve Latin colonies (about two-fifths) pleaded for relaxation. The Senate, besides needing men badly, was alarmed by the precedent and the evidence of collusion —the one thing it had always sought to prevent—and as soon as it could safely do so disciplined them severely, demanding both regular census figures and the novelty of direct taxation. The drift to Rome made it impossible for the allies to find enough men, especially as their proportion to Romans in the legions was being raised; so in 187, by mutual consent, all their people made Roman citizens since 204 were repatriated. After the Hannibalic War was over, five thousand allies were kept under arms, while the Roman legionaries were released. The nastier enemies, such as the northern Boii, were left to the allies. The distinction became even more glaring when citizen soldiers were exempted from being scourged and allowed to appeal against military death sentences. Romans also began to take the lion's share of booty and captured land. Perhaps much of the trouble arose because the Italians wanted more land now that cash-cropping had become lucrative, but the boundaries between their territory and the domain of the Roman people were ill-defined. Each new land bill that was passed at Rome would seem to them to be a further sign that a policy of encroachment was being followed. Finally, the allies wanted to be able to vote at Rome, even though they would have to trek many miles to do so. True, they would only attend for vital issues; but the reality of the privilege was shown when citizens flocked to the capital from far and wide to elect Gaius Gracchus tribune, and again to vote his measures.

Gracchus was, it can plausibly be inferred (though details are obscure), proposing to upgrade Latins to full citizenship and Italians to the privileged Latin status, and to exempt Italian soldiers from scourging. Their bitterness was all the greater when the Senate and People refused. Since 200 there had been no good reason why all Italians should not be made citizens; instead, in 128 the full liberty of allies to migrate to Rome was curtailed, and noncitizens were expelled in 122. The need for protection against abuses by Roman officials made citizenship more and more desirable. If Praeneste had accepted citizenship when it was offered in 216, she would have been able to set the tribunes onto Lucius Postumius. In 125 the famous and historically loyal Latin colony of Fregellae, goaded into rebellion, was crushed. Rome's attitude progressively infuriated the Italians. When the younger Drusus, the latest advocate of their enfranchisement, was murdered in 91 the Marsians and Samnites raised a wholesale rebellion, the Social (i.e., of the Socii, or Allies) War, and succeeded in extorting citizenship for all free men in Italy south of the Po. Sulla, however reactionary, did at least confirm this, though not without laying Samnium waste for ages to come. At first the rebels had thought of establishing their own state, with its capital at Corfinium, renamed Italia. But many of the institutions they adopted were reflections of those at Rome, and in the end they wisely decided that they could not do without her. Coins struck after the war showed Italia, bearing a cornucopia, joining hands with Roma, diademed, and resting her foot on the globe.

The Italian burghers were good stock, generally superior in culture, in Cicero's opinion, to the Romans of the capital (he was one of them by origin). They were proud to wear the toga, and they shared in the advantages of empire. Indeed many of them emigrated, not only to the East but to Gaul, or spent the best years of their lives in trading abroad, where they stuck together in clubs. But at home also they provided industrial strength. Already in Cato's list of the best places to get various agricultural implements Rome had figured as only one of a number of centers in Italy. Julius Caesar saw the empire as a whole, with Rome as its cosmopolitan capital. Augustus, whether from original choice or because he was pushed into it by Antony's easternizing policy attuned to Cleopatra, saw the Italian nation, the manly West, as chosen by destiny to prevail over the decadent East. Vergil's *Georgics* is the great poem of Italian sentiment at its best, love of the land in all its rich variety, nostalgia for peasant life, and admiration for the works of Roman hands. In the *Aeneid* he portrayed Augustus at Actium as leading the Italians into battle backed by all the powers of Roman, Ennian tradition against a motley horde of degenerate barbarians (regardless of the fact that three hundred senators were with Antony). The second half of his epic foreshadows the Social War, the struggle that had to occur before a synthesis of Trojan (i.e., Roman) and Italian virtues could emerge.

Constitutional Changes

In 287 B.C., by the *Lex Hortensia,* the Roman plebs had won the constitutional right that the decisions of its Assembly, *plebiscita,* should have the force of law. But this did not lead, as one might expect, to democracy, because the Assembly could only vote yes or no to proposals put to it by the presiding tribune, and normally he was acting on behalf of the Senate. Important spheres of policy also, such as foreign affairs and finance, were by custom left to the Senate. The Concilium Plebis, primarily a city-state assembly, consisting as it did of the urban commoners near enough to attend regularly without the inconvenience of several days' journey, was indeed unsuited to govern. Tiberius Gracchus was revolutionary because he broke the consensus and applied the constitution logically. Further, he induced the plebs to depose a tribune who was lawfully using his right of veto, which was another of the Senate's safeguards against mob rule. And finally, at a time when the Senate had taken fresh precautions against the emergence of a dominator by letting the office of dictator fall into disuse and by enacting the policy that no one should be consul twice at all, let alone after a period of ten years, he stood in defiance of established custom for reelection as tribune for a successive year to give himself time to carry out his program. His brother Gaius saw that this was the essential means for any reformer who wished to impose his policy. When speaking from the Rostra he pointedly faced the People, not the Senate as was customary.

To deal with Gaius Gracchus the Senate devised a partial substitute for dictatorship that would be more under their control, the "ultimate decree," which invited the consuls to impose martial law. It was by means of this power that Cicero summarily executed the Catilinarians. But the Gracchi had shown how the stranglehold of the nobles might be broken; and there now began the years of struggle between the *Optimates*, the inner ring of the Senate supported by the propertied interests, and the *Populares*, politicians who sought to break the ring and get their way by manipulating the Popular Assembly. How strongly the Optimates were entrenched can be seen from the fact that between 264 and 134 B.C., out of 262 consuls elected, only 16 were "new men." Power was in the hands of about twenty noble families. The chief reason why Rome never achieved democracy was the inequitable voting system, but another was a genuine confidence in the superior competence of the Senate. There were, however, according to Cicero, three places where popular opinion could make itself felt: when a magistrate summoned the People to give it an address (*contio*); in the voting assemblies (and after 139 the ballot was secret); and by applause or withholding applause for individuals entering the auditorium at public shows or at the theater, where the audience often perceived that lines could have a topical application and applauded them with an alertness that did credit to its intelligence. There was no "Popularis" party, let alone a democratic party (which Rome never produced), though the Populares might support popular measures—whether for their own sake or to get popular backing for other ends —such as small parcels of land for the landless, corn subsidies, debt relief, a secret ballot, and personal protection for citizens and provincials. The first great Popularis was Tiberius Gracchus, his greater successors Marius, Pompey (from 70 to about 53), and Caesar.

As for the publicani, Gaius Gracchus integrated them with the Equites, the old elite cavalry of well-to-do citizens,[1] whose favor he courted by handing over to them the jury courts and the right to contract, in competitive companies, for the lucrative concession of farming the taxes in the rich province of Asia (after the manner of the Hellenistic monarchs they superseded). He made them conscious of their identity. Their potential threat as rivals of the Senate is indicated by the fact that Sulla was concerned to get rid of sixteen hundred of them by proscription, though the mere wealth of some would also make them a tempting prey to him, there being no Claudian Law in reverse to prevent Equites from investing in land, the senators' domain. In fact most Equites were landowners in Italian towns, though they were not nearly so rich

---

[1] The usage of *Eques* is confusing. Generally it refers to an *Eques Romanus*, any citizen below a senator (including those of Italian communities) who qualified by census of wealth, including any young men of senatorial family not yet in the Senate. The censors of 70 distinguished the old *elite* from *nouveaux riches* equites by the old title of *Eques Equo Publico*.

as senators. The ex-Eques Cicero, in the crisis of the Catilinarian conspiracy, succeeded in allying them with the Senate; but his dream of making such an alliance the permanent basis of the state, though possibly the best hope for Rome, was frustrated by the inveterate jealousy of the Optimates both of the Equites and of him in particular. Their influence was often felt, but mainly behind the scenes. It is noteworthy that in his work *De Republica* (*On the Republic*) Cicero makes no mention of the Equites as an estate of the commonwealth; yet his own bosom friend Atticus was an Eques and a man of great influence.

Between the two great military crises caused by the disasters of Cannae (216) and Arausio (105) only Fabius Cunctator was consul for more than one year at a time (even Africanus' command against Antiochus had to be informal). But Marius then held the consulship for five successive years, and this set the precedent for the war lords of the first century. The Senate never contemplated the radical administrative reform and heavy taxation that would have been needed to keep the raising of forces and the pensioning of veterans in its own hands. The war lords showed that power lay with the man who had a professional army of the Marian kind attached to him by long service, interested in his success, and dependent on him for retirement benefits. At first they were not constitutional revolutionaries, though Marius took it upon himself on the field of Vercellae to grant Roman citizenship to two brave Italian cohorts. Sulla, having revived the dictatorship in order to impose his reforms in the interests of the Senate, retired into private life. Pompey, returning from the East with greater prestige and popular support than any Roman general had ever enjoyed, disbanded his legions. But Caesar, who remarked once that Sulla showed by retiring that he did not know the first thing about life, took measures first to prolong and then to perpetuate his own dictatorship, apparently envisaging a Gracchantype monarchy. The Triumvirate who achieved power after his murder were ostensibly preparing the way for the restoration of republican government; but by the time Caesar (Octavian) emerged as the survivor, he did not really mean to restore it, and by then many senators were actually afraid he might. Thus began the principate; and such, in brief, was the Roman constitutional revolution.

Growth of Imperialism

The Romans acquired their empire piecemeal and for various reasons. Even Polybius could see no justification for their seizure in 238 of Sardinia, which was to become, with Sicily, the granary of their forces. In the western Mediterranean it was a case of taking over what had been the Carthaginian empire with an eye to security; but in the eastern Mediterranean it had been one of gradually being drawn into a power vacuum created largely by themselves through mistrust of the kings of Macedon and Syria. Wars so occasioned might be profitable, but there was as yet no idea of permanently exploiting the provinces. The Senate wanted to preserve the city-state character of Rome and not to have to garrison places abroad with reluctant citizens of her own. It sought control without annexation. Even after it perceived that direct rule was inevitable, it made no overall plan, created no administrative service: it simply improvised. Nor did it anticipate expansion. When Sulla enlarged the number of praetors and quaestors, he provided only for the provinces then existing. Even when the rich, ripe plum of Egypt was offered to Rome by the will of King Ptolemy Alexander I in 88, she did nothing to take up the legacy—on the contrary, she interested herself in the restoration of claimants to its throne. And there is little evidence for the old idea that the Equites promoted imperialism for commercial purposes.

And yet, by custom, down to the late second century the censors regularly prayed to the gods for an increase in Rome's possessions, until Scipio Aemilianus changed this prayer to one for preservation. It was the people who became greedy for the spoils of conquest. When Tiberius Gracchus was at a loss as how to finance his land policy (since finance was a senatorial preserve), he seized upon a chance windfall, the legacy of the kingdom of Pergamum to Rome by Attalus III. This was doubly untraditional, since foreign affairs were also a senatorial preserve; but it put ideas into the heads of the people. Until now provinces had, apart from Sicily, barely paid their way. But Attalus' kingdom, now organized as the province of Asia, was overflowing with wealth. Gaius Gracchus roundly declared the whole empire to be the property of the Roman people, for whose benefit he designed to exploit it, though with safeguards for the inhabitants. He was also the first to distribute provincial land for the benefit of the Roman poor and would have gone further if he had not been struck down. A generation later large numbers of Marius' veterans were settled in Africa.

But the big change in the Roman attitude toward empire came after the Social War of 90–89. Wealthy Italians, now enfranchised, swelled the ranks of the Equites. In the provinces Italians became very influential because they provided continuity, expertise, and local knowledge for the guidance of constantly changing governors. Rome settled down to fleecing her subjects as she had never done before, the supreme organizer of this policy being Pompey. Opportunities for profit were now deliberately sought. The demagogic Clodius in 58 proposed to finance his distribution of free corn by the annexation of Cyprus. The Roman masses were now participating in the benefits. Their self-esteem was also fed by triumphs: if they were insignificant individually as citizens of Rome, worth little more than a vote, they were collectively the lords of the earth.

In Asia at least oppression by taxgatherers and moneylenders became terrible. Exorbitant usury drove communities to sell public buildings, works of art, and jewelry, and even parents to sell their children. Unscrupulous governors levied blackmail, sold favors, and exacted fantastic sums for the expenses of themselves and their staffs. Roman nobles had become much more arrogant, whether as triumph hunters in making war on barbarians or as governors of civilized provinces where their heads were turned by adulation previously accorded to Hellenistic monarchs. They became immensely rich (none richer than Pompey and Caesar) and were expected to help Roman citizens to wealth. Cicero, as governor of Cilicia, found that he was expected to press the people of Salamis in Cyprus to pay arrears of interest at 48 percent. He refused and was then mortified to find that the usurer was his friend the virtuous Brutus, acting through cover agents; but he still refused. Cicero was a good governor himself; but how bad they could be is evident from the case of Verres, on the prosecution of whom Cicero's reputation as an orator was founded—and not all bad governors were impeached. The trouble lay in the system, by which ex-magistrates were appointed for one year only, so that they could not get to know their province well, while they relied on their year as governor to recoup by monstrous exactions the expenses already incurred on bribery in their campaign for election to their magistracy. Nor were the juries of Equites always the safeguard they were supposed to be. Publius Rutilius Rufus had been an exemplary legate to Scaevola in Asia in 94, protecting the province from the publicani. Convicted on his return on a trumped-up charge of extortion, he chose to spend his consequent exile at Smyrna, among his alleged victims. In a speech made four years after those against Verres, Cicero said, "It is hard to express, Romans, the extent to which we are hated by foreign peoples"; and in a dispatch to the magistrates and Senate from his province he referred to the difficulty of raising auxiliary troops from allies "owing to the harshness and injustice of our rule."

When a province was annexed it received a constitution. After that each governor was supreme. Only Roman citizens there remained under the *ius civile.* The incoming governor, like the praetor at Rome, issued an edict based on his predecessor's, embodying some local peculiarities and any variations he liked. Thus Cicero was pleased to borrow a clause from the edict for Asia of his old mentor Scaevola designed to give his subjects some feeling of independence, that in suits where all parties were Greeks they could use their own law. For the rest the Romans allowed local differences in religion, language, and culture to persist so long as they did not endanger security, showing only a prejudice for urbanization as against tribal systems, and for timocracy, the oligarchy of the wealthier, against democracy. But gradually an Italo-Hellenic culture spread over the empire. In Spain, distinguished teachers of Greek settled on the Baetis (Guadalquivir), and Greek was taught as well as Latin in Sertorius' school for the sons of Spanish notables at Osca (Huesca). The old Greek idea of a family, however quarrelsome, of free states gave way eventually to the Eastern idea of a world state of uniform culture under one ruler exemplified in Alexander's empire. Julius Caesar was the new Alexander. He saw Rome as a cosmopolitan city, *prima inter pares,* capital of the inhabited world (*ecumene*). Determined as he was that the Senate should in the future be powerless, he had no scruples about enrolling Gauls and Spaniards into it; and this Supreme Pontiff tolerated Egyptian cults at Rome and especially protected the Jews.

The western empire (Sicily, Sardinia with Corsica, and Spain) had been annexed for reasons of security. This was not so with the Hellenistic East, where it was rather a question of meddling that led to exasperation. Polybius might express surprise that the Macedonians were not content to live more securely under Roman rule; but it was left for his Stoic friend Panaetius in the circle of Scipio Aemilianus to propound a philosophy of imperialism that could satisfy his thoughtful friends in high places. Carneades, as we saw, took the opportunity of telling the Romans that their empire was based on wisdom (i.e., self-interest), not justice. He was the first person we know to have applied to Rome the doctrine of Thrasymachus in Plato's *Republic,* that might is right: justice was not natural but relative, different for each state. Panaetius, impressed like Polybius by his Roman associates, argued that nature had given power to the best (rather than strongest) for the good of the inferior. Rome had a civilizing mission and a right to subdue peoples who could not see where their own good lay. As God rules man, mind rules body, and reason rules desire, so the best rule the worst. This idea probably came to him from Aristotle, who used it to justify slavery; only to Aristotle the Greeks with their superior philosophy of life were the master race, the barbarians natural slaves. It was far from being an orthodox Stoic idea, for the Stoics believed in the brotherhood of man. It was a Panaetian heresy, though one that seems to have been accepted by his greater pupil Posidonius, that the Romans were nature's master race, who should be taught by philosophers to be worthy of their destiny. It was admitted into Cicero's *De Republica* and also into Augustan thinking. Hence Juno's fiat in Horace, *triumphatisque possit / Roma ferox dare iura Medis* ("and may warlike Rome be enabled to deal laws to vanquished Medes"); and Vergil's conception of Rome's mission *paci imponere morem* ("to build morality on peace").

But the doctrine carried with it the obligation to see that the conquered really were better off. Cicero, on his way to his province, declared that he felt himself to have given a surety consisting of six books (the *De Republica*), and he was as good as his word. But Julius Caesar, who as consul in 59 had promoted laws against extortion, as governor of Gaul proved "the greatest brigand of them all"; and it was only with the Augustan reforms that the provinces began to revive.

Weaknesses of the Late Republic

It is not difficult, with hindsight, to diagnose some of the diseases of the late republic. Patriotism had declined. Whereas in the Hannibalic War public reserves had not been touched until private resources had been exhausted, in the Social War public reserves were used first, then public sites sold and temples stripped of treasures in preference to taxing citizens. The Senate had once been so admirable that people like the younger Cato, himself a byword for scrupulous integrity, could not bring themselves to believe that it could not become so again. "The capital, my dear Caelius, the capital! Stay there, and enjoy a place in the sun. All residence abroad . . . is dim and sordid for those whose industry can confer luster at Rome": this from Cicero, the upright and popular governor of Cilicia, who in reality had for more than five years been able to do no public service at Rome beyond dancing to the tune of Caesar and Pompey, whom he had rashly attempted to cross. The glamour of the Forum and innate conservatism blinded senators to the fact that their city-state institutions were quite unsuitable for governing a far-flung empire. Besides, in recent times they had either been insanely ambitious for the insignia of office or absorbed in the fine produce of their fishponds. Politics fell into the hands of clandestine clubs, *collegia* (first legislated against in 64), which rigged elections and through which votes, verdicts, and violence were bought and sold. In 54 the first voting division alone absorbed ten million sesterces in bribes. The Equites, though primarily landowners like the senators, seem to have been largely devoted to making money, not always by scrupulous means. At Rome (as distinct from the rest of Italy) there was nothing between absentee landowners and rich businessmen on the one hand and the urban poor and slaves on the other. There were, of course, high-grade clerks in the Treasury (the poet Horace was to be one at the time when he was writing his *Satires* and *Epodes*). They used their expertise to lead by the nose the youthful quaestors set over them year by year till they met their match in the younger Cato, who made himself an expert and dealt severely with the malpractices he unearthed. But conservatism prevented the Romans from establishing what expansion had made imperative, a full-scale professional civil service.

Nor was there any proper police. In the fifties of the first century organized and political gangsterism grew so flagrant that Pompey had to be made sole consul for 52 to put it down. There was also no provision for economic expansion. Industry was developed mainly for internal consumption: there was not enough export trade; and if there had been, the profits would hardly have found their way into the pockets of the poor. Naturally no one thought of anything so unfamiliar as representative government or so utterly unimaginable as the abolition of slavery. Meanwhile the urban plebs, unable to govern but able to be manipulated, had been made conscious of their power, though they soon forgot to worry about the loss of it when Caesar sweetened that loss with largesses.

In view of all this, many scholars have reflected, if more palely, the blaze of Mommsen's enthusiasm for anyone bold enough to grasp at monarchy—for Caesar, in fact. He got things done. Certainly in his short dictatorship his practical genius helped him to accomplish a remarkable amount of reform, such as that of the calendar; and we may suppose he would have undertaken more if he had not been struck down. But the price was loss of liberty, which should be paramount in any state, even if it is, as at Rome and so often elsewhere, little more than liberty for a limited class. One can only sympathize with Livy, who wrote in his preface, "We have got to such a pitch that we can tolerate neither our evils nor their remedies." This ultimate impasse had perhaps become inevitable long before.

Cultural Revolution

Philosophy and Religion

In the realm of ideas the individualism encouraged by contact with Greece expressed itself in adoption of the individualistic philosophies of the Hellenistic world. The dominant influence in the period we are considering was the Stoicism embraced by the Scipionic circle. It was an influence almost wholly for good because its emphasis on morality was what the affluent age most badly needed. It gave a man something to live for, moral self-respect, and encouraged him to see himself as having a place in a universe divinely ordered for the benefit of man. The influence was exercised mainly through the presence and works of Panaetius (see p. 67). Whether the changes he made in the Old Stoicism were due to association with those Romans who were experienced in governing or to his own predisposition, it is clear that his version suited the Roman temperament. He was not interested in the paradoxes and impracticalities of his predecessors, such as the concept of the Stoic Sage, an impossible kind of saint, as an ideal for all. He preached not absolute virtue but progress toward virtue. For him goodness was different for each individual, since it meant realizing one's own particular potentialities to the full. He was skeptical about astrology and divination and about an afterlife. Nor did he require the suppression of emotion, only a reasonable self-restraint. His philosophy was, in fact, more this-worldly, more sensible, more humane; and most important, it allowed a more positive value to politics. When Cicero came to compose, ostensibly for his son, his treatise on moral duties (*De Officiis*), destined to have enormous influence centuries later, he chose Panaetius as his guide.

We have seen that contact with the Greeks encouraged rationalistic questioning of the old Roman religion; but it must not be supposed that even educated Romans become agnostics overnight. Sulla, just as much as Marius, believed in omens and oracles. Marius, the man of the people, who despised Greek, was particularly superstitious, consulting a Syrian prophetess called Martha as to how to beat the Cimbrians and undertaking a pilgrimage to the shrine of the orgiastic Cybele in Phyrgia. As late as 57 B.C. a proposal to send an army to Egypt could be dropped on the pretext that the Sibylline Books pronounced it impious. At the same time Oriental cults, such as those of Isis and Osiris from Egypt, having gained ground in the time of Sulla among the masses, threatened to settle even on the Capitol, and were with difficulty confined to the suburbs. When the Senate ordered their temples within the walls to be destroyed, the consul had to take the ax himself to strike the first blow, since no workman dared. Stoicism was only for the educated intellectual: it did not encourage the gentleness and philanthropy that the age also badly needed; it had less appeal to women and children, no gospel of hope, and no missionary spirit. But these Eastern religions seemed to care about the soul of even the humblest. No wonder they caught on.

Outwardly the pieties were observed. The speeches of the elder Cato and the Gracchi, like the Senate's agenda, began with the gods. Whenever a new colony was founded, a code for its *ius divinum* was meticulously laid down, and this practice was continued even by Julius Caesar. But cracks were beginning to appear in the monolithic edifice of the state religion. When so obvious an ill omen as a peal of thunder occurred during an election, Saturninus, with a gibe at the Senate, ordered voting to continue. When Bibulus as consul in 59 tried to suspend the Senate's business by announcing that he was going to observe the sky for omens, his colleague Caesar took no notice, and next year Caesar's agent Clodius got this traditional obstructive maneuver formally abolished. By the end of the republic many temples in Rome were visibly falling into neglected ruin. No Flamen Dialis (see p. 21) was appointed between 89 and 11 B.C.; and by A.D. 5 Augustus had to allow even freedmen's daughters to be eligible for a place among the six Vestal Virgins, who were originally all patricians.

At the beginning of the first century Quintus Mucius Scaevola, the Supreme Pontiff, taking his cue from Panaetius, formulated what many educated Romans must have felt instinctively about religion. There were three traditional kinds: that of the poets, that of the philosophers, and that of the statesmen. Dismissing the first as inconsequential, he pronounced the second to be partly irrelevant to the state and partly dangerous. This kind the pontiff-statesman would keep from the masses, not because he thought it false, but because he considered it expedient for the state that its citizens should be deceived. In this he agreed with Polybius (see p. 6); and his trichotomy was later reaffirmed by Cicero's friend, the extremely learned Varro.

Cicero himself, who had completed his apprenticeship in the Forum under the aegis of this Scaevola, illustrates perfectly such a state of mind. As to the religion of the poets, the fragments of the poems he wrote in heroic hexameters about his own exploits show that he indulged in the full epic paraphernalia of omens and divine machinery; we gather indeed that he depicted himself as being received by Jupiter into the council of the gods and taught the arts by Minerva. That was what was expected in the genre. He could jokingly in a letter to Atticus refer to some of his lines as having been dictated to him by the Muse Calliope herself.

The statesman's religion appears not only in his appeals to the gods in his public speeches but in the dialogue *On the Laws*, which was the companion work to his *On the Republic*. Book 2 embodies, with only small improvements of his own, what we can check from other sources as being an accurate account of the Roman state religion as it was. "We must persuade our citizens," he says, "that there are gods who govern all things, benefactors of mankind, who observe the character, acts, and intentions of individuals and their piety or impiety." "Who will deny that such beliefs are useful," he adds, "when he remembers how often oaths are used to confirm agreements, how important is the sanctity of treaties, how many persons are deterred from crime by fear of divine punishment?" He himself was proud to belong to the prestigious college of sixteen augurs, whose ostensible function was to determine by the flights of birds whether a projected course had the approval of the gods; not surprisingly, since apart from Marius he was the only "new man" for two hundred years to hold a major priesthood.

To pass from the *Laws* to the series of philosophical works he composed in the last two years of his life is to move into a different compartment of his mind. As a philosopher he had attached himself, when on a youthful visit to Athens, to the civilized and tolerant New Academy, which held that absolute truth was unattainable, but that probability was a sufficient guide for life. On all matters, not excluding religion, the right course was to give a fair hearing to the various schools of thought and then form your own opinion. A man's philosophy of life should be an eclectic affair conditioned by his own temperament: it was wrong to subscribe to anyone else's authority. In his dialogue *On the Nature of the Gods* he has the chief speaker, a pontiff called Cotta, announce that on matters of religion he would follow the great pontiffs, not the great philosophers: in his position he must accept the opinions of his ancestors and most solemnly maintain public rites and ceremonies. Having said so much, he asks another speaker to give him, as a philosopher, arguments for the existence of gods, on which he has many disturbing doubts.

Cicero's work *On Divination* is even more surprising. For here this augur allots the part of defending official divination to his brother, and himself demolishes it—omens, prodigies, prophetic dreams, the Delphic oracle, astrology—in Book 2 with a relish worthy of Lucretius. Whereas in the *Laws* he solemnly asserted divination to be a true art and not a mere expedient of state, he here says the opposite, scornfully recalling that Caesar, Pompey, and Crassus had each been falsely assured by soothsayers that he would die in his bed. "We are alone," he says, "so we can seek truth without prejudice." St. Augustine commented that Cicero would not have dared to breathe in a public speech what he proclaims here so eloquently. There was no mass media to give him away: only the ruling class read literature.

What then did Cicero really believe? The letters, so many of them intimate, rarely refer to religious observances, which he seems to leave, like housekeeping, to his wife. This negative evidence is highly significant. The impression we get from the dialogues, confirmed by the *De Officiis,* is that philosophically he believed in "natural religion." He was clearly impressed by the argument from design, by the regular procession of the seasons and of the bodies in "the spacious firmament on high." He was also predisposed to believe that the divine creator was good (like the Demiurge in Plato's *Timaeus,* a dialogue he translated); and a good god must be providential. In the same age his friend Varro was able, by Stoic syncretism, a rather uncritical synthesis of beliefs, to identify the Jupiter of the Capitol not only with the Stoic world soul but with the Jewish Yahweh. Summing up at the end of *On Divination,* Cicero insists that he has been arguing against superstition, not against religion, which he considers to be true to this extent as well as beneficial to the state, the sole sanction for the great concepts of *pietas, fides,* and *iustitia.* What he disliked about all claims to foretell the future was that they conflicted with his belief in free will as the basis of individual morality. We may take his word for it that he shared the belief that men have souls, and that the individual soul was a spark of the fiery divine soul. Being a man of strong moral sense, he felt that conscience must be explicable. It was the foundation not only of all good conduct but of all true law. It must be divine: *divina mens summa lex* (the divine mind is the highest law).

What of an afterlife for the soul? Educated Romans were profoundly impressed by the *Phaedo* of Plato, which has Socrates putting forward arguments for the immortality of the soul while awaiting imminent execution. The younger Cato read through that dialogue twice before falling on his sword. Cicero puts the arguments in the first book of his *Tusculan Disputations,* but without dogmatism. His beloved daughter Tullia had just died, and he could not bear to think of her as nonexistent. He made elaborate plans to erect a shrine for her and for what he called an "apotheosis" or deification.

To sum up, Cicero, though he proclaimed reason to be the highest faculty of man, was himself emotional, and, as happened with many other Romans, his emotions sometimes conflicted.[2] He was also an advocate used to speaking with apparent sincerity on whatever line suited his cause, a literary artist with an eye for what would be most effective, and a statesman accustomed to take into account the public effect of his words. No wonder his tenets are not clear-cut. And he may have been not untypical of his class. As an eclectic sworn to no master but believing whatever his own nature prompted, he was to have a counterpart in the poet Horace at a time when Stoicism seems to have been gaining on Epicureanism.

There was one Stoic par excellence in the late republic, the younger Cato, who consciously emulated the conspicuous uprightness of his great-grandfather and wedded it to that philosophy. He seems to have been a conceited prig, apt to speak of himself in the third person when holding himself up as a standard; and Cicero at least deplored his rigidity when he disrupted the promising policy of *concordia ordinum* ("concord of the orders") by persuading the Senate to hold a company of Equites to a contract for taxgathering, obtained as usual by auction, that proved to be unprofitable. Yet it was invaluable to the state to have a paragon to shame the unprincipled. Nor was he inhuman, like the most orthodox Stoics; by sharing the hardships of his soldiers and talking to them individually, not by indulging them, he won their affection almost unawares. He deeply loved his brother Caepio and mourned him in a most unstoical way. He was considerate and magnanimous to subordinate peoples and individuals. And however determined to save his own honor by suicide, he did everything he

---

[2] Sulla, who plundered Delphi, yet carried a little image of Apollo that he kissed and prayed to in crises.

could to enable other defeated Pompeians to escape. By being willing to die for his principles he became a martyr and a symbol, his memory kept alive by the encomiums of Cicero and Brutus, which Caesar's intemperate counterblast failed to discredit.

Among the systematic philosophies there was only one real rival to Stoicism, Epicureanism. Cicero, who had no use for it though he tolerated it amiably in his friend Atticus, declared that it had taken hold of the whole of Italy, but this may be an exaggeration. It appealed to two kinds of people. On the one hand were those who found in its ideal of the quiet garden a refuge from the turmoil and horrors of the revolutionary period. On the other were men like Caesar and Cassius, far from quietists, who were attracted by the rationalistic hard-headedness of its philosophy founded on atomistic materialism.[3] Its prophet, though he may not have been widely read, was Lucretius, the great poet who was un-Epicurean enough to conceive a passionate mission to preach this philosophy as a release from fear of the gods, of death, and of what was fabled to happen to people after death. It is this sense of urgency, combined with a pictorial, imaginative grasp, that so often quickens his exposition of physical science into poetry. It is a relief to find someone prepared to sweep away the cobwebs of Roman religion: "it is no kind of *pietas* to be seen often turning veiled toward a stone and approaching every altar."

The common view of philosophers was that death was either extinction or a release of the soul to a higher life. We may doubt whether even ordinary people believed in the underworld of Greek mythology. But although there was no orthodox dogma attached to the February Parentalia, a cheerful and orderly renewal of the rites of burial, or the more shadowy Lemuria of May, when ghosts were propitiated, in this age of perpetual danger there seems to have been a particular obsession with death. Among the educated it might take the form of Neo-Pythagoreanism, with its belief in the transmigration of souls. Panaetius had reasserted the distinction of soul from body, and his follower Posidonius had seized upon this distinction to develop a mystical kind of Stoicism, which in turn opened the way of such beliefs. Among the masses, longing for a life beyond the drab miseries of this one was catered to by the mystery religions of the East. Here tombstones of the imperial period, as contrasted with the republican, tell their tale by their references to survival.

Literature
The new individualism made itself felt also in literature, and again through the Scipionic circle. Gaius Lucilius, who continued to live and write for a quarter of a century after Scipio's death in 129, was a Roman Eques from South Italy, and a man of means. Before Lucilius poets at Rome had been humble employees,

---

[3] Cassius explained away in most sensible terms Brutus' vision before the Battle of Philippi of his "bad angel" *(kakos daimon),* which Shakespeare made into Caesar's ghost. The Epicureans believed that everything, including the soul, was material—being composed of atoms.

however much valued when they were successful, and not purveyors of original subject matter. The freest of them, Naevius, was imprisoned when he dared to speak out. Lucilius, on the contrary, consorted on equal terms with the Roman aristocracy. Indeed he became Pompey's great-uncle. He vindicated freedom of speech for literature. Being of a censorious temperament, he "flayed the town," as Horace said, and especially the opponents of Scipio, claiming to be "the enemy of all but the good." It was he who imparted to satire, originally a dramatic medley, the quality that has come to be called satirical. Though his personal attacks were no doubt pointed and salutary, to us he appeals as the general scourge of such aberrations as superstition, pomposity, and pettifogging philosophy. In particular he inveighed against the incoming tide of luxury.

Being also an irrepressible egoist, he poured out, never blotting a line, his views on anything that interested him and his reactions to anything that happened to him, besides experiments in objective genres. He was thus also the pioneer of personal verse in Latin. It was the realization that Lucilius had spontaneously left a complete revelation of his life, and that this was, as much as anything, what made him readable, which encouraged Horace, his inferior in status, to do the same, though Horace's self-revelation is more knowingly contrived. Not that Lucilius was naive: he was steeped in Greek literature and Hellenistic philosophy. His verse was enlivened by Greek words and Latin words given a Greek twist. After experimenting in various meters he settled for the stately hexameters, which enabled him to be mock-heroic when he chose, and his example made this meter the canonical vehicle of Roman verse satire. Unfortunately, like Ennius, he was a genius born before his time, before his meters, borrowed from Greek, had been fully adapted to the differences in Latin and so to Roman ears. He thus seemed uncouth to later critics acclimatized to the improvements introduced by others (it was this that gave Horace the courage to emulate him); and neglected, for this reason among others, by the schoolmasters of the empire, he survives only in numerous short quotations, often picked out by grammarians to illustrate some verbal peculiarity.

By the end of the second century Roman aristocrats were trying their hand at making Latin versions of Hellenistic verse epigrams. But it was not until the middle of the first century that there arose a coterie of highly individualistic poets, some of them at least of the first order. They were called *Neoteroi* (modernists); and nearly all of them except Calvus came originally from north or west of the Po, from beyond the political frontiers of Italy. Perhaps this made it easier for them to attach themselves, not to the grand Roman tradition stemming from Ennius, but to the sophisticated one of the Hellenistic East stemming from the third-century Alexandrian Callimachus. Each of them tried composing a short, highly wrought, narrative poem on a mythological subject. But for us it is more interesting that they composed, in various meters, occasional poems, reckless in their expression of love, hatred, amusement, joy, or sorrow, ostensibly thrown off for the benefit of intimates, yet artfully contrived and not unconscious of a potentially wider audience, if we may judge from the extant collection of

Catullus, preserved through the Middle Ages by a single manuscript at his native Verona.

But in one way Catullus is unique and vitally important. He fell passionately in love with a fascinating married woman some ten years older than himself, Clodia, to whom he gave the sobriquet Lesbia. Her superiority in both age and station led him to adopt toward her an attitude of worship never quite paralleled in the affairs between young men and courtesans of New Comedy and of Hellenistic epigram. For the first time a poet calls his beloved his mistress (*era*). She is "my shining goddess." With her he makes "an eternal compact of love." In Greek literature lyric had been the genre for passionate love poetry, notably in Catullus' favorite Sappho. But so overpowering was his passion for Lesbia that not only in epigrams but in two longer poems it overflowed into a genre that in Greek, so far as we know, had dealt with love only objectively—the elegiac. Thus began at Rome a new genre, the subjective love elegy. The four books of Vergil's friend Gallus about his mistress Lycoris, a well-known stage artiste, are lost; but he handed on the torch lit by Catullus to the elegists of the Augustan age, whose mistresses were of similar station to Lycoris, gifted and well-educated courtesans.

Catullus was something of a rebel, with his defiance as a lover of "the talk of censorious old men," his Callimachean scorn of the grand epic tradition, and his railing against Pompey and Caesar, who as governor of Cisalpine Gaul used to stay with Catullus' parents at Verona. This nonconformist attitude passed to the Augustan elegists. They set up a new ideal, the life of the young poet-lover as against the traditional ones of statesman, advocate, merchant, or soldier. They paraded their *nequitia* (naughtiness) like some French poet of the nineteenth century. Among them was a woman of the highest rank, Messalla's niece Sulpicia. In one of six spirited and passionate epigrams she glories in having got her man and avows she would be more ashamed to conceal than to boast of *peccasse* (living in sin).

The tender, fragile elegists would have nothing to do with any warfare but that of love. Propertius, who, though adopted into the Augustan circle of Maecenas, had suffered grievous family losses from Caesarian troops in the civil war around his native Asisium (Assisi), goes beyond the milder Tibullus in his irony about patriotic expeditions, his joy at the withdrawal of legislation that would have disrupted his love life, and his implied contempt for the Augustan moral crusade. There is no reason to doubt the reality, at least initially, of the passion of this exciting genius for the mistress he called Cynthia. Yet even his first book is a contrived work of art; and from then on he is more of a dramatist, portraying in his own *persona* the varied situations of a love affair. The occasional glimpses of autobiography give an air of reality, but they cannot be aligned into a consistent story. By the end he has become a brilliant narrator, who has prepared the way for the great entertainer in the field of love, Ovid (whose mistress Corinna is almost certainly a fiction), Ovid, the witty connoisseur of psychology, both male and female, whose *nequitia* eventually got him into trouble.

So much the Roman genius and Latin language in alliance were able to achieve, working mainly within the tradition of Hellenistic literature and philosophy. But Cicero at least, however much use he made of Greek originals, was inspired by Roman patriotism; and in this he was the forerunner of the true Augustans, Vergil, Horace, and Livy.

Chapter Five
AUGUSTANISM

Transition to Empire

For fourteen years after the murder of Julius Caesar in 44 B.C. by aristocrats bent on restoring republican institutions, war was almost incessant in the Roman world. The formation of the Second Triumvirate—Antony, Lepidus, and Octavian—was followed by ruthless proscriptions of which Cicero was among the victims, and many Equites suffered for their wealth as well as senators for their politics. After defeating Brutus and Cassius at Philippi in 42 the triumvirs still had to eliminate Pompey's son Sextus, who had many adherents and whose control of the sea caused famine. Numerous peasants were uprooted to accommodate their veterans, including Vergil's Mantuan neighbors, Horace's father, and Propertius' family. By 36 Sextus was defeated and Lepidus ceased to count, but Antony and the young Octavian, each considering himself the heir to the Caesarian cause, remained, colleagues but incompatible. The marriage of the latter's good and beautiful sister Octavia to Antony, which was designed to seal their reconciliation at Brundisium in 40, foundered when he succumbed again to Cleopatra. And so what began as a division of responsibility —Octavian to supervise the settling of the veterans in Italy, Antony to cope with the continued threat from the Parthians in Asia Minor—issued in 33 in a war in which Octavian figured, with suitable propaganda, as the champion of the manly, Italic West against Cleopatra and her Roman slave with all the rabble of the decadent East. No wonder Horace and Vergil, looking on from the side of their patron, Maecenas, Octavian's great supporter, felt as though Rome must be under some primal curse of original sin.

These events and their sequel in Octavian's victory at Actium and Alexandria are familiar. In 29 he celebrated a great triumph, and the cool, calculating, ambitious triumvir showed himself, after declaring an amnesty, the statesman who was soon to be known for all time as Augustus, a name with religious associations given him in 27. There was little opposition among the survivors, only revulsion from civil war and profound relief that there were no proscriptions this time. The rule of one man was accepted as inevitable. Octavian had already shown, after Sextus' defeat, remarkable ability and energy in putting down the brigandage that was making life in Rome and Italy intolerable, whereas Antony had failed to secure Asia Minor, in which so much Italian capital was invested. He now came forward with a concerted program of reform based on a return to the virtues and pieties of the old days and animated by the Romano-Italian patriotism that had become a genuine sentiment for some since the unification of Italy that followed the Social War.

In temperament he was different from his great-uncle. His new approach was not due, we may surmise, merely to wariness of the mistakes that had proved fatal to Julius. Whereas the latter was an intellectual, a farsighted innovator contemptuous of conservatism as of omens, however horrific, Augustus had more sympathy with the ordinary man, putting on great games for him and, unlike Julius, watching them attentively. And perhaps more genuinely than Julius, he had a love of Rome's antique customs and the *mores* that, in common with men like Cicero, he believed to have been a cause of her rise to greatness. Patient and conciliatory as well as shrewd and enlightened once he had come to power—though still ruthless when he thought it necessary—he ruled for forty-four years, during which the empire had time to consolidate a new stability. He was no general: others won his victories. Nor was his health good. But his statues credit him with a calm dignity and he had the authority and magnetism to inspire selfless devotion in men as different as Agrippa and Maecenas. Agrippa, once his schoolmate, was a plain, honest man of humble origin, a highly competent admiral and general, and a great constructor of roads and naval bases, aqueducts (possibly including the Pont du Gard) and drainage, as well as of the first public baths at Rome and the original Pantheon. Maecenas was a Roman Eques (though proud of royal Etruscan descent) who preferred to enhance the prestige of his order by not seeking promotion out of it, one whose luxurious tastes and foppery in dress and literary style, so blatantly un-Augustan, belied great administrative ability and incessant hard work. A genial personality, he was immensely valuable as the sympathetic patron of a brilliant circle of poets in which class counted for nothing. To encourage Vergil to write the *Georgics* and to give Horace that peaceful Sabine farm showed a touch of imagination.

Some distinguished Romans retired from public life under the principate. One was Asinius Pollio, man of action as well as letters, tragedian and historian of the civil wars, Vergil's patron in his *Eclogues* period, who started the first public library and the social recitations of poetry to which attendance was to become so irksome a duty. Another was Messalla, also a patron of poets, whose circle included Tibullus and Ovid. After sharing the consulship with Octavian in the year of Actium he kept in the background, though he lived to propose for him twenty-nine years later the title "Father of his Country." Though Pollio, perhaps himself disillusioned and even embittered, did attract some dissidents and kept alive the name of liberty, such men took no part in the occasional conspiracies—five at least—that were hatched against the princeps. As for the common people, at home and abroad, they venerated him; and the severe discipline he imposed on his soldiers seems only to have confirmed their loyalty.

Augustus was at pains to ease the political transition by preserving the outward forms of the republic. His appellation "princeps" (cf. Duce, Führer) carried with it no special office or dress. He wished to seem only *primus inter pares,* first among equals: in the reliefs on the Altar of Peace he is distinguished only unobtrusively. His position was sanctioned by a "spontaneous" oath of allegiance taken by all Italy in 33 and later administered to the Western provinces, the consulship for the first six years, and after that proconsular *imperium* and sacrosanct tribunician power, which included that of veto. The gradual stages conveyed an impression that the arrangements were somehow provisional. The Senate still met to sponsor the measures he proposed to it, the people to pass those measures, the Assemblies to elect his candidates. But despite appearances Augustan Rome was no more a republic than the republic had been a democracy; for Augustus' real power was secured by his command of the armies. *Imperator,* was a title his immediate successors dropped as being offensive to the Senate.

This command was firmly in his hands because of the ingenious arrangement by which he retained the frontier provinces, where most of the legions were stationed, under his control, with hand-picked senators acting as his deputies, while the rest remained the responsibility of the Senate. The extent of the empire came to be restricted by the limit of volunteer soldiers available, by finance, and by the defensibility of frontiers. A show of power sufficed to settle the old score with the Parthians; but withdrawal from Germany beyond the Rhine had profound consequences for the future history of that country. By his political testament Augustus recommended that the empire should be extended no further. Apart from Claudius' annexation of Mauretania, Thrace, and part of Britain and Trajan's of Dacia (roughly Transylvania), his boundaries were those that ultimately crystallized.

Effects on the Social Classes

Julius Caesar had shown little regard for the feelings of the aristocracy; Augustus saw that it could be kept contented by enhancing its self-respect in proportion to its loss of power. Unlike Caesar (whose memory seems to have been played down somewhat after the settlement of 27) Augustus was a hardener of distinctions. He more than once purged the Senate of unworthy elements (unworthiness including deficiency of wealth for qualification). On the other hand he used his power of nomination to give more openings to "new men" as well as to sons of senators who seemed promising, distinguished Equites, and Italian (not provincial) municipals from all sides. He wanted the Senate to feel itself an elite, a caste apart. Thus he prohibited not only senators, but their sons, grandsons, and great-grandsons from marrying freedwomen. The old republican magistracies retained their attraction and glamour to a surprising degree. A law to curb electoral bribery had to be passed in 18 B.C., and another in A.D. 4. Great were the congratulations and rejoicings at the sacrifices made on the Capitol by the successful candidate, even after the consulship had been devalued in A.D. 2 to a tenure of six months. The consuls, representatives of the other magistrates, and fifteen senators chosen afresh by lot for six-month shifts formed the advisory council of the princeps that prepared business for the Senate. Besides providing him with a sounding-board of senatorial opinion, this arrangement was no doubt designed to give the impression that the Senate was involved in policy making. But what Augustus allowed it to share was work, not power.

His own power was indeed so absolute that there was no effective freedom of speech. Though he made the Senate meet twice a month, with fines for unexcused absence, though he invited debate, seldom used his right to speak first, and did not punish outspokenness if ever it occurred, it is unlikely that any motion he disapproved of ever got passed, and attendance naturally dropped off. As time went on the senators themselves began to resent any outspokenness. Augustus himself had to veto a proposed measure to prevent attacks on him in wills. Senators began to know less and less about what was going on: in 14 B.C. Agrippa set a precedent for reporting to the emperor alone. Rumors, skepticism, and apathy were the results. He for his part got to know more and more through his agents, open and secret. The infamous system of rewarding informers out of the property of their victims grew; and the crime of treason (*minuta maiestas*) against the state was enlarged to include offenses against the emperor and even his statues. The machinery was thus created for the terrors of succeeding reigns. Senators were prohibited from leaving Italy without permission and particularly from visiting the land of Egypt, vital as being Rome's chief source of grain. One role and safeguard the Senate did however acquire: it became a court of criminal jurisdiction for trying its own members accused of treason or other offenses against the state and thus became immune from juries with equestrian participation, which it hated.

The Equestrian order also retained its glamour and privileges—the right, for instance, to wear a gold ring and a special tunic and to sit in the theater in the first fourteen rows behind the senators. Equites, like senators, became disqualified if they lost the means to keep up an establishment commensurate with their dignity. Equites "with public horse" could be tacitly purged at their annual parade simply by omission from the roll call. Yet during Augustus' principate their numbers rose to five thousand. Equestrian families led the aristocracy of many Italian towns. In Padua alone there were at one time five hundred who qualified. From such stock had come Cicero of Arpinum, and now came the poets Tibullus of Pedum, Propertius of Assisi, and Ovid of Sulmo. The Equites were given new roles, in the service of the state instead of themselves. A period of service in the army was made compulsory for them, and they became the source of a regular officer corps. And besides remaining the private agents of senators, they were entrusted with offices personal to the emperor—financial and administrative, civil and military—including some in the new provinces. A pyramidal career structure for them emerged. At the apex was the governorship of Egypt, which became the emperor's domain, being too vital to be put under any senator. In 2 B.C. there was created what was to become an even more powerful office for Equites, the dual prefecture of the Praetorian Guard. Another Eques commanded the paramilitary *Vigiles* (police and fire brigade), seven thousand strong. When, in about A.D. 8, a special commission was set up to safeguard the corn supply and end the recurrence of famines at Rome, it was again an Eques who was put in charge.

The primacy of Italy was reasserted and emphasized on coins. The legions, now a standing army of up to 150,000 men, were confined to Italians, provincials providing auxiliaries to about the same number. Italian towns had become microcosms of Rome, often borrowing her street names and boasting a Forum, sometimes a Capitol, where the local Senate met. Life there, if duller and more old-fashioned than in the capital, may perhaps have been less corrupt.

The transformation of the plebeian order by foreign elements was slowed down through restrictions on the freeing of slaves. It was quite unsuitable for governing an empire and was soon deprived of even the pretense of passing laws. Augustus made it happy with an initial largesse and a fourfold increase in the corn dole and kept it so by shows such as a mock naval battle in which thirty ships and three thousand men took part. He records his uncharacteristic lavishness over these spectacles in his *Acts.* The investment was unfortunate, since without escalation it would show diminishing returns in gratitude. But it certainly paid immediate dividends. A popular riot that took place in 22 B.C. was not against him but in support of his being granted perpetual dictatorship.

The republican notion that no gentleman should receive direct payment for services, public or private, was lofty in conception, but besides leading to devious abuses it left no reward for humdrum tasks or for virtue displayed away from the limelight. A salaried service was a great improvement; and both at home and abroad it was supported by a growing bureaucracy, recruited largely from freedmen. Augustus inspired it from the start with his own exceptional sense of duty.

The provinces gained enormously from the mere establishment of peace. There Augustus was a name to conjure with. Exactions for military billeting and supplies ceased, and taxes were stabilized. Though he had no special economic policy, the relics of great building schemes testify to increasing prosperity. Governors, besides being under the overriding command of the emperor, were now salaried, though there is evidence of continuing extortion, to finance the extravagances of life at Rome; also they could, in the imperial provinces, be kept in office for more than a year, thus having a chance to become interested in and to understand local conditions. For the rest, though the provinces remained technically "estates of the Roman people," they had local self-government. In the West the most striking change was from village and tribal to town-centered life. Mérida, Saragossa, Nîmes, Avignon, Trier, and Turin are among Augustus' foundations.

Religion

As soon as he became princeps Augustus also put in motion a scheme for the restoration of eighty-two temples in the city whose ruinous condition was a palpable symptom of religious as well as economic decay. The revival of religion was fundamental to his conception of the regeneration of Rome. It was by no means dead in the small towns and countryside, as abundant inscriptions show: Faunus, Silvanus, and the Lares were still real to country people. Horace's "rustic Phidyle" with her sacrificial mite was no doubt typical. But it was the old state religion, as we have seen, that had weakened in the enlightenment; and it was this that so many thinkers—Polybius, Scaevola, Varro, Cicero—had considered essential to political stability. Augustus accordingly revived old priesthoods, induced senators to participate, and enrolled himself among them. The ostensible object was to reestablish the old "divine law" as the means of preserving the *pax deorum* ("peace of the gods"), especially through cults connected with the prosperity and fertility of men and their farms. On the *pax deorum* depended also the security of the empire. But Augustus himself had from the first a particular devotion to Apollo. Already in 36 he had vowed a temple to him, and before it was built on the Palatine there came an added stimulus from the victory of Actium, won beneath a promontory on which that god had a temple. The library and the portico with fine Greek sculpture that were attached to it betokened his feeling for the Apolline element of beauty and civilization in Greek sensibility. It was these ideas that were emphasized in the three-day Centennial Festival (*Ludi Saeculares*) of 17 B.C., which marked the apogee of Augustanism, embodied in the hymn composed by Horace for the occasion and soon after in the dignified sculptures on the Altar of Augustan Peace erected in 13–9 B.C., substantial fragments of which survive. The mythical Golden Age was said to be returning. Augustus' successors, especially Tiberius, were generally scrupulous in maintaining his religious policy.

We may doubt whether many citizens of the capital, at least among the educated, became naive enough to believe any more than previously in the efficacy of the rites. Nevertheless, they may well have recovered the Scaevolan belief in the political importance of maintaining them, and it remains an astonishing fact that an act of policy gave the old religion sufficient fresh impetus to survive for several centuries more and to be a serious target for the attacks of the Christian Fathers, notably Augustine. The inclination must have been there, only waiting for encouragement from above.

The Eastern cities, long accustomed to paying divine honors to their kings, had often transferred these tributes to their Roman governors, but in republican Rome itself such a thing was unheard of. The fact that Julius Caesar, on his return from Cleopatra's Alexandria, seemed prepared to accept them was one thing that led to his downfall. But after his death he was officially deified, popular credulity being fortified by the chance appearance of a comet during the games instituted by him in honor of his supposed ancestor, Venus Genetrix, which his heir and great-nephew celebrated, since transference to the stars was a way for great men to achieve immortality long recognized in the Hellenistic world. In addition, there was widespread yearning at this time for a savior. In the surge of enthusiasm that followed Octavian's final triumph there was a disposition, noticeable in what Vergil and Horace wrote at the time, to pay divine honors to him also; but warned by Caesar's fate he pertinaciously resisted this as far as Italy was concerned, apart from allowing the cult of his *genius* to be associated with that of the district Lares, while in the provinces he prescribed that his worship should be associated with that of Roma. He was however by adoption the son of the deified Julius, *divi filius* (son of a god), and after his death he was formally deified, as most of his successors were to be. That was an idea not alien to Rome: from early times it was believed that certain men had been raised to the status of demigods for their services to mankind, namely, those mentioned by Horace in his fifth "Roman" ode (3. 5) in the context of Augustus' future elevation—Castor and Pollux, Hercules, Liber (Bacchus), and Romulus —with the addition of Aesculapius.

Morality

The revival of religion was part of the general move to reinstate the *mores* of the idealized past. Augustus in effect took over Caesar's "care of morals," though he retained the Republican medium of laws passed by the Assembly. His prime object was to reestablish the integrity of the family. Long before the end of the republic the religious form of marriage had gone out of fashion. The bride no longer passed into the legal control of her husband: she remained, nominally at least, in that of her father or a guardian appointed in his will. This meant that she could have her own property, and her husband only had the usufruct of her dowry. She could also divorce him, as easily as he could divorce her, if he deserted her, for instance, or became a prisoner, or was convicted of certain crimes. Divorce became commonplace. Cicero, after thirty years of married life, divorced Terentia. He then married his ward, Publilia, a mere girl; but she, naturally jealous of his continued absorption in her much older stepdaughter Tullia, was in turn put away for failure to conceal her pleasure when Tullia died. The most astonishing story is of that paragon of virtue, Cato. To oblige Hortensius, who aspired to a connection with him, he gave him his wife, Marcia, and later remarried her as a wealthy widow. We must of course beware of assuming that divorce was equally common all down the social scale.

One of the chief grounds for divorce was adultery, though Augustus did remove a frequent occasion of it by allowing wives to accompany their husbands on missions abroad. Roman custom was very unfair to wives, presumably in part because confusion of paternity might be involved. Only the Stoics protested. Not until Constantine could a wife take legal action against an unfaithful husband, whereas a husband could divorce an adulterous wife and retain part of her dowry. Indeed under the republic he had the legal right, if he caught her in the act, to kill either her or her lover or both; and in any divorce the husband retained custody of the children. The Julian Law of 18 B.C. set up a permanent court to try cases against adulterous wives and their lovers. If convicted they were heavily fined and banished to different islands. Divorce followed automatically, and the woman, never allowed to marry again, had to wear a short tunic and toga like a prostitute. There being no public prosecutor, the initiative was left to informers. A married man also now became liable to prosecution if he seduced another man's wife and was cited as corespondent, even if her husband openly connived at it. Nor was the legislation merely concerned with behavior within marriage: this was a crusade against sexual irregularity of all kinds (*stuprum*), which included homosexual practices and even having a mistress who was not a registered prostitute (though it is hard to conceive that this was seriously enforceable). No wonder this part of Augustus' program provoked bitter resistance, not the less bitter because rumors of adulteries on his own part went the rounds.

The object of the legislation was not only moral: it was also to recruit the citizen body, sadly reduced not only by the civil war, during which many died, many were long absent from home, while many emigrated in search of a better life, but by a long-standing reluctance to rear children (which will be discussed later). Bachelors between the ages of twenty-five and sixty and spinsters between twenty and fifty (there must have been very few: there is no Latin word for "spinster") were disqualified from inheriting property from outside their family and from attending public games. Any stipulation by a testator that an heir remain celibate was made legally null. Divorcees had to remarry within six months, widows within twelve. No wonder marriage brokers flourished. If a father or guardian refused consent to a marriage, the young couple could go to law. There were also incentives: privileges were given to the parents of three or more children and to married freedwomen who had children. The latter were now permitted to marry any citizen except senators and their progeny, and their existing children were legitimized.

The Arts

The cult of antiquity was symbolized by the statues of more than a hundred old Roman worthies, erected by the emperor, with inscribed eulogies, in colonnades around his new forum. It is perhaps significant that he chose as tutor for his two grandsons, Lucius and Gaius, the antiquarian lexicographer Verrius Flaccus, who collected a great deal of information about old Roman customs and religion, public and private life. Another expert on the old religious rites was Ateius Capito, consultant for the Centennial Festival. An attempt was made to revive the drama of the second century, but this was unsuccessful. The wearing of the toga on formal occasions, including attendance at spectacles, was revived.

The city of Rome itself had until the middle of the first century B.C. been no match for several in the Hellenistic East, or even Capua in South Italy. Julius Caesar had begun to transform it into something there had never been before, a capital of the world. After Octavian's victory wealth had poured in, so that in 29 the rate of interest fell from 12 to 4 percent. In his own words, he "found the city of brick and turned it into marble." In the old part indeed the thorough-fares remained alleys winding up the hills from the fora, too narrow for the height of the buildings, which he restricted henceforward to seventy feet on the frontage; but in the Campus Martius, the large flat field in the bend of the Tiber, which was now properly embanked, the portion away from the river became a network of broad piazzas and long colonnades, more like a Hellenistic city. Besides the works of Agrippa already mentioned there were an additional forum with its temple of Mars the Avenger, the shrine of Apollo on the Palatine with its porticoes, the Theater of Marcellus in the handsome new building material, travertine, basilicas and colonnades, and paving for the streets. The aqueducts also made Rome, as it is today, a city of fountains. All this must have aroused a sense of pride and purpose, pride not only in the city itself, but in the empire depicted on the huge annotated map that Agrippa caused to be prominently displayed.

The glory of the Augustan Age, however, was its literature. Thanks partly to enlightened patronage, the dozen years following Actium surpassed, one may hold, any other period of the same length in its output of first-rate works. Much has been lost, most regrettably the work of Vergil's intimate friend Varius, also an epic poet; but of what is extant there appeared in those years Vergil's *Georgics* and *Aeneid;* Horace's *Epodes,* his second book of *Satires,* the first three books of his *Odes,* his first book of *Epistles* and possibly the *Ars Poetica;* and in elegy the first three books of Propertius, the two books of Tibullus, and perhaps some of Ovid's earliest work; while in prose Livy was beginning his monumental his-tory. The excitement must have been intense, especially as these masterpieces would generally be revealed to friends gathered together before they were circulated in book form.

Not all of this work was in tune with Augustanism. Most of elegy, as we have seen, and a considerable part of Horace's odes were in the Hellenistic tradition of individualistic hedonism, precisely that against which Augustus was setting his face. But Maecenas had the grace to see that literature should be encouraged even if it had no propaganda value, and Messalla was not a committed Augus-tan. What concerns us here, however, is the specifically Augustan element, as found in Horace, Vergil, and Livy.

Horace's engaging vein of ironical self-depreciation should not beguile us into forgetting that he struck people in his own day as a quite exceptionally able person, even apart from his poetry. His father, a freedman in the remote "heel" of Italy, took him to Rome himself to put him under the best schoolteacher of the day, then sent him on to study philosophy at Athens. There Brutus, in ostensibly unambitious retirement after liberating Rome from Caesar, was so much impressed that, when war broke out between the republicans and the triumvirs, he gave his twenty-two-year-old fellow student high rank in a legion. And years later, long after Vergil and Varius had obtained for this "wing-clipped" ex-republican the entree to Maecenas' circle, the emperor tried unsuccessfully to persuade him to be his private secretary. There was only one effective social barrier: a freedman's son could hardly marry into the class with which he now associated, and to marry beneath it would have ended the association. That is probably why, despite the Augustan campaign, he remained a bachelor.

Several times, in satire, ode, and epistle, he excused himself from celebrating Augustus' martial deeds: his Muse was unpretentious, he said, though elsewhere he showed full awareness that his fame would be worldwide and immortal. There are, however, a number of poems in Books 1–3 of the *Odes,* notably the six weighty "Roman" odes at the beginning of Book 3, that are definitely in tune with Augustan policy, and more in Book 4, written after the commission to compose the *Carmen Saeculare* had brought him back to lyric poetry after a six-year abstention. Where he can sublimate the present into myth, as in Juno's Ennian speech to the gods in 3. 3, the "Battle of the Gods and Giants" in 3. 4, the story of Regulus in 3. 5, or Hannibal's soliloquy in 4. 4, he achieves grandeur. Where Augustan policy coincides with his own opinions, as in the protest against extravagant private palaces in 3. 1, or where Augustus figures as peacebringer, his sympathy makes itself felt in his poetry. But on other occasions, notably in the *Carmen Saeculare,* he writes only like a skilled laureate competently doing a job. Even Propertius, though occasionally with an irony that has only recently been recognized, even Ovid with his *Fasti,* a poem about old legends and festivals structured on the calendar, sometimes wrote works that could be held to further Augustan aims.

Vergil had a personal reason for being attached to Octavian: the young triumvir appears to have ordered his family's farm near Mantua to be spared during the evictions of 41 B.C. for the settlement of veterans. Soon after that we find him with Varius in the circle of Maecenas, with whose encouragement he embarked on the *Georgics.* Quite apart from the rather extravagant eulogies of Octavian in the proems to Books 1 and 3 and in the epilogue, this is a work inspired before the principate ever began by what was to become Augustanism. Its total effect was to commend, without false idealization, a life of hard work in the country that was its own reward, by contrast with that of the hectic city; and country life had long been associated with virtues of which old Cato's Sabines were the embodiment.

The *Georgics* had just been completed when Octavian celebrated his Triumph in 29. The thoughts of the poet were already turning toward epic. It is a good thing that he abandoned the idea of a work celebrating his leader's deeds directly, a kind of poem for which there were Roman precedents from Ennius onward. Instead he wrote the *Aeneid*. It is not an allegory but a story molded from legend yet full of contemporary relevance. A Trojan prince, son of Venus by Anchises, individualistic as any Homeric hero, received a divine command to abandon the past, the burning city, and with his father and household goods to sail away and found a new Troy in the West. As in Yahweh's promises to Abraham, the location and future significance of the promised land is revealed to him ever more clearly in prophecies and oracles. In his experience with Dido, the love and apparent prospect of happiness he is forced to abandon, he learns the pain for self and others that sacrifice of individualism for a higher end entails. When he finally reaches Italy and in his mystic visit to the underworld is shown by his now dead father a visionary pageant of the future greatness of Rome, he no longer merely obeys; his imagination at last takes fire, and he goes forward with no further hesitation to the heavy and often heartbreaking task of warring to establish the new Italy, in which the Trojans, symbolic of the future Romans, may blend their manners, civilized but with a tendency to decadence, with the virtues of the Italians, virile but with a tendency to brutality: *sit Romana potens Itala virtute propago* ("May the Roman stock be mighty through Italian manliness"). The outstanding men of the republic, such as Pompey or Caesar, had been, like Homeric chiefs, primarily concerned for their personal honor (*dignitas*). Such a man was the Italian leader Turnus in the *Aeneid*. Aeneas represents the new type of hero, concerned with his country's honor and welfare, not with self-aggrandizement.

The *Aeneid* is far the greatest embodiment of Augustanism. From us, with our modern revulsion against imperialism, it demands a special effort of historical imagination. Vergil, looking forward, had faith that the Roman Empire would be a blessing to mankind: we, looking back, must acknowledge to ourselves that it was so. As the young E. M. Forster, no imperialist, put it: "The modern reader sometimes wonders why a poem that is patriotic rather than human should have held humanity so long. One reason, perhaps, is that we can read the *Aeneid* as patriots. Our civilization comes from Rome, and it concerns us personally that she once became great." Another reason is the sheer grandeur of the conception and of the verbal execution.

The other great Augustan literary monument is Livy's history of Rome down to his own times. Unfortunately we possess only thirty-five books, apart from summaries, out of 142. These cover the periods from the foundation to about 300, largely sheer legend or fiction, and from 218 to 167, that is, from the outbreak of the Second Punic War to the Triumph of Aemilius Paullus. The legendary parts (and patriotic legends invented or fostered by the ruling class took the place of indigenous mythology at Rome) are in a way better reading than the historical; for Livy, a great stylist, is an admirable storyteller, best when he is uncramped by his annalistic method and a historian's conscientiousness that was yet too feeble to make him a good historian. We would give a lot to have the part, carried down to 9 B.C., that covered his own lifetime; for there he must surely have told the truth as he saw it. We know that he was more sympathetic to Pompey than to Caesar, yet this did not prevent his being a friend of Caesar Augustus. No wonder; for nothing could be more in tune with Augustanism than this prose epic of the Roman people, so nostalgic for the *mores* of bygone centuries. But prose, however good, cannot carry the reader along as poetry does; and in ploughing through the quarter of the work that has survived, even with due recognition that it is epic rather than history, the mind flags because of a certain sameness.

Lasting Results

How shall we assess Augustanism? In its early days it must have substituted hope for generation-long despair. It restored law and order and national self-respect, imparted an efficiency unknown before, and made spectacular improvements in the sphere of architecture, town planning, and communications. So far as much could be said for Mussolini's Italy. But its effect abroad was much greater than that of Fascism, inasmuch as Rome was already mistress of the world. And this effect survived, whereas Mussolini had to throw in his lot with a greater and still more evil power that involved him in ultimate ruin. Nor did Fascism inspire any great literature. Finally, it is undeniable that Augustanism was preferable to the anarchy and violence it replaced—indeed there was no practical alternative to some form of monarchy—and that many of Augustus' provisions were wise and humane.

Nevertheless, with the hindsight of two thousand years' experience, we can see that what was lost was vital, and in the past this has not been sufficiently emphasized. There was no substitute for political liberty, even if exercised in practice only by a small class. Even juries liable to bribery were better than subservient courts. There was no substitute for freedom of thought and speech. The Scaevolan maxim that "it is expedient that in matters of religion the people should be deceived" is degrading and ultimately self-defeating. The generation at Rome that grew up not having known the relief of the ending of civil war was apt to be irreverent about such things as the campaign for morality, perhaps even defiant. But the banishment of the genial poet of the *Art of Love* to a Black Sea outpost on the confines of the barbarian world was an act of political and personal petulance that hardened into cruelty as the years went by and Ovid's pleas for recall went unheeded. Literature wilted under the empire (except for such retrospective satire as could appear when there was a temporary thaw), as much from inanition as repression.

The outlook for the future was also inevitably darkened by the problem of succession. If the principate was to be permanent there were two policies that had a chance of success, though where power is practically absolute there can be no reliable safeguard. The first was election by the Senate. In Augustus' time this would have seemed too like a return to the dissensions of the recent past.

It did happen eighty-two years after his death, when the Senate elected Nerva to succeed the murdered Domitian, and the result was a liberal thaw. But by then the authority of the principate depended on army support, and this Nerva did not command. He survived only by promptly adopting a great soldier, Trajan.

This other policy, of the emperor adopting a successor-designate, depended on the monarchy being an accepted institution. Augustus had not that advantage. Whoever he adopted, others might feel they had an equal claim. He decided therefore to limit invidious competition by keeping the succession within his own family. Already in 9 B.C., on the Altar of Peace, there appear amid the public officials children of what was already coming to be thought of as the imperial family. The imposing rotunda he erected as a mausoleum for himself and his family contrasted with the markedly modest residence he had occupied on the Palatine. But there was always the risk that at any time the family might contain no one suitable. Extraordinary bad luck gave the policy an inauspicious start. Augustus had no son. His first choice fell on Marcellus, the son of his sister Octavia. But it was only after the untimely death of four other intended heirs that Augustus fell back on his stepson Tiberius, whom he had compelled after Agrippa's death to divorce his deeply loved wife (Agrippa's daughter Agrippina) and marry his own daughter, Marcellus' and Agrippa's widow, Julia. And even so Tiberius only succeeded to the principate in A.D. 14 after an embarrassing discussion in the Senate, a middle-aged man embittered by having been so often passed over despite brilliant military achievements, and by the misconduct of his enforced wife. The hereditary principle (which apparently appealed especially to soldiers) inflicted on Rome, Caligula, Claudius, Nero, and Domitian; and though the election of Nerva and his adoption of Trajan did at least usher in a golden period of eighty years, this came to an abrupt end when Marcus Aurelius, himself adopted by his predecessor (four emperors on end having had no son), perhaps inevitably designated as his successor his own disastrous son Commodus.

Chapter Six

PRIVATE AND SOCIAL LIFE IN THE CICERONIAN AND AUGUSTAN AGES

Let us now turn to the private and social life of our central period, the Ciceronian and Augustan ages. For this we have, in addition to the later historians, a uniquely authentic and copious source in the letters that Cicero himself, mainly in the twenty years that separated his consulship and his death, poured out to Atticus, his "other self," and his correspondence with many others, including the most influential figures of the day. We have also the informative satires and epistles of Horace. From the time of Lucilius onward there were individuals who presumed that others would like to know about them. The first letters circulated were those of Cornelia, mother of the Gracchi. Sulla wrote his memoirs, and many followed suit. Plutarch, for his great series of lives, often had biographies, if not autobiographies, to hand (the extant life of Atticus by the contemporary historian Cornelius Nepos is a valuable specimen). But we must always bear in mind that what our literary sources reveal is chiefly the life of the upper crust in the capital. On the mass of people, at Rome and in the provinces, they throw only incidental sidelights, which we must inadequately supplement from such evidence as that of inscriptions.

Daily Life of the Upper Class

By the time of Julius Caesar's murder there were over a hundred private houses in Rome that were on a grand scale. Their magnificence would not be apparent from the narrow, blind, crowded streets. It was only when you got into the courtyard and the peristyle beyond that you would begin to appreciate the comparative peace and luxury. Horace speaks several times of the trees that diversified the network of buildings. Rich men also acquired gardens in the less central districts—Julius Caesar beyond the Tiber, the historian Sallust in the dip between the Quirinal and Pincian hills. But life in the city was hectic. A leading citizen would get up at first light and busy himself with such things as private correspondence until the sun rose and the crowd of callers began to pour in. Friends would be received in an inner room; clients and the like would wait on benches in the courtyard until he came out to greet them. Then, after a hasty breakfast of bread dipped in wine or eaten with honey, olives, or cheese, he would sally out into the street, bound no doubt for the Forum, trailing behind him his crowd of clients. He would generally walk: the streets were so narrow that Julius Caesar had had to ban vehicular traffic from the city within the hours of daylight save for that of building contractors and occasional public processions.

When his business was done, he might wish to attend some public entertainment. Most forms of this, having been originally part of religious festivals, were financed by the state; but gladiatorial shows were put on by rich individuals, and the other shows were subsidized by the aedile responsible, in a spirit of escalating competitiveness and with an eye to popularity and electoral success. The shows were therefore free and open to all. In most the staleness of repetition could be avoided only by novelty—Caesar's giraffes, for instance; or intensification—Caelius must produce more panthers than Curio, more pairs of gladiators must be matched. There was also the spice of partisanship. A gladiator could be as popular as a film star today. Horace represents discussion of gladiators' form as typical of the kind of small-talk he might have with Maecenas. "Celadus the Thracian is the girls' heart-throb (suspirium)" reads a graffito at Pompeii. Or it could be faction partisanship: already the red and white teams had their respective supporters, self-appointed at whim, among the 150,000 spectators at the chariot races; and under the empire, with the blues and greens added, this rivalry was to become fanaticism. Boxing too was always popular with the plebs, though the Greek competitive athletics only became so a century later.

Amid all this the legitimate stage could compete only by lowering its standards, especially as the populace was becoming more of a cosmopolitan rabble. Ironically, Rome acquired her first permanent theater, from Pompey, at a time when the great period of the stage had passed, the period of the masters of tragic and comic acting, Aesopus and Roscius, who gave Cicero tips for *actio* in oratory. Drama was driven to spectacle in an effort to keep its audience: six hundred mules in the *Clytaemestra,* three thousand wine bowls in *The Trojan Horse!* Horace endorses this complaint of Cicero: whole squadrons of cavalry and infantry, in variegated uniforms, and lavish scenery that evokes wild applause before the actor has spoken a word! Classical tragedies and comedies were still in the repertoire, but few new ones were staged. One of these was Varius' *Thyestes,* first performed at Octavian's triumphal games in 29. It is not known whether Ovid's much-praised *Medea* was ever staged, since drama was on the way to becoming purely reading matter, though we know of a new play produced under Claudius. But farces continued to be produced, not only the old "Atellane" type (the Roman "Punch-and-Judy") but the new verse mimes, which must have had merits to interest Julius Caesar and amuse Cicero and were serious enough to provide copybook maxims for schoolchildren, but were also salacious and had the novelty of female actors, naked to the waist. These in turn yielded the palm of popularity to the masked pantomime actor, who gestured in silent ballet while an orchestra played and a chorus sang or recited a libretto of a mythical or historical nature.

If he were not going to some such entertainment, our Roman might not be too late to return home for a light midday lunch, followed by a bath more elaborate than we are used to and a siesta. Dinner was the chief meal of the day, taken in the late afternoon. If he was entertaining, the party would be for nine (or multiples of nine), this being the number held by the couches that faced three sides of each table. There they might continue reclining until a late hour, drinking and talking or watching a performance of some sort. Outside the streets were dark: there was no public night life, only the rumbling of supply wagons and an occasional guest returning home with a slave carrying a torch before him.

The day of a Roman woman of the upper class may strike us as ordinary, but that is because of her emancipation—far from ordinary in antiquity. She might go out paying calls, perhaps in a sedan chair, her matron's gown ensuring respect from the passers-by; or to a temple (women tended to favor the more exotic deities). She might then go to the circus, where she could sit with men and watch the chariot races; or to the amphitheater or theater, where Augustus ruled she must sit aloft behind them; or to games (but only when the athletics and boxing were over). Later, after her bath, she might accompany her husband to a dinner party. At home she might play with her children—and a daughter would be on particularly intimate terms with her. On them she could be an educational influence: the Stoics (and Quintilian) thought it important that both parents should be as cultured as possible. Hence reading and playing music might occupy part of her time. For the rest, she might write letters or spend some time on her own business affairs, consulting with the appropriate freedman. Under the republic it was customary for the mistress to supervise the spinning and weaving by daughters and slaves, which went into clothes for the whole household. This activity had a certain moral aura—it kept women out of mischief; and the Empress Livia, at least to some extent, still set an example in maintaining it, though with the increase in sophistication it was already dying out. No wonder Augustus' daughter Julia kicked over the traces. A woman's husband, on the other hand, might expect her to ignore, if not facilitate, his amours, as Livia again is said to have done (unlike her predecessor). But, apart from the periodic anguish inevitable in any community where child mortality is high, there was no reason why she should not have a full and happy life.

Nevertheless, the more the city grew, the more people tried to get away, especially in the hot malarial months, from "the smoke and wealth and noise of Rome." It was Varro who said that "God made the country, but man made the town." Those who could afford it acquired country houses, "villas" (Cicero had six or seven—"the jewels of Italy"), especially at the seaside toward the south, where even people of modest means like Horace frequented resorts such as Baiae on the Gulf of Naples and the Tarentine riviera. Some of the grander villas were built out over the sea, like the piers with concert halls that are the indispensable attraction of an English seaside resort. There were also inland resorts in the foothills, such as Tibur (Tivoli) with its great waterfall, and cool Praeneste (Palestrina). It is clear from the sites of their villas, and still more from those of their temples, like that of Jupiter Latiaris on the summit of the three-thousand-foot Alban Mount and that of Jupiter Anxur on the commanding cliff top above Terracina, that the Romans were exhilarated by coastal scenery and panorama just as we are, and no less by inland hill scenery and woodland. Catullus hymns Diana as mistress of the mountains and green forests, hidden valleys, and echoing torrents. Horace claims, "the waters that flow past fertile Tibur and the thick foliage of the woods shall mold me into a poet famed for Aeolian song." There is even today an extraordinary peace and calm about the situation of the farm amid the Sabine hills, some fifteen miles beyond Tibur, that was given to him by Maecenas. In a rare romantic passage he associates the feelings he has when in the remote country he "wonders at the hillsides and the solitary woods" not only with fresh poetic inspiration but with the ecstasy of a Bacchant at night on a Balkan mountain "gazing out over the river Hebrus, and Thrace white with snow, and Rhodope trodden by barbarian feet." "One can believe," says Seneca, "in the presence of God in some lonely, lofty forest; or a mountain cave may thrill your heart with an intimation of religion." Where the Romans differ from us is in not thrilling to the gothic "horror" of wild and rugged peaks and precipices. Distant ranges might form an effective backdrop to a panorama of rich country, as in Vergil's *First Eclogue:* "and now far off the rooftops of the villas are smoking, and shadows fall longer from the high mountains"; but the Alpine passes were simply obstacles to travel, to be sur-mounted as expeditiously as possible, and ancient botanists knew nothing of Alpine flowers. The only peak regularly climbed was Etna, and that apparently less for the views than for the interest of its smouldering crater.

Upper-Class Family Life

The family, the basis of life in the early republic, no doubt retained its hold on many, especially outside fashionable circles at Rome, perhaps even its religious sentiment of Vesta, Lares, and Penates and the presiding, all-pervading *genius* of the paterfamilias. It was not merely a matter of blood relations but of the whole household, sometimes so large and diversified in functions as to be almost a self-supporting unit. But of course the spirit would depend on the feeling for each other of the family in our sense of the word. And here we encounter something quite alien to our own culture. The modal age of first marriage for an upper-class girl seems to have been twelve to fifteen. As far back as Augustus the minimum age for marriage was twelve for girls, fourteen for boys, and in practice a girl could be married at eleven. The idea seems to have been that the bride should be untouched and malleable. Puberty in girls was generally supposed to occur in the fourteenth year, and the evidence is that intercourse took place irrespective of it immediately on marriage. The natural result would be, as Plutarch realized, that fear would be the dominant emotion of many a tender bride, handed over by her parents to a man who might be years older than herself at an age when she was not yet capable of truly enjoying sexuality.

Once married, however, the bride became *domina* in the house and shared her husband's status. The fact that the marriage had been arranged by the parents would be no bar to the development of affection, as we know from some modern societies. The bridegroom was also accepted into the bride's family: it is striking that Catullus should say to his Lesbia, "I loved you then . . . as a father loves his sons and sons-in-law." When Lucretius thinks of what an ordinary man is reluctant to lose by death, *uxor optima* (excellent wife) is in the forefront, as *placens uxor* (pleasing wife) is in Horace's similar evocation. There never was such a marriage of convenience as that of Pompey to Caesar's daughter Julia, designed to cement the First Triumvirate; yet he soon came to love her deeply and would spend long summer days talking to her in the gardens of their villas, to the neglect of public business. Augustus' last words to Livia were an exhortation not to forget the happiness of their fifty-one years of married life. His stepson Drusus referred in the Senate to "my wife, whom both for her own sake and for our children's I love so much"; and Valeria, mother of the poet Sulpicia, said of her dead husband, "As far as I am concerned he is still alive and always will be." Augustus' laws designed to induce widows to remarry infringed the deep-seated Roman respect for women who only married once *(univirae)*. Vergil expected his readers to understand Dido's feeling of guilt because for Aeneas' sake she had broken her vow of fidelity to the memory of Sychaeus, her dead husband.

Two salient examples, one from life and one from literature, will suffice to show how selflessly devoted such love could be. The first is from the inscription known as the Praise of Turia, put up by a senatorial widower. He tells of her splendid courage and loyalty in early crises (in this she resembled most wives of the proscribed) and their forty-one years of happy life together, and recalls how shocked he had been at her unselfish suggestion that because they were childless he should divorce her and marry someone else while letting her remain like a sister to him and a second mother to any children he might have.

The other example is from the noble elegy that Propertius wrote on Cornelia, daughter of that Scribonia who was once wife of the future Augustus, cast in the form of an apologia for her life made by her to the judges of the underworld. At the end he pictures her as addressing her second husband and committing their children to his sole care: let him now be mother as well as father to them, hide his grief when he kisses them, and talk to her in the privacy of his dreams as though she could answer. Then she turns to her children. If their father should marry again, they must not mind, but show approval: their stepmother will be won by their ways and surrender her heart to them; only they must be careful not to hurt her by tactless praise of their mother. Or if he is content not to marry again, but to live on memories of herself, they must realize that he will soon be old, and growing up the more quickly cheer him and stop up every avenue that could lead to the sorrows of widowerhood. It does not matter that the scene is imaginary: it shows how a sensitive poet thought a great Roman lady should and would feel and behave toward her husband.

But the mention of Scribonia is enough to remind us of the other side of the coin. Octavian had divorced her, the mother of what was to prove his only child, after little more than a year of marriage, and had then prevailed on Tiberius Nero to surrender to him his wife Livia, though she had borne him one son, the future emperor Tiberius, and was pregnant with another. We had a glimpse of (p. 107) the misery that enjoined divorce and remarriage was to cause this younger Tiberius. Women, whose status and influence at Rome were so high, were all the more liable to be treated as pawns in the political game.

Family life must have been seriously disrupted by such treatment of wives, even though there were women as noble as Octavia, who when Antony deserted her brought up his son by Fulvia and even his daughter by Cleopatra as though they were her own. But to what extent were there children to be involved? Julius Caesar had only one child, a daughter, by his three wives.[1] We here come face to face with a remarkable fact, the smallness of Roman families, which led Augustus to introduce those privileges for parents of three or more.

The old Roman marriage contract specified that the aim was procreation of children. As early as 403 the censors had rebuked and seriously fined elderly bachelors. But by the second century self-regard prevailed over public spirit. Meanwhile Roman citizens were losing one of the old incentives to rear a family, religious anxiety for the upkeep of rites due to themselves after death. The poor might be reluctant to raise children for economic reasons; but with the richer classes another factor at Rome, as in contemporary Greece, was loss of interest in perpetuating one's family, class, or nation, and consequent reluctance on the part of parents to undertake the responsibility of rearing children or, in the wife's case, the trouble of pregnancy, the pain and danger of childbirth, and the disfigurement these caused (in what was now a sexually competitive world), especially as adoption was an easy alternative.

The Stoic Seneca scorned the idea of marrying to have children, to perpetuate one's name, to secure a support for old age or an heir. As early as 131 B.C. the censor Metellus Macedonicus, himself irreproachable, had made a wry appeal to his fellow citizens: "If we were able to endure life without a wife, we should all avoid the trouble. But since nature has ordained that we can neither live comfortably with them nor at all without them, we should consult our future welfare rather than our immediate pleasure." Augustus quoted this old speech to a far from receptive Senate.

Another limiting factor was consideration for one's children. A custom had grown up of leaving legacies to many friends and even mere acquaintances, till

---

[1] Gossip credited him however with fathering Brutus from Servilia and Caesarion from Cleopatra.

omission became almost a snub. For reasons of vanity as well as cupidity men angled for these legacies, and while their blandishments might encourage testa- tors to gratify them by remaining celibate, the effect in the case of married men would be to curtail the amount available for the family heirs. There was also no tradition of primogeniture: the family members were coheirs of what was left after specific legacies; and in intestacy all a man's relations got a share. The status of a son would depend on his property and competitive expenditure, while a daughter's expectations would depend on the size of her dowry. Hence the ideal family number to aim for, anticipating some deaths in childhood, was one like Cicero's, a daughter and a son; or, if the son was born first, the daughter might be omitted.

But Romans' family planning was far from scientific. They had no statistics, no clear conception of probabilities, only casual observation of individual cases. Infant mortality seems to have been about 20 percent, and only about two- thirds of those born reached reproductive age. Indeed all the ten siblings of the Gracchi died young save one. Over 80 percent of the people whose death records have been found at Ostia were under thirty. Of the five sons of Marcus Aurelius only Commodus survived. The number of three children set by Augustus as a minimum for privileges was a minimum indeed: more would be required if the survival of a male heir to breeding age was to be a fair chance. This number applied only to Rome itself; and even there it was four for freedwomen, as in the rest of Italy, while in the provinces it was five. Perhaps he was limiting his sights to the attainable. In fact families died out right and left. Under Augustus there were seventy-seven senators of patrician family, under Nero twenty, by A.D. 96 only four. The number of wills preserved that leave everything to freedmen testifies to the prevalence of childlessness. Four successive emperors from Nerva had no son. Pliny's three marriages produced no heir.

How was fertility restricted? Contrary to what is sometimes said, there is positive evidence that Romans, at least under the empire, did to some extent use contraceptives such as we find recommended by their Greek doctors. Some of these—alum, vinegar, brine—were promising enough to be still recommended by the English scientist and birth-control advocate Dr. Marie Stopes in 1927; but some were of dubious or negligible efficacy, some mere magic. The lore of "safe periods" was also prevalent but unreliable. There was no method of assessing efficacy, a difficult enough task even in an age of organized science. Augustine (who had lived for thirteen years with a concubine and somehow managed to have only one son by her) is unique in classical antiquity in men- tioning coitus interruptus, as a practice of some sectaries, though we find tech- niques recommended that were designed to have a similar effect. It is likely enough that unreproductive modes of sexual intercourse were widely practiced. Abortion too was apparently quite common. The fetus was regarded as simply part of the mother: Stoic doctrine was that the soul entered only at birth. Whether recourse should be had to abortion was officially decided by the husband; but Seneca praised his mother for not practicing it.

There remains infanticide, which was also at the husband's discretion. In the case of deformed children this was actually enjoined by the Twelve Tables and still casually approved five centuries later by Seneca: "We drown children born weakly or abnormal." Illegitimate children also had no such status as they have in some other societies, and indeed are hardly ever mentioned. They appear to have been generally suppressed. Nor did infanticide stop there. The drowning, strangling, or exposing of normal infants is naturally a topic about which there would be reticence at Rome, as there was in Greece and is in India. We know of cases of exposure besides such fictional ones as those of Longus' Daphnis and Chloe. The parents of Gaius Melissus, an Augustan literary man, exposed him because they were at loggerheads, but he survived. (No doubt many foundling infants were, like him, reared and sold as slaves.) Augustus forbade the child born to his granddaughter Julia after her disgrace to be reared. He himself was reported to have narrowly escaped such a fate, an astrologer having given him a bad forecast at his birth. Claudius ordered the child of his divorced wife, begotten by a freedman, to be exposed at her door. In the same century Musonius Rufus, a philosopher who also deprecated contraceptives and abortion, expressly condemns rich people for sometimes refusing to rear infants so that the prospects of existing children may not suffer. In this he anticipated the Christians, the frequency of whose denunciations has led to unjustified assumptions that what they were attacking was something new.

Finally there was a quite different factor. A Roman man, married in the first instance to someone chosen not by himself, might well prefer to take his sexual pleasure outside the marriage bed. Indeed passionate sexual love was not considered in those days to be appropriate in marriage either by Romans like Lucretius and Seneca or by Greeks like Plutarch, who when advising a newly married couple tells the wife not to mind, but to be grateful, if her husband, out of respect for her, works his passions off on a courtesan or slave. Horace in a Lucilian-type satire remarks on the convenience sometimes of having a slave girl or boy at hand. Of course in second or further marriages, where the partners had more choice, sexual attraction might play a greater part. Poor Tullia was infatuated with the glamorous adventurer Dolabella, whom she married as her third husband to the dismay of her father Cicero, abroad governing Cilicia; and the future Augustus married Livia for love. But widowers, from the Elder Cato to Marcus Aurelius, often took a concubine instead of a new wife, and no stigma was attached to this. One object might be to avoid saddling sons with a stepmother, another to be able to choose from any class without interference from a paterfamilias.

In the early Republic education was a family affair; and even later the mothers of the Gracchi, Julius Caesar, and Octavian were reputed to have been a strong influence on their children. But education by skilled slaves encroached and in some aristocratic families long remained the rule. Meanwhile ordinary boys and girls went together to a primary school from the age of seven to learn reading, writing, and arithmetic, and a small proportion of them to a secondary school to learn literature. It was primarily Greek literature, for education was bilingual and Ennius and Terence were no match for Homer and Menander as classics. But in 26 B.C. one Quintus Caecilius Epirota, a Greek freedman of Atticus who had been an intimate of the poet Gallus, began teaching the poetry of the modernists, including the *Eclogues,* possibly even the *Georgics,* of Vergil. Cicero and Vergil provided the Romans with classics of their own, and Sallust also, who was later preferred as a writer of history even to Livy and Tacitus. But the method of teaching, though it resulted in familiarity with the classics, sought to impart comprehension and stylistic awareness rather than literary apprecia- tion in the wider sense.

At sixteen an aristocratic boy had a year of political apprenticeship in the Forum, as it was called, watching some eminent friend of his family, after which he did his military service for another year or so, at first in the ranks though still with a tutor, then as an officer on someone's staff. After this interruption came three years or so of rhetoric, which was not confined to aristocrats (Vergil tried it). Rhetoric at least taught a boy to marshal and express his thoughts effectively. The fact that the subjects of exercises were fantastic or historical rather than "relevant" caused some disapproval in antiquity, which modern critics have echoed. But all education need not be directly utilitarian; what harm if it was amusing and imaginative? The curriculum is more to be criticized for its narrowness: it bred no thoughts worth such choice expression. The nine- subject syllabus advocated by Varro never got off the ground. If you wanted to learn higher mathematics or even music you had to go to a private tutor, and the natural sciences were simply neglected. If you wanted philosophy you could go to some authority in Italy, as Vergil went to Siro at Naples for Epicureanism; but generally, if you could afford it, you went like Cicero's son and Horace to Athens, where there was more choice, or to some other center in the Greek world. Otherwise you could study jurisprudence at Rome. But the advocacy by Cicero, and Quintilian more than a century later, of a broad curriculum under the umbrella of rhetoric came to nothing: narrow utilitarianism was too strong. Jurisprudence was something you could not get in Greece; otherwise Roman schools were replicas of Hellenistic ones. The state played no part in their organization, until Vespasian, toward the end of the first century, began reward- ing teachers with privileges and establishing chairs for professors.

Schooling apart, there was physical education. Under Augustus aristocratic youth clubs like the Greek *ephebia* were founded, first in Rome and central Italy, then more widely. For young Romans he favored games with a practical, even military, turn. Horace, who in an early satire had represented himself as enjoy- ing a ball game called *trigon* in the Campus Martius, where such activities took place, in his Augustan vein chides the young for rolling Greek hoops and reproaches Lydia for spoiling Sybaris, who ought to be riding, wrestling, and throwing the javelin or discus with the other cadets and plunging afterward into the Tiber. Augustus favored games that were not Greek-style competitions for individuals but collective exhibitions like the displays at modern military tournaments, giving scope for the Roman flair for disciplined movement. In particular he promoted the famous Troy Game, an intricate equestrian maneuver outlined in the fifth book of the *Aeneid.*

Greek athletics had been introduced to Rome in 186 B.C., but only as a foreign spectacle. What precluded Roman participation was the nakedness. Ennius wrote "the beginning of shame is to strip before fellow citizens"; Lucilius, "seeing others naked in the origin of vice"; and Cicero quoted both with approval. With this proviso Augustus encouraged athletic displays. Indeed he founded Greek games at Actium to commemorate his victory there as well as four-yearly games at Rome. But sober Romans remained suspicious of the Greek gymnasia, regarding them as hotbeds of pederasty.

The attitude of Romans to homosexuality is indeed hard to discern. They certainly did not regard it, like the Platonic philosopher Polemo, as "a dispensation of the gods for the care and protection of the young." The nearest to that relationship we find is in Vergil's Nisus and Euryalus, *amor pius.* Yet neither was it a forbidden topic; the lyric and elegiac poets, not to mention Petronius, treat even its most crudely physical manifestations as a matter of course, Ovid alone disclaiming interest in pederasty for the sympathetic reason that sexual enjoyment should be mutual. But the poets also protested that their morals must not be judged by their poems, which were to be recognized as written in Greek tradition. It was also common form to accuse any enemy of sexual abnormalities, and the fact that political opponents thought this worthwhile indicates their estimate of public opinion. The old Republican *Lex Scantinia* forbade homosexual acts between free citizens, so often condemned as *stuprum;* and the disapproval of Scipio Aemilianus was echoed by Cicero. Nevertheless in a world in which nothing was unmentionable and slaves abounded, it is likely that no sexual deviation went unsatisfied. The odd thing is that we hear so little of lesbianism, perhaps because, apart from Sappho herself, Greece provided no literary precedents and Rome few female poets; and in any case women seem to be more reticent.

Outside the family friendship played a great part in Roman life, partly no doubt for the simple reason that the city provided such a social center. Many upper-class citizens were attracted to Epicureanism, which reckoned the cultivation of friendship to be the chief thing that made life worth living in a materialist world. It is true that the word *amicitia* had a wide spectrum of meaning, and historians with political interests have tended to stress that which implied political alliance and a calculus of benefits. But the similar convention by which British parliamentarians refer to a member of their party as "my friend" does not debase the normal associations of the word; and the Romans were well aware that true friendship was based on natural affection, mutual good faith, mutual respect, and similarity of character and interests, as Cicero described it in a charming little work with an abundance of native instances, of which the intimacy of Scipio Aemilianus and Laelius was the most conspicuous. He himself had in Atticus an *alter ego,* always ready to help, always forbearing, and utterly discreet in a dangerous world. And yet, in a society in which general affability was an essential, as we have mentioned, could not an expansive cult of friendships involve disloyalties? The Epicurean Atticus would probably have said, if he had been pressed, that his most intimate friend was Cicero. It is therefore a shock to find him on friendly terms with the triumvirs who had been responsible for Cicero's death. To be "all things to all men" is not really compatible with true affection *(caritas),* which, as Cicero said in the *De Amicitia,* composed at this same Atticus' request and addressed to him, can unite only two people, or at most a few.

Life Among the Lower Classes of Freemen

So much for the upper crust of a few thousand senatorial and equestrian families. But what of the remaining inhabitants of Rome, totaling up to a million? These classes were separated from one another by a social gulf. It was a serious offense for an ordinary citizen to insult a senator or an Eques. We know all too little about their life: literature seldom took account of them. Cicero, though he might in his study be carried away by Stoic thoughts of Nature disposing men to love and help one another, left all that behind when he went down to the Senate House; and no doubt he was typical of his class.

Snobbery played a considerable part in Roman society. In the late republic there remained about twenty patrician families, some claiming their ancestors "came over with the Trojans." Patricians were still to sport their special red boots with the crescent-shaped ivory buckle two centuries and more after their status had ceased to carry any function beyond the holding of a few decreasingly prestigious priesthoods. More formidable was the snobbery of the nobles in general. Cicero, the "new man," suffered from it. He tried to keep up with the Metelluses by buying the villa at Tusculum that had belonged to a Catulus and before him to the great Cornelius Sulla himself, and a house on the fashionable Palatine that had belonged to Crassus. They only cold-shouldered him the more, and when he tried to stiffen their resistance to the First Triumvirate, abandoned him and let him be exiled, not (as he thought) without some gloating. The Romans were too much dazzled also by the glamour of the Triumph. Thus Cicero himself, when he had to make the agonizing choice between Caesar and Pompey, had his judgment partially confused by fears that he might forfeit this reward (which was always in doubt) for a minor defeat of a mountain tribe that had disturbed his province of Cilicia.

Yet there was always a mystique about being a Roman citizen of any grade. "The person of a freeman," says the lawyer Ulpian, "is beyond price." He had from time immemorial the right to appeal to the people against condemnation on certain capital charges. In any case a citizen was rarely executed, but allowed to escape into exile. Even among deserters in war, as we saw, Aemilius Paullus had discriminated: the Roman citizens were not to be trampled by elephants. We saw also that one of the grievances that led to the Social War was that citizen soldiers, unlike allies, could not be scourged with rods.

In a well-known passage Cicero expounds the traditional attitude to various occupations, illogically based in some cases not on the value of the worker but on the character of the work. Farming is by far the most gentlemanly. A successful large-scale merchant might pass muster if he made enough to retire to a country estate and so justify having engaged in an occupation sordid if pursued on a smaller scale. Law usurers were naturally unpopular and so despised, as were taxgatherers, the "publicans" of the New Testament. Architecture, medicine, and secondary-school teaching were all right for those whose status they befitted (i.e., not gentlemen; mostly Greeks, in fact). Retail tradesmen and middlemen were suspect: could they combine success with honesty? Lowest of these were such as cater to sensual pleasures, selling food or perfumes, with whom are classed dancers and cabaret performers. The village blacksmith was not idealized. On the contrary craftsmen and mechanics were belittled: who would choose to spend his time in a workshop? Lowest of all were unskilled manual laborers, as their pay indicated. Their work was indistinguishable from that of slaves.

We can supplement this tariff of snobbery from other sources. Law was prestigious, the only profession in which senators and Equites competed with plebeians. Auctioneers and undertakers were for some reason debarred by Julius Caesar from holding municipal office. The trade of miller-baker was despised for being dirty (but that did not deter one Marcus Vergilius Eurysaces from causing its processes to be depicted on his imposing tomb, still to be seen just outside the Porta Maggiore). Primary-school teachers were despised; and fencers and prostitutes were classed with pantomime actors. Astrology was illegal but irrepressible, winked at so long as it kept clear of state affairs. What the authorities would not tolerate was the sort of astrologer who went about saying, "Where is he who is born King of the Jews, for we have seen his star in the East?" It should be added however that the snobbery of the Ciceronian Age began to weaken under Augustus, and that it seems to have been in any case largely an upper-class foible.

On the land there were the peasant proprietors outside the large estates, many of them ex-soldiers. The latter, if they did not want to cultivate their land themselves, might leave an evicted peasant to do so on commission, as in the case of the miserable Moeris in Vergil's *Ninth Eclogue* or the philosophic Ofellus in Horace's *Satire* 2. 2. There were tenant farmers, such as Horace's "five good fathers" who attended the Senate at the local center of Varia. Poorer peasants could hire out their families and themselves at vintage and harvest time. On the large estates, according to Caesar's prescribed proportion, one-third of the laborers were freemen. The life of the freeman on the land will have been on the eternal pattern, with its hardships, limitations, and compensations, enshrined by Vergil in his *Georgics* and Gray in his *Elegy*.

Apart from agriculture, the chief honorable employment of the free Roman citizen was soldiering, a voluntary one except in severe crises, and soldiers included craftsmen of many kinds. On his return from pacifying Spain in 13 B.C. Augustus retained as a standing army twenty-eight legions of about fifty-five hundred men each, with as many auxiliaries drawn from the provinces. The officers were still young aristocrats—a potential source of weakness doubtless defended on grounds of education in patriotism. Other ranks signed on for a period of twenty years including four as a privileged veteran, raised in A.D. 6 to twenty-five including five with that privileged status. Soldiers up to the rank of centurion (centurions were commissioned officers, mostly promoted from the ranks) were forbidden by Augustus to marry, a rule that stood for two centuries: they must be dedicated to the service and ready to move anywhere without reluctance. They were however allowed to keep concubines, whose sons could legitimize themselves by enlisting in due course. Since the latter often took advantage of this, the army acquired elements of a hereditary profession. On retiring a soldier was given a pension of land or money. Senior centurions often began a new life as civil servants.

As for the urban plebs, the number poor enough to qualify for the corn dole had risen by 2 B.C. to 250,000 from the 150,000 to which Caesar had reduced it. Augustus brought it down to 200,000. But these could not have lived on corn alone: they must have supplemented it by working for hire, perhaps as dockers, for instance, navigation being undertaken from March 5 to November 11 only. And of those not poor enough to be eligible, between a quarter and a third of the total, many must also have worked.

Ancient society did not put capital to work to increase productivity. There was no mass-productive industry for export trade (the city was a parasite on the empire), though Italy did export—mainly to Gaul—wine, olive oil, lead pipes, glass, lamps, and the pottery of Arretium (Arezzo). But there was employment for all, for a workday of six hours or so (few worked in the afternoon). The trade routes, newly secured by two standing fleets under Augustus, brought in local specialties and abundant raw materials that had to be processed or distributed to meet the demands of a higher standard of living. The great new building projects must have absorbed many. Where vehicular traffic was so limited, there must have been thousands of porters. Many more must have been engaged in retail trade, whether as employees or on their own. And finally there was the drab crowd of clients of the rich patrons who doled out a pittance daily. What we hear very little of is woman employees, apart from slaves: indeed it appears that, as in Moslem countries, men even did the ordinary shopping. Presumably women spun and did household chores.

To Cicero the city commoners were "the dregs of Romulus," and the mob that in the late republic listened to political harangues and rioted in the streets for Clodius or Milo, or when stirred up by Antony's speech about the murdered Caesar and the reading of his will, may have been much as it is represented by Shakespeare. But physical considerations alone are enough to suggest that it was only a small fraction of the citizen population. What proportion of a half million or more can a speaker reach? The great majority will have been going about their business of eking out a precarious living.

The poor Roman subsisted on what could be made out of about three pounds of corn a day, cooked into bread, scones or a kind of porridge, with herbs and vegetables, and olive oil, perhaps occasionally a little cheese or dried salt fish, still less often meat in the form of pork. (Sheep were kept for wool, milk, and cheese, goats for milk and cheese, cattle for leather rather than milk, and for ploughing and draft, though all of these were eaten after sacrifice.) At least there was plenty of good, fresh water, especially after Agrippa's activities, and there was rough wine to dilute with it. Sweaty togas could also be washed in it by fullers for those who could afford their services. And the public baths, for which a small fee was charged, were popular centers of varied recreation. But piped water was only for those who could pay a water rate based on the size of the pipe, and only on ground floors.

The poor city-dweller could rarely enjoy family life. He probably lived in the open air as much as he could, returning only for meals and at night to a low room in a tall tenement block owned by some rich man like Crassus, where he slept in constant fear of fire or collapse, with no toilet facilities beyond a covered chamber pot, no heating beyond a charcoal brazier. Nor was there any security for his person until Agrippa instituted a police force, raised in 6 A.D. to seven cohorts of a thousand each, the watch who patrolled at night to guard against fire and burglary.

There was as yet no organized charity, only an occasional ostentatious meal, such as that for 200,000 given by Caesar at his Triumph, or an occasional largesse, such as that he provided for in his will and those of which Augustus boasted in his *Acts,* and the regular dole of patrons to poor clients. Indeed there was no ideological motivation for it. Charity was not a religious duty to Romans, as to Jews and Egyptians; and the Stoics, whose doctrine of the brotherhood of man might have inspired it, conveniently believed at the same time that virtue consisted in making the best of one's destined lot and that happiness was independent of externals. You were lucky if you had relatives who would tend you when sick or old and if you were not thrown out eventually into one of the common paupers' grave-pits outside the walls. Did no one care? Yes, the more sensitive poets, occasionally at least. Vergil congratulates the countryman on not having to suffer through pity of the poor as well as envy of the rich. "Why is anyone in need while you are wealthy?" Horace makes Ofellus inquire. This might be mere conventional philosophy; but not his vignette of the peasant family evicted by a grasping landlord: "Out they are driven, wife and man, clutching their fathers' gods and their ragged children"; nor his wistful coda on Death: "He, to relieve the poor man whose working life is done, summoned— or unsummoned—consents." We do however hear from Augustan times onward of endowed provision for poor children, both by private individuals such as Pliny and by emperors such as Trajan, who had a scheme to finance it and help farmers at the same time by mortgages offered at half the standard rate.

One deterrent was the absence in law of any guarantee of continuity for a foundation. Not until the Flavian emperors were municipalities empowered to receive inheritances and trusts. There was however the ingenious device of assigning fines for misuse of endowments to the public treasury, which thereby acquired an interest in enforcement.

What could a poor freeman have to live for beyond the contacts with friends that drew together all but the most abject? The old guilds of craftsmen are heard of after a long silence in 64 B.C., but then as being suppressed because they were a cover for political activities, being convenient units for bribery and subversion. But they were too deep-rooted to die, and Augustus tolerated them so long as they were licensed. Apart from this, there was the excitement and partisanship of the free games and spectacles, an occasional *festa* such as that of Anna Perenna on the Ides of March, a "pop festival" in the fields outside the Flaminian Gate. A client might take a partisan interest in his patron's fortunes. Perhaps the poor Roman was also sustained by pride in his city, the metropolis of the world. And at least in his case there was no consideration of family interests to prevent his marrying for love.

Slaves

It is remarkable that never—to our knowledge—did the freeborn worker complain of competition from slaves and freedmen. Slavery was taken for granted in antiquity; society was unthinkable without it, and much of the work that the rich might otherwise have provided for the freeman went on out of sight within the walls of mansions or villas. Even St. Paul, pleading to Philemon to spare the returning runaway Onesimus, does not question the institution. And to the life of slaves and freedmen we now turn.

The Romans were conscious of living amid disaffection: *quot servi tot hostes* ("you have as many enemies as you have slaves"). Even good masters, Seneca and Pliny, confirm this. The memory of the great slave risings in Sicily and the more recent, more protracted, and nearly successful one organized by Spartacus nearer home haunted their minds. Slaves were not distinguished by dress, lest they become conscious of their numerical strength—perhaps 400,000 in a city population of about a million—and so more capable of combining. Care was taken not to have too many compatriots within a household. The arming of runaway slaves in civil war was considered a terrible crime; and when Octavian recovered the large numbers recruited by Sextus Pompeius, he returned twenty-four thousand for punishment to their owners (for a slave was always treated as private property), and crucified the six thousand whose owners could not be traced. A slave who posed as a citizen—tried to enlist as a soldier, for instance

—was liable to execution. Individual runaways were hunted down: Cicero alerted provincial governors in two known cases.

By an old custom, if a master was murdered by a slave, all his slaves were put to death (which, at the lowest consideration, seems hard on his heir). This was modified in A.D. 10, when it was laid down that all slaves within the house —or if the murder took place outside, all slaves who were present—should be tortured, but only those actually participating should be put to death. Nevertheless, and in the teeth of popular protest, four hundred were executed as a warning in A.D. 61 in the particular case of a murdered city prefect. So deep was the feeling of the ruling class that the whole of society depended on a deterrent that was absolute.

In the late Republic most slaves were still obtained as prisoners of war. Caesar is said to have captured up to a million in Gaul. The first agony must have been severance forever from home and shrines. Horace had the imagination to envisage this: "What barbarian girl, her betrothed slain, shall be your slave? What palace-bred boy, brought up to shoot arrows from his father's bow, shall stand with scented locks to serve your wine?" he asked a friend setting out to plunder Arabia. After capture, there were vast differences in conditions. The worst slavery was in mines and quarries, backbreaking work in dangerous or unsanitary conditions to which criminals (other than ex-soldiers) could also be condemned for periods. Work on large estates in chain gangs, herded at night into half-underground jails, was almost as bad. Vital but menial jobs like distributing water in tenement blocks were done by slaves. In industry, in which a great expansion began under Augustus, slaves worked side by side with freemen, and there was probably little difference in their conditions on the shop floor.

The Romans also took over from the Greeks the extraordinary idea that slaves would give reliable evidence only under torture, though Augustus restricted this practice to capital cases and those where the man's evidence was crucial. In law a slave was a chattel, defined by Varro as "a talking instrument." In theory he could be killed by his master, but no one, except in a fury, would be likely to destroy his own property. He might, in practice, until Domitian's time, be mutilated (he was often branded as a matter of course), and there are many stories, told in disapproval, of wanton cruelty and outrageous punishment. He (or she) could also be used sexually at will, but there were limits to this: Augustus exonerated some slaves who killed a notoriously uninhibited master.

In domestic slavery much would depend on the character of the master. There were of course good ones, as there were some good employers before labor unions arose. But absolute authority too often leads to callousness, if not actual cruelty; and consciousness of past unkindnesses would breed fear of revenge and a further spiral of severity. There was a juristic debate as to whether a slave for sale could be called sound if his tongue had been cut out. The story is well known of Vedius Pollio, who ordered a slave to be thrown to his voracious lampreys for breaking a crystal dish. Augustus, being present and appealed to by the slave, ordered that he should be freed, all Vedius' crystal broken, and the fishpond filled up. Such stories indicate what could happen, but they are only told because people were revolted.

Obsequiousness was equally demoralizing to both parties: "nothing is disgraceful that the master orders." Menial services were also degrading. Petronius' Trimalchio had a boy with a mop of hair standing by for him to wipe his sweaty hands on when playing ball—a caricature, but it shows what tendencies were. The use of slaves in education had already seemed a scandal to old Cato: how could he allow his son either to be punished by a slave or to owe a slave anything so precious? Horace, telling us how his own father acted as his *paedogogus* (escort) at Rome, adds the significant epithet *incorruptissimus:* a slave was often in a position to be corrupted and to corrupt.

Slavery, then, was a great evil; but it was by no means an unmitigated one. In many ways a domestic slave was better off physically, and even psychologically, than a needy freeman. He was clothed, fed, and housed, and, at least as long as he was useful, insured against anxiety about these basic needs. The law may also have been harsher than the reality: Varro's precepts show that he knew better than to treat slaves merely as "talking instruments." Humanity will out. Censors took cognizance of cruelty to slaves. Though a slave could not officially marry, he could have a concubine. He was allowed to make and save money and to receive legacies from outside the family. For a start, he could sell part of his food allowance. A clever slave, trained by his master, was allowed to exploit his skill by working for hire, in his spare time or on an agreed commission. He could rent land (on a farm he could have a plot and a beast or two). He could lease a business, a shop, or a ship, employ agents, and even have slaves of his own who called him "master." There were public slaves, both in Rome and other towns, who did responsible work and had status accordingly; and Augustus used these, together with his own ones, on a greatly increased scale as the lower grades of his new civil service. A slave could belong, with his master's leave, to a club or guild, including religious ones. Religion was most important to him.[2] It enabled him to keep in touch with those from the same homeland. It gave him self-respect as an individual, which was otherwise denied to him, another plane of existence. Within a household a slave could enjoy comradeship: "Papas all his life was dear to his fellow slaves," runs an inscription. At the Saturnalia he was waited on by his master and could (subject to prudent thought for the future) say things he had to bottle up during the rest of the year. He could attend some public games and spectacles, though not the circus races; and the forty-five brothels of Rome were largely patronized by slaves. Above all, if he was thrifty (not to mention dishonest, for he notoriously had ample opportunity to steal),

[2] How important emerged clearly in the Sicilian slave risings of the second century B.C. Eunus, leader of the first, represented himself as inspired by the Syrian goddess Atargatis. The second was planned within the precincts of the Palici, underground deities believed to champion the oppressed. The slaves elected as king one Salvius, a dancing dervish devoted to female divinities. Spartacus' concubine was a Bacchant prophetess.

he could save up in a reasonable time enough to buy his freedom, even if he was not freed by the indulgence of his master. This was an incentive, prudently provided, to hard work, efficiency, willingness, and at least the appearance of honesty.

From the time of the Punic Wars onward most slaves were foreigners captured in war or kidnaped by traders or pirates, sold to middlemen at a depot such as Delos or Capua, and retailed, with descriptive labels attached, in the Forum at the Temple of Castor. Their destination would depend on their aptitude. A herdsman in wild country had to be strong and swift, unfettered, armed, and even mounted. He would generally be a Gaul or Spaniard. The stoutest support for Spartacus' revolt had come from Germanic prisoners working on the land. Caesar had thirty-five thousand Germans and Gauls trained as gladiators, distributing many more as slaves among his soldiers. Thracians were the best gladiators however. On the other hand for posts requiring more refined skill and culture the Hellenistic world was the obvious source. Even household physicians were slaves. But the true distinction was not between nationalities, still less between such vague categories as "Orientals" and "Westerners," but between civilized and uncivilized. Plenty of Gauls were talented, plenty of Greeks stupid.

After the Augustan pacification however there were fewer accessions by capture in war, though many still no doubt through purchase by traders in remote parts. The *verna,* the slave born in the family, became relatively commoner than the ex-enemy and more important. This led to progressive amelioration of conditions, partly in that slaves were now encouraged to mate and rear slave children (the parents would have an increased sense of belonging), partly in that normal masters could hardly fail, even if half-ashamedly, to have a soft spot for characters they had seen toddling and growing up about the place. Atticus' household consisted entirely of *vernae,* many of them highly trained for book production. "My reader Sositheus, a delightful fellow, has died," writes Cicero in a letter, "and I am more upset than perhaps I ought to be over the death of a slave." He mentions casually to Atticus that he will avoid arriving at Pompey's villa at the Compitalia because it would not be fair to the slaves, who have a holiday that day. When the proscriptions came, with the offer of liberty and ten thousand drachmas to any slave who betrayed his master, the slaves of Marcus Cicero were even ready to defend him from his pursuers, whereas those of his brother Quintus betrayed him. Which was the more typical case, who can say? Inscriptions naturally record only happy relationships. A boy of sixteen is described as "slave and yet son." Some masters even formally adopted a slave. By tradition slaves shared in the family tomb, until they became too numerous for this to be feasible.

To see the relationship at its best we may take two people we know well, Cicero and Horace. Tiro, Cicero's remarkably versatile secretary, was as indispensable as he was beloved. When, aged hardly more than thirty, he was freed, Cicero's brother Quintus wrote from Britain, "I jumped with joy when I heard that Tiro was to be our friend instead of a slave." When Tiro had to be left ill at Patras, Marcus' letters to him are full of solicitude, and the frankness with which he reveals his disapproval of Caesar, who had just crossed the Rubicon, shows absolute trust. Young Marcus, writing to him as a student from Athens, congratulates him on buying a farm:

So you're now a man of property! You'll have to drop those town manners: you've become a Roman country gentleman now. How clearly I can see your dear old face before me as I write. I can just imagine you buying your equipment, talking to your foreman, and saving the seeds at dessert to put in your pocket.

Horace, himself the son of an admirable father who had begun life as a slave, had eight slaves on his Sabine farm. Amid the tiresomeness of Rome he thinks of them. "O those nights and feasts divine when I sit and eat with my friends before my own Lares and hand down helpings from my dishes to my saucy *vernae*." In the next satire he represents Davus, one of his town slaves, as using the license of the Saturnalia to point out to him that he is himself just as much a slave—to his own way of life. And when he wants to commend country life as against urban, he does it in the form of a chatty, intimate letter to his slave foreman. This is literature, of course, but the attitudes and relationships it represents are surely real.

Freedmen

We have seen that Roman citizenship was much prized, and not only because it carried certain rights: even on his deathbed a man was glad to receive it. It is an extraordinary thing that from early times at Rome a slave who was freed became forthwith a citizen, and further, that a master could free his slaves, until the time of Augustus, regardless of national interest or policy. The interest of the state in the transaction was limited to a 5 percent tax on the slave's value, one of the few sources of revenue from Italy that remained in the first century B.C. Things got out of hand when prisoners from all over the Mediterranean world came to Rome as slaves and were subsequently freed. Already Scipio Aemilianus was able to call the plebs "the stepchildren of Italy." Though numbers are hard to calculate, it is clear that by the end of the Republic freedmen predominated in the upper section of the urban plebs that was above qualifying for the corn dole. Rome was thus a city of extraordinarily mixed population to which the nearest modern analogy is perhaps New York, a microcosm of the known world, which could be described in 69 B.C. as "a community made up of a coming together of the nations." We hear twenty-five years later that Caesar's murder was mourned by the various nations according to their customs, especially the Jews. The schoolmasters who insisted on teaching grammar strictly by rule instead of according to popular usage had a point: they were the guardians of *Latinitas*.

Motives for private manumission were various. To begin with the lowest, informers were often rewarded with freedom. Then it paid to get rid of a slave who was old or ill: Augustus had to take measures to prevent masters from relying on the corn dole available to freemen to relieve them of their responsibility for maintaining useless slaves. It paid also to receive purchase money for freedom, and this was one of the commonest motives. Vanity was another—the desire to be seen with as many clients as possible, or if manumission was by testament, to have as many mourners as possible in your funeral procession. Prudence was still another—the provision of a standing incentive to all your slaves. Still higher comes recognition of merit: threatened by exile, Cicero advised Terentia, if confiscation seemed imminent, to free all her slaves who deserved it. Public slaves could also be freed for good service.[3] Allied to this is the genuine Roman humility in face of superior culture, which made some ashamed to keep Greeks in servitude. But from what we know it seems likely that the desire to be liked or at least kindly remembered, or sheer good nature, was often the motive; and in some at least the true Roman *humanitas,* fostered progressively by the spread of Stoicism.

The status of a freedman was however subject to certain restrictions. As regards his former master, now patron, he was freed subject to an oath to render specified services *(operae)* for a certain number of days per year. Their extent was governed by reasonableness: they must not prevent him from earning his living. Their fulfillment was governed by good faith, *fides:* he must show his gratitude by a proper loyalty *(obsequium).* In some cases the patron (or patroness) and his immediate descendants had a right to half the freedman's estate. He could not, without the praetor's permission, bring a lawsuit against his patron; and any injury he did him could be punished by penal servitude in the mines. If he were caught in adultery with his patron's wife, he could be killed by his patron, though a wife could not kill a freedwoman she caught with her husband. Nor could a freedwoman married to her patron obtain a divorce and remarry without his permission.

As regards the state, a freedman had considerable disabilities. He could not become a senator or an Eques or hold office in Rome or any town other than colonies. As a voter he was confined to one of the four city "tribes" (registration divisions), so that collectively the freedman vote had very restricted weight. Nevertheless, in the Forum the influence of freedmen was recognized to be considerable through the inside knowledge they might possess as members of noble households and because, having generally been freed on account of their personal merits, they tended to be men of more than average gifts and personality. A freedman could not serve in the legions or the Praetorian Guard or be a priest of any Roman deity. Under judicial examination he was still liable to

---

[3] Indeed only on the land, where they had less chance of catching the master's eye, was manumission rare. The acclimatization of exotic fruits such as the cherry, imported by Lucullus, was thus probably owed to skilled men who remained slaves.

torture. To have been a slave at all carried a stigma, and "servile" was a term of abuse as applied to occupations as well as people. Attempts were made to persuade citizens intending to free and marry a slave woman to take her as a concubine instead of making her *domina*. (This was snobbish rather than rational.) A freedman's origin was not forgotten: though he was endowed with his master's name, he still retained his original name as well, for example, Marcus Tullius Tiro. He wore his "cap of liberty" on such occasions as his patron's funeral. At dinner parties of the upper classes he occupied a lower seat and was served with inferior food; indeed Augustus would not have freedmen at his table. In fact he was tolerated in society so long as he knew his place. But if he was successful, he was a target for the envy of satirical writers and their readers. Horace counterattacked those who backbit him at one time because, a freedman's son, he commanded a legion and later because he was a friend of Maecenas, who was above such prejudice. He boldly claimed credit for his father and himself for having raised themselves by their own merits. (Italian and provincial towns seem to have been free from this snobbery, to judge from appreciative inscriptions.) A freedman's son born after manumission was apparently exempt from his father's legal disabilities except as to voting tribe; he could have a thoroughly Roman name like Quintus Horatius Flaccus; and his father could buy for him offices to which he was not initially entitled, though only the next generation could aspire to be magistrate or senator.

Dionysius of Halicarnassus, the Greek historian who resided at Rome during the first half of Augustus' principate, was impressed by the danger to her national character from the flood of indiscriminate manumission. In 2 B.C. Augustus decided that action was called for. He established a sliding scale for manumissions. If you had two slaves, you could free both; if you had three to ten, you could free half; and so on. No one was to free more than a hundred all together. He also blocked up some undesirable loopholes. But he took care not to be inhumanly repressive. For instance, while a master under the age of twenty was to be forbidden to free a slave unless for good cause approved by a special council, permissible cases might include freeing a devoted and loved nurse or *paedagogus,* or wishing to marry a slave woman with whom he had fallen in love. Or a freedman could purchase the freedom of his parents or siblings. Augustus also tightened up existing regulations about eligibility of freedmen for public office; but to offset this he founded a special office for them at Rome and in all municipalities, that of *Severi Augustales,* a board of six whose official duty was to superintend the cult of the local Lares, but whose real function was to provide from private wealth (thus relieving public funds) spectacles leading to prestige and popularity. Finally, he formalized the loyalty previously left to *fides* by enacting that a patron could banish an ungrateful freedman to a distance of a hundred miles from Rome.

So much for disabilities: what of the positive advantages? The relationship of patron to freedman was conceived of as analogous to that of father to son. One token of this was that they could not be required to give evidence against each other, except in the overriding case of treason. The law did what it could to strengthen this relationship. Often a freedman would go on living in the household of his patron, among people he knew and liked, perhaps in some responsible position such as butler or chef, secretary or tutor. Or the patron would set him up in business, perhaps on condition of sharing in the profits, or make him his political or business agent when he was abroad. Abundant inscriptions testify to gratitude and affection: *sibi et patrono* ("to himself and his patron") is the dedication on some tombs. The Elder Pliny tells of a freedman, left sole heir, who preferred to throw himself onto his patron's pyre.

Outside the family there were many openings for freedmen (and for freedwomen, source of the talented courtesan-entertainers with whom much of Latin erotic poetry is concerned). They could serve in the auxiliary forces, police, and fire brigade. Often they were foremen in factories—in the ratio of about one to every twenty slaves, to judge from signed bricks. In some professions—medicine, philosophy, and teaching, the fine arts—they seem to have been overshadowed by free Greek residents, to some of whom Caesar gave citizenship; in others —architecture, for instance—by freeborn Romans also, such as Vitruvius. But they dominated trade and industry, where there was no snobbery; and a good career was opened to them by Augustus' new civil service. In guilds and clubs, where there was also no snobbery, they played a great part, as well as in religious communities: "the synogogue of the freedmen" is mentioned in the Acts of the Apostles. Thoroughly Romanized, they could congratulate themselves by comparison with the relatives they had left behind in the province of their origin, who had to pay tribute.

They could become rich, either by exploiting their patron's status, like Sulla's notorious Chrysogonus and several agents of the triumvirs, or by becoming his heir, or by their own talents in business. (Petronius' fictional freedman Trimalchio, after retiring from active business, financed other freedmen; and a real one at Venusia who had made his fortune in perfume freed all his slaves in his will and apparently left them his money.) Besides including some of the most powerful men in Rome, they provided some of the most cultivated. Such were Tyrannio, a distinguished scholar captured in the Mithridatic War, who arranged Cicero's library at Antium, tutored his nephew Quintus, and wrote a book on accents; the poet Parthenius, captured in the same war and freed by the family of Cinna the poet, who is said to have taught Vergil Greek and who certainly helped the other modernist poets, for we possess a collection of love stories about heroines that he made for Gallus; and Hyginus, an encyclopedic writer, whom Augustus put in charge of the new Palatine Library.

Whether, given the slave system, Roman custom (it can hardly be called policy) concerning manumission was wise is a question we cannot answer. It was certainly both wiser and more humane than any attempt to make slavery perpetual as well as hereditary. When Juvenal complains that he cannot bear the city gone Greek, and that the Orontes (Antioch's river) has flowed into the Tiber, he is merely xenophobic (and misleading, for the population was not predominantly Oriental). For three centuries and more there had been no racial purity to pollute, and Rome was at least innocent of color prejudice. We must take more seriously the opinion of an unprejudiced foreigner like Dionysius of Halicarnassus about the deleterious effect of indiscriminate manumission on national character. No doubt many of those who came from the North and West had a strain of barbarity, as those who came from the long-established Hellenistic monarchies were liable to have a habit of servile deceit; and the very experience of slavery must have corrupted in many the sense of values. Some successful freedmen may have been as vulgar as Petronius' Trimalchio. But giving freedmen citizen rights without effective vote can have done no harm, and it seems to have turned many into cooperative and patriotic Romans. Without them the great administrative machinery of the empire, to which we now come, would have been unthinkable.

CHAPTER SEVEN

THE EMPIRE IN THE
FIRST TWO CENTURIES

In the two centuries that separate the accession of Augustus in 27 B.C. and the death of Marcus Aurelius in A.D. 180 the framework constructed by Augustus remained remarkably firm. There was even a fair degree of monetary stability, as is shown by the fact that the only change in soldiers' pay was a rise of one-third under Domitian. In this chapter we shall see how the experience of the Roman people was intensified or varied within this period from what has been described in the past two chapters. By "the Roman people" we mean all those, bond or free, who lived in the Roman Empire; but more especially the citizen body, as distinct from foreigners (*peregrini*). The citizens numbered something over four million when Augustus came to power, and despite his checks the citizen body was expanded, with corresponding dilution of privileges, until, by the Edict of Caracalla in 212, practically all freeborn men in the empire acquired Roman citizenship in addition to that of their home.

Relations Among the Peoples of the Empire

In the lands bordering the western Mediterranean and to the north Romanization was fairly rapid. The Italians retained for some time the special position safeguarded for them by Augustus. The only taxes they paid were 5 percent on inheritances and on manumissions and sales of slaves, one percent on market sales, and customs duties. They still had a majority among senators and consuls. They provided the Praetorian Guard, the privileged elite corps that acquired unhealthy power after Tiberius' minister Sejanus established a permanent camp for it beneath the walls of the capital. But an enactment of Trajan, that senators must invest one-third of their income in Italy, shows what anxieties were felt. "Italy lived on the empire, and died of it." By the end of the first century Gaul was producing competitive pottery, glass, and plain textiles, and Domitian had tried ineffectively to ban provincial winegrowing in the face of competition from Bordeaux, Burgundy, the Rhine, and the Moselle. Cheaper oil was now imported: a hill 140 feet high in what was the mercantile quarter of ancient Rome, the Monte Testaccio, consists entirely of fragments of African, Spanish, and Gallic jars dating from the early empire.

What the provinces derived in turn from Roman influence is indicated by such monuments as the theater at Orange on the Rhône, the bridge at Alcantara (subscribed for by eleven communities), the Pont du Gard (just part of an aqueduct for the town of Nîmes), and the baths at Bath in Somerset. What had been essentially tribal centers (Caesar, for instance, knew Paris as "Lutetia of the Parisians") became towns on the Italian pattern, like Vienne, in southeastern France, where all the chiefs of the Allobroges went to live. The seeds of education sown in Spain by Sertorius eventually bore fruit in writers such as Lucan, the Senecas, Columella the agriculturalist, Quintilian, and Martial, and in two of the greatest emperors, Trajan and Hadrian. By the second century the Italian race was of dwindling significance. By A.D. 56 many Equites and even senators were descendants of slaves. To be a Roman meant nothing racial, but to be the proud possessor of Roman citizenship, to be able like St. Paul to appeal to Caesar, and, in the West, to follow Roman customs; and, if you were educated, to speak Latin as well as your native tongue and to nourish your Roman patriotism on the reading of Cicero, Vergil, and Livy. The hopes and wishes of the central government were signified and spread by an ever-changing coinage bearing inscriptions and symbolic emblems that were apparently well understood.

From at least the time of Claudius auxiliary soldiers to the number of about five thousand a year became citizens automatically on retirement. Again, where Rome planted a military colony any natives already on the site were given citizenship. Cologne (Colonia Agrippinensis) was founded by Claudius in 50 among German Ubii whom Agrippa had brought over for their safety to the west bank of the Rhine. When in 69–70 Civilis from the Low Countries tried to establish a breakaway "Empire of the Gauls," these Germans refused to massacre the Romans, "our relatives." They returned to their allegiance as soon as the revolt was quelled. The Greek geographer Strabo noted that the Romanized Turdetani of Spain wore the toga, spoke Latin, and produced literature, while the Lusitanians beyond them lived on acorn bread and water, slept on the ground in their day clothes, exposed their sick, stoned criminals, and maimed captives and disembowelled them for purposes of divination.

In the countries around the eastern Mediterranean the situation was different. Their Hellenistic civilization was the parent, not the offspring, of the Roman. The "Common" Greek they spoke was recognized as an official language, on a par with Latin except in the army; and although there were those who followed Polybius in their admiration for Roman institutions, from Strabo and Dionysius under Augustus to Plutarch and to Aelius Aristides after him, most Greeks apparently took little trouble to learn Latin and to get to know a literature now far superior to what they were producing themselves. It was some time before Vergil was translated into Greek, whereas Aelian chose to write in Greek though he came from Praeneste, near Rome.

But good roads and safeguarded seas facilitated travel all over the empire. Horace and Propertius could anticipate being read in the remotest parts. The latest speech of Pliny or epigram of Martial would be delivered everywhere along with the *Daily Chronicle* from Rome. Syrians penetrated into the far north and west, trading and introducing their invention of translucent glass; and there are tombstones at Bath, for instance, of soldiers who had been born on the Rhine and the Moselle, in southern Gaul, and in Spain. Most of the victims of the great persecution of Christians at Lyon in 177 were Greeks. Tourism also was one of the great pleasures of the age. People went to Gades (Cádiz) or Gaul to see the wonder of the Atlantic tides. Plutarch once encountered at Delphi two men of whom one had just been to the Persian Gulf and the other to the islands beyond Britain. But chiefly Greek lands were visited. Tourists were not much interested in local customs, which in this area did not differ greatly. There were a certain number of natural phenomena worth seeing; but the works of man were the chief attraction. Young men like Ovid and Horace's friend Bullatius made the grand tour of the Greek cities around the Aegean. There was still plenty of Greek art that had not been carried off to Italy, not to mention great works of architecture: Phidias' Zeus could be seen at Olympia, Praxiteles' Aphrodite at Cnidos. A race of guides sprang up. Temples were museums in which you could see such things as outsize elephant tusks or historical relics. The Emperor Vitellius presented to a temple of Mars at Cologne the dagger with which Otho, his predecessor, had killed himself. At Sparta you could see an egg laid by Leda herself (perhaps an ostrich's). Marsyas' skin and the cauldron in which Pelias was boiled had a special appeal. Indeed one has the impression that, apart from Egypt, people visited these lands more for their connections with history or legend than for their glories of art or architecture, however conscientiously checked off. Though to Propertius the prospect of a visit to Athens had held hopes of artistic enjoyment, Atticus, who lived there, valued its human associations more. Some went to Marathon or followed the footsteps of Alexander. Some sought initiation at Eleusis, questioned the oracle at Delphi, or even sacrificed on the site of Hercules' pyre on the summit of Mount Oeta. There was not so much exploration, though Nero shared the perennial curiosity about the source of the Nile, and in his reign an Eques who penetrated barbarian country to the Baltic brought back a quantity of amber. Conversely, Roman objects have been found in tombs in Norway by Trondhjem Fjord and in Finland, a Roman lamp a thousand miles south of Algiers, and pots from Arretium in Pondicherry in southeastern India and in Hertfordshire in Britain. Merchants pushed along the trade route that brought the silks of the Far East to the warehouses of Syria and Egypt, India was reached by land, and finally in 166 Marcus Aurelius sent a trade mission to the Chinese court by sea. (The Chinese noted that they were honest in their transactions and had no double prices—the old *fides* seems to have still been operative.) A more regular luxury trade with southern India by sea, already considerable in Augustus' time, increased greatly after Hippalus ascertained the habits of the monsoon.

The Romans, despite occasional recognition of "hearts dedicated to dying free" (in Horace's phrase) and Caesar's unique crediting of greatness of spirit to the Nervii, and despite Tacitus' attribution to the Briton Calgacus of the famous epigram "they make a solitude and call it peace," were confident in general that they had a mission "to give laws" (*dare iura*) to undisciplined lesser breeds, and that barbarians should be grateful to be under their rule in a culture based on urban life. Tacitus attributes to the Roman commander Cerialis, on the occasion of the quelling of Civilis' revolt, a speech at Trier in which he put it to the rebels that, whatever their transient grievances, they were permanently better off under the Pax Romana than they would be amid the incessant local feuds that independence would let loose again. The northern Gauls they found backward rather than savage, and they had an irrational contempt for their trousers. Indeed that people proved slow to achieve the highest rank, one of the first to do so being Vindex, who in 68 took the initiative that eventually toppled Nero. Germans they found very different. If they apparently resented their superior stature, it was a remarkable compliment that Augustus should choose to recruit his personal bodyguard from among this brave, loyal, uncomplicated people. Tacitus picked out for praise such of their customs and characteristics as could be used as a reproach to his own countrymen. Similarly Horace, following Greek tradition, had alleged, in contrast with contemporary Roman tendencies, "The Scythians of the Steppes do better . . ."; and the Elder Pliny idealized the Ceylonese for having no slaves (a most rare acknowledgment of the unthinkable) and no civil lawsuits. Interest in barbarian peoples as they really were emerges in the markedly differentiated types shown in the reliefs on Trajan's column.

Though moralists like Tacitus and Juvenal, nostalgic for the old Catonian type of Roman, tended to look askance at "Greeklings" as decadent, the animosity of Juvenal at least may have sprung from jealousy of success. In general the Romans were laudably tolerant of divergences, short of the human sacrifices perpetrated by the Celtic Druids and the Cypriots. They even made exceptions to accommodate Jewish peculiarities. Augustus changed the day of the corn dole to avoid their sabbath. Jews all over the empire were allowed to contribute half a shekel yearly to the Temple at Jerusalem. They were exempt from military service. Their religious and judicial affairs were left to the High Priest and his Council. They also had their own coinage, bearing no graven image of the emperor. Julius Caesar protected them, grateful for their having saved him from a tight corner at Alexandria; so did Agrippa when he visited the East in 14 B.C., moved by the advocacy of one Nicolaus, the spokesman of his own friend Herod. Nicolaus pleaded the Roman principle of religious freedom. This freedom however presupposed the idea countenanced by Stoicism, that all religions were embodiments, varying in purity, of religion in general, in which spirit Augustus and Livia caused offerings to be made daily in their name in the Temple at Jerusalem. This idea the Jews utterly rejected. Their tribal Jehovah was the only true God. They made converts (possibly even Nero's Poppaea).

Their neglect of the state religion infringed the "peace of the gods." They refused to accept the symbolic act of allegiance performed by all other provincial Roman subjects, emperor worship. Trouble was bound to come, and when it did it was of exceptional violence. Tiberius transported four thousand Jewish freedmen to Sardinia as conscripts, though Claudius reaffirmed their privileges and refused to take sides against them over riots at Alexandria. Judaea rebelled in 66, and in 70 Titus captured Jerusalem, pillaging the Temple. The heroic mass suicide at Masada followed three years later. Even this was not the end: there remained six or seven million Jews scattered all over the empire. Vespasian diverted their annual half-shekel donations to rebuilding the Temple of Capitoline Jupiter, destroyed in the upheaval of 69. But meanwhile the remnants of Jerusalem were becoming reinhabited.

Caution on the Use of Sources

The popular image of the early Roman Empire is probably a distorted one in which, owing to the nature of our literary sources, emperors loom too large and extravagance is exaggerated. One cause is the survival of Suetonius' *Twelve Caesars,* important because, as Hadrian's secretary, he had access to imperial archives, but interlarded with gossip uncritically purveyed. Another is the dramatic and satirical genius of Tacitus and Juvenal. The historians tend to see things in the light of senatorial tradition. Surviving literature, apart from the novels of Petronius and Apuleius, deals mainly with the comparatively small upper classes. Were it not for the wealth of inscriptions and papyri we should know even less than we do of the life of the common man. Thus inscriptions show that the office of Seviri Augustales was the pride of innumerable freedmen, whereas in literature we meet it only in the person of Petronius' Trimalchio and his guest Hermeros.

Our literary authorities also tend to be stern moralists. They indulge in the rhetorical exercise of "abuse of the present age," prominent already in Sallust, and unrealistic nostalgia for Catonian simplicity. Imbued with Stoic preaching of the virtues of a life according to Nature, the Elder Pliny deplored the cultivation of cabbages, artichokes, and asparagus, which she had intended to grow wild. Marble should not be used in building: Nature had put it where she wanted it. Indeed earthquakes and conflagrations were probably divine vengeance for the luxury of great houses. And "no greater inroads have been made on our morals than by the consumption of shellfish." The luxuries of one age are the necessities of the next. The neurasthenic Seneca likewise condemned central heating, hothouse flowers, potted plants on roofs, roses procured out of season, dyed fabrics, and of course seafaring and the mining of jewels and metals. Later Apuleius was accused, among other things, of advocating the use of toothpowder; and as for Caracalla, Dio accuses him of indulging in soft living at Antioch even to the extent of having his whole chin shaved. The Elder Pliny also deplored the innovations of senators sitting on cushions and wearing sun hats in the theater. Moralists made no distinctions: Sallust was equally shocked at Roman soldiers' becoming corrupted by the luxury of the East and at their admiring Greek works of art. Seneca speaks contemptuously of those who fill their houses with beautiful objects, while Juvenal jumbles breaches of convention with what we would consider real immorality.

Probably no one took these flourishes very seriously; nor should we. It is true that the gap between rich and poor was shamefully great. It is true that the proliferation of slaves led to absurd specialization. Hadrian's country seat below Tibur (Tivoli) is of fantastic extent, yet smaller than the palace of Charles IV at Caserta. And who are we, for instance, to call the Romans gluttonous? They imported rare delicatessen: so do we. They had about seven courses at their dinner parties: the Edwardian English often had twelve. "Turtle heads, part of fins and green fat; capons, turkeys, pullets, pheasants, partridges, pigeons, snipe, woodcock (of all these only two small *noix* from each side of the back); plovers, grouse, quails, stuffed larks, ortolans; garniture of cockscombs, truffles, mushrooms, crawfish, olives, sweetbreads, green mangoes" were the ingredients of a great dish prepared, not for Vitellius, but for Queen Victoria's Albert and some fellow diners at York. The moralists often cite headline cases as if they were the rule. To do so is indeed the stock in trade of satire. We must remember also that, unlike many of us, the Romans had only one main meal a day.

The Emperors

Let us consider the emperors first. Partly because what has survived of Tacitus' *Annals* largely concerns Tiberius and Nero, an impression may have been created that reigns of terror were frequent. In fact the term could justly be applied only to the last few years of Tiberius, Caligula, Nero, and Domitian, perhaps a total of about twenty years out of the two centuries from Augustus to Marcus Aurelius. During most of those centuries there appears to have been good government. Tiberius, though lacking in the graces, was a man of outstanding ability, and in his honesty a change from Augustus, whose ill usage of him is enough to account for his ultimate obsessions. Some of Claudius' actions do not suggest the freak he was supposed to be. Justice and the provinces were well administered under Domitian, a stern puritan who was yet popular enough with the Roman plebs and the army. To some extent the character of emperors affected fashion. Thus Nero gave a temporary boost to declamation and to the arts (witness his marvelous coinage), Marcus Aurelius to philosophy; and upper-class life became simpler under the Sabine Vespasian, who regularly revisited his unaltered ancestral farm, and who filled the gaps made in the Senate by the slaughter of 68–69 with solid Italian burghers. A good deal depended also on what advisers an emperor had. Claudius was unfortunately under the thumb of his wives and freedman secretaries; whereas Seneca and Burrus guided the young Nero wisely in the early, happy years of his reign. Power went to the head of Caligula, apparently a psychopath, who was fortunately murdered before, for instance, he achieved his maniac desire to foist his statue on the Temple at Jerusalem; and of Nero, whose reckless expenditure after the fire of 64 nearly bankrupted the treasury. Domitian required to be addressed as "Lord and God." But what must be emphasized is that on the whole, changes of emperor made far more difference to upper-class circles at Rome than to the empire as a whole.

The city populace judged emperors largely by their showing at the spectacles in circus, arena, and theater, where it was showered with gifts and lottery tickets. Julius Caesar having given offense by patently attending to paperwork in his box, Augustus took care to give no such impression of indifference. Tiberius was positively hostile to the spectacles, cut them down, and absented himself more and more. Caligula on the contrary was a fanatical supporter of the green faction of chariot racers, whose colors he wore, while Vitellius acted as a groom for the blues. Claudius was actually criticized for excessive zeal in securing "criminals" to throw to the beasts, and Tacitus alleges that he amassed nineteen thousand for each side of his naval battle on the Fucine Lake. But Nero most captured the imagination of the populace, driving a racing chariot himself and appearing on the stage to mime sensational scenes from tragedy or to play the lyre and sing songs he had composed himself, sometimes highly original, which achieved sufficient popularity to be sung at wayside inns. He even toured Greece, seeking a more sympathetic and discriminating audience to supplement his organized claque, the Augustani, whom he took with him. There he arranged for all the four ancient games to be held in one year so that he could compete (if it could be called competition). Finally, a new Flamininus, he proclaimed at the Isthmian games that all mainland Greece (Achaea) was to be free and exempt from taxes (Vespasian was to cancel this a few years later). Back at Rome he instituted four-yearly games on Greek lines, at which many wore Greek clothes, and got distinguished Romans to compete with him, besides encouraging Greek athletics as healthy exercise for the young. All this shocked the majority of respectable Italians, especially his stage appearances (acting was by tradition a "disreputable" profession, though several emperors had actor favorites); but such was the impression he made on ordinary people, and especially on Greeks, that when he died many could not or would not believe the news, and of three impostors one held out for some time with Parthian support.[1]

Nero's games petered out after his death, but Domitian had much more success with the Capitoline games he founded: they were celebrated throughout antiquity, ranking with the Olympics and drawing competitors from all over the empire, and the winners were reckoned world champions. The area of his specially constructed stadium survives today as Piazza Navona. Music was performed before an audience of ten thousand in the Odeum built for the purpose by Apollodorus of Damascus, reputedly the most beautiful building in

[1] As late as the eleventh century there were those who looked for his return.

Rome. A unique feature was the competition in Greek and Latin poetry. Clad in Greek clothes (everything was Greek) and wearing the innovation of a golden crown, the emperor himself decorated the winners with a wreath of oak leaves on the Capitol, a ceremony revived for Petrarch in 1341.

An account of the Roman experience must have regard to individual emperors only as they affected that experience. But one of them is so interesting in himself, so all-embracing in his activities, and so central to this period that we may use him, as we used the Scipios and Cato, as a paradigm—Hadrian (117–138). He shows how much difference an active emperor could make.

Hadrian was born in Spain in A.D. 76. His father having died when he was ten, he was brought up by his cousin Trajan and well educated, mainly in Domitian's Rome. At the age of seventeen he was sent on military service to Aquincum (Budapest), and thus early became acquainted with frontier conditions. He was twenty-one and stationed in Germany when he was chosen by his fellow officers as the obvious person to go to Cologne and convey their congratulations to Trajan on his adoption by Nerva. Within a year Trajan was emperor, and he and his wife Plotina, whose affection Hadrian reciprocated, arranged in Roman fashion that their young protégé should marry a great-niece of his, Sabina. Whether the childless marriage proved happy is dubious, but at least there was no outward sign to the contrary during their thirty-seven years together. Consul at thirty-three and presented with a ring that Nerva had given his successor, Hadrian might well think himself the heir apparent. Whether others agreed, or Trajan intended so, remains unclear.

One late favor Trajan did, however, do his young cousin: he put him in command of the major military province of Syria while he himself campaigned against the kingdom of Parthia. On his return, the Mesopotamian conquests already in revolt, Trajan died in Cilicia; and Hadrian learned (or alleged he had learned) that he was his successor by a deathbed adoption. He wrote modestly to the Senate and caused a great Triumph to be celebrated at Rome in his predecessor's name; but several of Trajan's most influential military advisers were put to death, ostensibly for plotting against the new man, and it was on a wave of unpopularity that Hadrian finally arrived in the capital in 118. He had to bid for favor with huge games, twice the usual present given by a new emperor to the soldiers, and the cancellation of very large outstanding debts to the treasury.

The style of his reign soon became apparent: it was to be like that of Augustus. Already he had withdrawn, as Augustus would have advised, from Trajan's conquests beyond the Euphrates: the ancient Parthian culture was not assimilable. (The annexation of Dacia, with its new settlers, not to mention its mineral wealth, was a *fait accompli,* though he is said to have consulted his privy council even on this.) His coins proclaim his policy: "The Liberality of Augustus," "The Discipline of Augustus," or simply "Hadrian Augustus." At Rome senators and Equites were reminded to wear the toga on formal occasions.

The reforms he instituted in the army were to stand the test of 150 years. Discipline as to leave was tightened up. Soldiers were not to be recruited when too young nor kept on when too old. Promotion was to be by merit, and he himself scrutinized it down to centurion level. Camps were cleared of civilian traders. As in the case of Augustus, stricter discipline only increased the emperor's popularity with the soldiers. He knew as many of them as he could personally. He shared their life and rations, trudging thousands of miles at their head. An inscribed column at Lambaesis on the edge of the African desert, where he spent a fortnight in camp, records his commendations and admonitions. He paid attention to decorations and bonuses; and though marriage was still barred, he granted a place (not a high one) in the scale of intestate succession to a soldier's son born "in the camp."

Hadrian treated the Senate with deference, as Trajan had done; but in both theory and practice the emperor was much more truly an autocrat in his day than in that of Augustus. It was accepted that his word was law; and by the codification of the Praetor's Edict, carried out by his brilliant protégé Salvius Julianus (Julian), arguably the greatest of all Rome's jurists, he removed the last potentially independent source of legal change. Henceforward it must all come through the emperor and his council, and we hear no more of rival schools of jurisprudence. Law had become a part of bureaucracy.

Hadrian at his accession had already seen more of the empire than any previous emperor in his whole lifetime. Unlike Trajan, he was a cosmopolitan at heart. He wished the provinces, of whose individuality he was deeply conscious, to feel themselves partners rather than possessions. In one respect he recognized that things had changed since Augustus' time: Italy could no longer be conceded her old superiority. She now received circuit judges, as some provinces did; and the emperor's tours of inspection in Italy are commemorated on coins and inscriptions in the same terms as his provincial journeys.

The years 121–132 he spent mostly in travel. He began with the West and by 122 had created the fortification across Britain from the Tyne to the Solway that controlled the north and south passage and safeguarded east and west mobility of troops. From there he went south through Gaul and Spain. But by far the greatest part of his travels was in the Hellenized East, making good earthquake damage, reforming administration, hearing cases in court and complaints from his tenants, presenting an aqueduct here, a temple there, and founding various Adrianoples; for he was a passionate philhellene. His Mecca was the "free" city of Athens, free within the empire, which six years before he became emperor had elected him an archon, an honor granted to no previous foreigner save Domitian. The breastplate of his statue at Olympia showed Athena with her owl and snake being crowned by two Graces, with the Capitoline wolf suckling Romulus and Remus beneath. He reformed the city's laws and indulged her with a host of imposing structures: a porch with library, a gymnasium, and a whole new quarter surrounding the huge unfinished temple of Olympian Zeus. This temple was now at last completed; fifteen tall Corinthian columns still stand today out of more than a hundred. He also founded a Panhellenic Council of a cultural nature and presided over its meetings. At Athens he wore Greek clothes and talked in Greek, enjoying the company of the "Sophist" intellectuals who congregated there. Their discourse was, we may feel, banal compared with that we may attribute to their predecessors of five or six centuries before; but they thought they had revived the Greek genius, and their enthusiasm for artistic prose spread to the West. Hadrian was the first Roman emperor to cultivate a beard. Beards were the mark of philosophers.

It was as a philosopher (we should say "intellectual") that he liked to see himself, and "philosopher" meant also "man of letters." He shared and paraded the fashionable tastes of the age, such as rating the late epic poet Antimachus above Homer, Cato above Cicero, Ennius above Vergil. His ambition was to be the all-around man, combining Roman and Greek, soldier and aesthete. His passion for hunting and military exercises was matched by a passion for singing and lyre-playing; and much of his travel was pure tourism, in search of natural spectacles like the sunrise seen from the summit of Etna or Casius, or the sites of literature and history—Zama, Troy, the tombs of Ajax and Epaminondas and Pompey.

One of his acts, the placing of a white marble statue of Alcibiades (famous for his good looks) on his grave two hundred miles east of Ephesus, was perhaps motivated by another element in his psyche. It was while touring in Asia Minor that he met and fell in love with the beautiful Bithynian youth Antinoüs, who was his constant companion for nine years until he was drowned on an expedition up the Nile in 130. The grief of the emperor at this event pervaded the empire. Rumor had it that the boy had somehow sacrificed himself for his friend. The city of Antinoöpolis rose at the place where he died. He was deified and identified with Hermes, Apollo, Dionysus, or Osiris. A new-found star was claimed to be his soul. The passion of Antinoüs was the subject of a mystery play, and games were founded in his memory. A more lasting effect was the proliferation of portrait statues and busts of him; about five hundred survive, including the only important nudes produced under Rome (the nudity denoted deification). Some, such as the head at Olympia, may have been from life, though most are posthumous. His astonishing, melancholy, mysterious grace had inspired a direct apprehension of human beauty in art unknown since the time of Praxiteles five centuries before; and in the words of Kenneth Clark, "The physical character of Antinoüs is still perceptible when, after its long banishment, the Apollonian nude returns in the person of Donatello's David."

The reader will not be surprised to learn that Hadrian was a connoisseur of religions and a student of astrology and magic. One religion, however, he gravely failed to understand, that of the Jews. Jews and Greeks were perpetually at odds in the Near East, especially at Alexandria. In 115–116 the Jews of Cyrene had risen (for causes unknown) and massacred a quarter of a million Greeks (so Dio relates), and revolt had spread to Jews in other areas, though not to Palestine itself. Hadrian, reaching Jerusalem on his travels and desiring as ever to turn desolation into a flourishing community, converted the site of the Holy City, abandoned since its sack under the Flavians, into a splendid pagan Roman colony, to be called Aelia Capitolina. And this time the Jews of the homeland fought a last desperate guerrilla war under Rabbi Akiba and his proclaimed Messiah, Bar Kochba. They lost, of course.

Most of Hadrian's last six years were spent at Rome. There we encounter great monuments of his passion for building, which left its mark all over the empire in such examples as the baths in Leptis Magna and the basilica at Cyrene in North Africa, remains of which may still be seen. The fire that had devastated the greater part of the old city of Rome under Nero in 64 had given an opportunity to architects to develop on a grand scale the possibilities of a new kind of construction, Rome's great gift to the art of building, using brick and concrete with marble or stucco facings for apses, vaults, and domes and in general for the organization of space. First came Nero's own Golden House, on a site of 125 acres, soon obliterated by the baths of Titus and Trajan, while the Colosseum rose on the site of his ornamental lake. We know the name of Trajan's architect, who built a famous bridge over the Danube and the splendid forum that surrounded his column, the Apollodorus of Damascus already mentioned. (His banishment by Hadrian in 129 and subsequent execution are said to have been due to criticisms, tactlessly expressed, of the huge temple of Venus and Rome designed by the emperor himself, who was liable to sad lapses from grace.) Who the architect of the Pantheon was we do not know: the conception may have been Hadrian's own. The name of the original founder, Agrippa, was allowed to stand on the huge, incongruous portico that leads to the serene interior of what was until recently the largest dome in the world. The grandiosity of Nero's Golden House was surpassed in the palace that Hadrian built below Tibur on a site three-quarters the size of Rome. A sort of permanent exhibition of the empire with reproductions of places and buildings, mainly in Greece but including the Alexandrian Canopus, and of all kinds of statuary, it was perhaps somewhat vulgar in its conception though it is romantic today as a nexus of ruins. In one last emulation of Augustus, whose circular tomb by the Tiber bend had no more room for imperial remains, he reared on the opposite bank, led up to by a new bridge, his mausoleum (now Castel Sant' Angelo), the rotunda of which was originally crowned with statues and surmounted by a roof garden.

Hadrian was destined to die as he had come to the purple, "hated by all." With the people of Rome he was never truly popular, perhaps mainly because of his long absences. His own class disliked him, partly because of the executions with which his reign had begun and, it is fair to add, his firm hand with corrupt and inefficient administrators, but also perhaps because he was a "know-it-all," a "Greekling." And as a childless emperor he had always the problem of the succession hanging over him. There were plenty of possibilities. In 136 Hadrian, already a sick man, gave a totally unexpected answer, adopting as successor a certain Lucius Commodus, who had just reached the consulship.

His reason is unknown. Was Commodus his illegitimate son? Or another Antinoüs? Though not a fool, he was undistinguished, and his health was dubious. Worse, his elevation involved the execution of Hadrian's aged brother-in-law, Servianus, and Servianus' grandson, a possible successor. But for the empire the sequel was less tragic. Commodus died a natural death in 138, and Hadrian made another choice, a much wiser one, as it turned out, of Titus Antoninus (though at the time he was neither more popular nor more obvious). He was only just in time: by July of that year he was in agony, begging for release from life.

Hadrian had always been a versifier. Before he died he addressed to himself those wistful lines that once more bring home to us the fact that he was no ordinary Roman:

Little soul, little wayward favorite,
Guest and companion of my body,
Where will you be going to now,
So pale, so stark, so naked,
Forgetting all your fun?

The Senate wanted to undo his acts and deny him deification; but Antoninus Pius deterred them, paid him due honors, and laid him finally in his mausoleum.

The Position of the Upper Classes

In the making of emperors the Senate played only an apparent part, though it decided which were posthumously to be deified. By the time Augustus died fifty-five years had passed since the last effort of republicanism, at Philippi. On only one occasion, the murder of Caligula in 41, did the Senate seriously debate whether to restore the republic or elect a successor itself, and it proved to be deeply divided—only to find that it had no choice, the Praetorian Guard having meanwhile fixed on Claudius, who had set a disastrous precedent by promising them a donative equivalent to five years' pay. Worse still, the death of Nero and its sequel, the successful elevation of Vespasian as emperor by the legions in the East, "revealed the secret that an emperor could be made elsewhere than at Rome" (Tacitus). It is true that on Domitian's murder the Senate elected one of its number nominated by the murderers; but he was soon forced by the Praetorians to execute his nominators, and general revolt in the armies would probably have toppled Nerva, had he not prudently adopted in Trajan a great soldier to their liking and died soon after. With Trajan the Senate finally came to terms, preferring a good emperor to more upheavals.

Freedom of thought and speech was the great question of conscience and principle for senators and thinking people in general from the time of Augustus' accession. Though Augustus himself, despite the case of Ovid, seems to have inclined to tolerance, the majority of the Senate did not. Titus Labienus had attacked the upper classes indiscriminately. When giving readings of his history he would say, "the next bit can be read after my death," and pass on. The Senate ordered his books to be burned and drove him to suicide. Toward the end of the reign Cassius Severus was exiled, and his books also burned, under the blanket charge that was to become an instrument of terror in later reigns, *maiestas,* treason. The fact that Augustus' name had been involved led to his being held responsible in after years, and certainly he must have condoned the repression. Ultimately the Senate stood for "law and order," the protection of established authority against any kind of subversion. Tiberius tried in vain to defend freedom of thought and speech. Cremutius Cordus, who had praised Brutus and called Cassius "the last of the Romans," was driven to his death, and the Senate had his history burned. In the early empire there were spies and eavesdroppers everywhere. Politics was not discussed at dinner parties. Even in provincial towns a governor could be blackmailed with "If thou release this man thou art not Caesar's friend"; a teacher probed with such a question as "Ought one to pay tribute to Caesar?"

How could opinion make itself felt, with the Senate becoming more subservient and wary with each disciplining of a member by the emperor, each bout of persecution? (The extent of its impotence was revealed by its failure to make decisions when Tiberius retired to Capri.) The mildest and safest way was to praise rulers for doing what you hoped they would do, as did Seneca in his treatise *On Clemency,* dedicated to the youthful Nero, and Pliny in his panegyric of the new emperor Trajan. There was also the time-honored method of presenting petitions or demonstrating at the spectacles, and rising and waving handkerchiefs to greet personalities, or not rising. The Equites demonstrated in A.D. 9 against Augustus' marriage legislation. Tiberius, having moved to his palace Lysippus' statue of an athlete with a scraper, was constrained by clamor to restore it to its public position. Occasionally the common people were outraged beyond bearing, as when Nero banished his former wife Octavia on a trumped-up charge of adultery, or when all the four hundred slaves of the murdered prefect Pedanius Secundus were put to death, though in neither case did the protest achieve anything. Graffiti were rife as always: "Up with Nero" and "Down with Nero and Poppaea" we read at Pompeii. Pointed abstention from participating in meetings of the Senate was practiced under Augustus by Antistius Labeo, and with great effect for three years by Paetus Thrasea under Nero, who finally forbade it and drove him to suicide.

Thrasea was a Stoic, and it was from the philosophers that the chief opposition came in the period from Nero to Trajan. In principle the Stoics thought that a just monarch provided the best form of government. Thrasea and his associates were partly puritans protesting against a corrupt and luxurious court. But he was also republican enough to write a life of Cato and to celebrate the birthdays of Brutus and Cassius, and philosopher enough to associate with Musonius Rufus and befriend the young Stoic satirist Persius. The Stoic Seneca had hoped to make Nero a philosopher-king. When he failed, he took refuge in a more Epicureanlike retirement, professing gratitude for leisure to pursue less worldly things, and even in one mood suggesting that the younger Cato, hero of Lucan and the Stoics, and usually of himself, had been mistaken in attempting political action when it could no longer hope to succeed. Thrasea was the great Stoic martyr. The campaign was carried on even under the frugal Vespasian, who might have seemed a good enough ruler. Thrasea's fanatical son-in-law Helvidius Priscus preached outright republicanism, eventually forcing the emperor to grant him the martyrdom he probably suspected him of courting and to promote the harmless rhetoricians at the expense of the philosophers. One of Helvidius' complaints may have been against the hereditary principle. If so, he could have claimed that Vespasian's son Domitian proved his point. Domitian expelled philosophers as subversive, un-Roman intellectuals dangerously interested in political theory, with the support of the rhetorician Quintilian, whose educational ideas were otherwise so enlightened. One of them was the saintly Epictetus, who inherited from Thrasea the idea that the only freedom that mattered was moral: the Pax Romana could give outward but not inward peace, and the emperor, though he could kill the body, could not harm the soul.

Even under Trajan the philosophic opposition continued at first. But Tacitus at the beginning of his *Histories* spoke of "the rare happiness of these times, when you can think what you like and say what you think." "His heart," it has been said, "was on the side of the republican past, his head on that of the imperial present." Contemptuous of philosophy, he admired martyrs but thought martyrdom useless. The Greek East had for centuries looked to a ruler to be a benefactor, *euergetes*. By the end of the first century A.D. the Stoics had formulated the concept of the emperor as God's vicegerent on earth: in St. Paul's words, "the powers that be are ordained by God." "The glory of obedience" is a phrase used by a Roman Eques. The philosophers finally came into their own under Marcus Aurelius, who was glad to have learned "the conception of a state with one law for all based upon individual equality and freedom of speech and a sovereignty which values above everything the liberty of the subject." Fair enough: but he felt obliged to designate as his successor to sovereignty his own son Commodus, a man dedicated to shooting wild beasts in the arena, who was to spend more and more of his time with gladiators.

At Rome senators ran the municipal organization, the city prefect, a senator, increasingly having the chief jurisdiction in the capital. Abroad they commanded virtually all the legions. To be a praetor or consul was worthwhile only because it led to a genuine role, the governorship of a province, and the status of these offices was lowered by necessary multiplication. After Augustus the provinces required in any one year a total of nine ex-consuls and thirty-four ex-praetors. When Tiberius, for the good of the imperial provinces, prolonged their governors' appointments for up to ten years, the Senate was annoyed and suspected his motives: offices were for sharing around. However, in A.D. 65 of 390 known senators no less than 147 had governed provinces. A whole career could be made abroad, as in Britain by Tacitus' father-in-law, whose biography he wrote, Agricola. But there was always the danger of an emperor's jealousy: Nero forced Corbulo, the greatest general of his time, to commit suicide, and Domitian recalled Agricola.

In general the senators were not discontented, so long as their ancient dignity was outwardly respected. But they naturally felt degraded when they had to vote fulsome felicitations to Claudius' freedman Pallas, for instance; and Tacitus' remarks on the futility of martyrdom may have been prompted by his shame at having participated in subservience under Domitian. Nor did they relish the introduction of provincials into their ranks, on which Claudius made a very sensible speech to them (preserved in an inscription at Lyon, where he himself was born). The fewer the old nobility became, the more snobbery they attracted. But primarily senators were men of wealth, making money out of slave-run estates by agriculture, mining, and pottery, evading by the use of proxies the law that forbade them to trade. Magistrates, as such, were expected to defray the cost of putting on games. This could be crippling; but the provider, as he rode high in a chariot with his children from the Capitol after sacrifice to the circus or arena, where the whole crowd stood up to acclaim him as president for the day while the gorgeous procession carried around the images of the gods, must have felt almost like an ancient *triumphator*.

The Younger Pliny was not among the richest senators; but the impression gained from his letters is one of not unreasonable, though rather smug, satisfaction with the life he led under Trajan. On one occasion he and Tacitus were chosen as joint counsel for the provincials of Africa, impeaching their governor successfully before the Senate. He was an expert on finance and an able administrator (we shall come later to his special mission to Bithynia). Like other sensitive Romans he considered the Greeks to be men in the fullest sense of the word (*homines maxime homines*). A sociable man, he was exceptional in enjoying those social recitals of poetry, attending one of them almost daily during one April. Regarding them as incidentally a way of encouraging young writers, he deplored the difficulty in raising audiences and the way in which some guests gossiped in the antechamber and only came in late, while others left before the end, and not always surreptitiously. Fortunately for him he had a dearly loved wife who was enthusiastic over his writings. He has one dilemma. A candid friend having told him he reads badly, he proposes getting a freedman to do it standing beside him. But how should he himself behave throughout? Look disinterested, or react appropriately?

Though he was a person of imperial consequence, half his heart was clearly in his home town of Como at the foot of the Alps. He gave it many gifts, including an endowment for poor children, a library, and a temple of Ceres with a spacious colonnade to shelter the great crowds that congregated for the annual fair. Though childless, he took the initiative in organizing a secondary school there (until then boys had to board at Milan, eighty miles away, in order to attend one). He was anxious that parents should subscribe, so that they might feel they had a stake in it and might appoint the teachers themselves rather than leave this to local authorities; but he was prepared to put up one-third of the cost.

He had several villas around Lake Como, including two on the promontory at Bellagio where it divides, the higher called Tragedy, the lower Comedy. He describes more fully his Laurentian villa seventeen miles from Rome. The dining room has transparent windows with a sea view on three sides, the waves lapping against it when the wind is in the southwest. The baths are big enough, considering that the sea is there for bathing; and if you turn up unexpectedly, there are three public sets of baths in a nearby village, while town amenities are available at Ostia.

But many senators and Equites were probably less refined than Pliny, deserving the scorn of the Greek satirical writer Lucian, who in the Antonine Age attacked the vulgarity of the idle Roman rich and the venality of the Greeks who for the sake of luxurious living took service in their households.

The Place of Common People

So much for the upper classes, the privileged *honestiores.* What of the rest, the *humiliores?* We have very little evidence about the feelings of the silent majority who worked on the land. We also tend to forget that even when the Circus Maximus at Rome was filled to its capacity of about 190,000 (and the Colosseum held less than half that number), nearly a million inhabitants of Rome must have been going about their ordinary, unrecorded occupations, and the same applies proportionally to the towns of Italy and the empire.

Let us begin with the chief profession of the common man, about which we do know something, soldiering. Any freeborn citizen was eligible. Outside Italy there were plenty of volunteers until civilian life became too comfortable. The recruit had to pass an interview test and a medical inspection. A letter from someone of standing could also be a great help. Once enlisted, he was given three gold pieces as a starter and swore an oath, renewed at the beginning of every year, of allegiance to the emperor. Out of his pay he had to find his arms and his uniform, even his tent, which he would look after the more carefully. This absorbed as much as two-thirds. But if he became a "principal," he would get half as much pay again, if a "senior principal," double. There were also periodical donatives from emperors, half of which was banked with the standard-bearers as a pension fund in the vault under the shrine of the legion's sacred Eagle and other standards. These, which largely took the place of the old booty, could be as much as five years' pay. It is clear that soldiers (whose wills, incidentally, were free from restrictions and formalities) could save quite a lot, for the deposits of two legions at Mainz were enough to finance Saturninus' rebellion against Domitian, who thereafter imposed limits. Looting or commandeering to the value of one denarius a day was condoned, and it is clear that much more took place. Diet was good and varied: even in the context of the rare mutinies we hear no complaint about that. And scurvy was practically unknown. On the other hand the exaction from privates by centurions of bribes for exemption from the nastier fatigue duties was so widespread that, as a substitute for it, Otho had to agree to a disbursement to centurions from his treasury, which became a regular payment.

Apart from this the centurions were an admirable body. They were sixty to a legion, and its backbone, either directly commissioned, even from the Equites, or promoted from the ranks. To become one was the recruit's ambition. If he served with distinction to the age of fifty or sixty and became a top-rank centurion (*primipilaris*), the way to really high office was open. Centurions' records were kept at Rome, and their promotions were subject to the emperor's approval.

Under the Empire a soldier might complete his service without even seeing an enemy. Of course he had to practice the use of weapons, dig and construct fortifications, drill, march, jump, and ride. But he also had to be able to sow and reap, to fell trees, to survey, and to make dykes. Corbulo's troops dug a canal in Germany from the Maas to the Rhine; and the Carr Dyke in Britain may have been dug out in the second century by soldiers to bring corn to the northern forces. Centurions could have police and security functions, go on diplomatic missions, or arbitrate in boundary disputes. Army staff officers were largely responsible for administering justice in the imperial provinces. The technology for the great construction works of the empire was largely supplied by the armies.

Emotionally what held the legions together was their oath, their symbols (the Eagle with its battle honors and other standards), their pride, and loyalty to their general. Success was due to good principles rigorously applied. Discipline probably became less severe in practice than in theory as ideas in general became more humane. Take decimation, the stoning or clubbing to death of every tenth man, chosen by lot, in a cohort by the other cohorts. Octavian had applied it in 34 B.C. to ones that had given way in battle, and had fed the remaining nine-tenths on barley instead of wheat as a punishment. But now decimation became a rarity: the other troops were naturally reluctant to cooperate. Nor was sleeping at a post, or absence from it, so often punished by death. Loyalty to the general, who as a man picked from a hereditarily experienced caste was usually competent though rarely brilliant, had predominated since Sulla. Many praetorians killed themselves on Otho's corpse, and Vitellius' men fought bravely against Vespasian's men. Individual armies had esprit de corps, but not the army as a whole: inscriptions on coins of Nerva, after the clashes of 68–69, optimistically balanced "the forethought of the Senate" with "the concord of the armies."

Finally there was the soldier's religion. The official military cult was based firmly on the old state religion of Rome, particularly the Capitoline triad Jupiter, Juno, and Minerva, with the addition of such suitable deities as Valor, Victory, and Discipline, and also the goddess Roma, associated with the cult of the deified emperors. The annual round of dates and ceremonies, including ones personal to the emperor, must have had a great influence in Romanizing foreign soldiers. But there is plenty of evidence that these also brought with them gods from their distant homes, such as the Egyptian Serapis and the Syrian Goddess, or identified Roman gods with local ones, as a name such as Mars Thincsus indicates, or simply prayed to the *genius loci,* the spirit of the strange locality to which they found themselves posted. There were especially military gods, such as the ancient one from the Commagene iron field in what is now Southern Turkey, Romanized as Jupiter Dolichenus, and in particular the Persian Mithras. Mithraism attained great popularity with the armies in the second and third centuries. It was for men only, in small brotherly groups, with grades akin to military ranks. The mystique of Mithras' bull-slaying and the aroma of burnt pine pervading the cavelike temple as the rites were intoned seem to have had a strong appeal. And finally there was the cult of the Eagle, which bound the whole legion together. How much hold this had was revealed when in Claudius' time a revolt in Dalmatia petered out because of the ill omen that difficulty was experienced in adorning the Eagle and moving the standards from their sockets.

Apart from religious groups, soldiers in the ranks were not allowed to form *collegia,* presumably for fear they might hatch mutinies. But all belonged to a burial club financed by compulsory deductions from pay. Those killed in battle far from their base were cremated, where they were recoverable, and had their ashes brought back: so strong was the belief in the ancient world that somehow a man's welfare beyond the grave depended on the payment of due rites to his remains. Tacitus gives a dramatic account of how the soldiers of Germanicus, six years after, buried the remains of Varus' three legions, annihilated in the Teutoburg Forest.

Veterans however could form *collegia:* those of Augustus especially held together. When attempts were made to settle on land in Italy veterans from various armies, it did not work: there was no community spirit. Men preferred to retire in the places where they had served and struck roots, which might well be also their native country now that legions were more static, and from Hadrian's time onward this became normal.

Conditions of Slaves and Freedmen

The empire, particularly under Hadrian and the Antonines, saw a continued improvement in the lot of town and house slaves. This was due partly to the prevalence of Stoicism in the upper classes. There was a growing tendency to respect the integrity of a slave's family, even though in law he could not marry. Again, though in law he was simply his master's chattel, the state intervened progressively. A slave could not now be thrown to the beasts in the arena without condemnation by a judge. The law recognized his *manes,* his surviving spirit, and protected his tomb, if he had one. Ill-treated slaves could seek sanctuary at the emperor's statue. Nero, under Seneca's inspiration, allowed slaves at Rome to appeal to the city prefect against injustice. Hadrian banished a mistress for ill-treating her slaves for trivial reasons. Antonius Pius allowed slaves in municipalities to complain to a local judge of unfair treatment, with the possibility of compulsory sale to another master. Claudius enacted that any sick slave who was abandoned by his master on the Island of Aesculapius in the Tiber should be free if he recovered, and that any master who killed a slave as sick and therefore useless should be guilty of homicide. Protests against cruelty to slaves become more vocal, in Seneca particularly, but also in Pliny, Juvenal, and Martial. Pliny complained that doctors were more rough with slaves than with freemen. The protests bear witness to the abuses; but there are plenty of inscriptions and stories recording loyalty in slaves, such as the women who refused under torture to testify against Nero's wife Octavia; the man who tried to save his master, one of the Pisonian conspirators, by impersonating him; and the ex-slave Epicharis, who suffered extreme agonies for refusing to betray her accomplices in treason. Apuleius in his novel *The Golden Ass* could at least imagine what it was like to be a slave toiling with the asses in a flour mill; and in Photis he gives us our only real portrait of a slave woman, a maid-of-all-work, witty, beautiful, vivacious, impulsive, and penitent at having endangered her lover. People also came to realize that it paid to treat slaves better. Columella gave relief from work to any woman on his farm who had three children, freedom if she had a fourth; and masters were enjoined to inspect the gangs on their estates to see that no slave was being intolerably victimized by the foreman. Pliny could boast that the quarters for freedmen and slaves at his Laurentian villa could be used for guests in case of need. Seneca's friend Lucilius dined with his slaves, and Seneca approved.

It was the use made by emperors of their own household as public administrators that inaugurated for slaves a career open to talent, since freeborn Romans would not do domestic chores, even accountancy. Julius Caesar began it by appointing some of his slaves to offices in the mint. One of them, Licinus, ended as procurator of Gaul. Felix, Procurator of Judaea in the New Testament, was a freedman. The father of Claudius Etruscus, born at Smyrna and brought to Rome as a slave, was freed by Tiberius and held important bureaucratic posts, including that of financial secretary under ten emperors. Hardworking and frugal, he was made an Eques by Vespasian, and he showed his wealth only in the sumptuous funeral he gave his wife, a senator's daughter. The overriding power of freedmen began in Tiberius' last years, when he was in retirement at Capri, and reached its height under Claudius when, to the predictable resentment of aristocrats and plebs alike, Callistus, Narcissus, and Pallas, as holders of the supreme secretaryships, practically ruled the world. No doubt they were exceptionally efficient at their work; but they were equally efficient at enriching themselves by selling places, pardons, and civic rights. Narcissus was the richest man in antiquity known to us. The imperial bureaucracy usually survived from reign to reign. In Nero's early days the Senate had a debate on the insolence of freedmen. Even after Hadrian had transferred the chief posts to Equites, freedmen continued to occupy positions of influence and patronage. Though some became Equites themselves, most were content to have influence without status, and this they achieved by talent and personality.

The improved condition of imperial freedmen rubbed off onto ordinary ones. As a class indeed they had no political goal, though they could be manipulated politically. Their status depended on that of their patron. Some made money by doing jobs considered degrading, such as that of undertaker. Most secondary-school masters, and some other professional men such as architects and physicians as well as historians and philosophers, were freedmen. Many acquired wealth. Rich men's heirs were sometimes disappointed to find that most of their inheritance was willed to favorite freedmen such as Trimalchio in Petronius. Freedmen account for more than half of those tombs that line the roads to Rome. Pliny, unlike Augustus, dined with his freedmen, smugly letting it be known that he drank the same *vin ordinaire* as he provided for them.

As we have mentioned, there was a widespread idea in antiquity that to work for another's benefit was slavish. This put the peasant above not only the hired laborer, but the artisan and the retailer. Nevertheless there were towns rich in craftsmen and traders, such as Pompeii, and plenty of craftsmen were not ashamed of their profession, as the tombstones testify. A Crassus might employ five hundred carpenters and masons to repair the burnt or rickety buildings he bought cheap as ruins, but in general big business was slow to develop. All over the empire the pattern was of small craftsmen employing a few slaves or freedmen. These craftsmen used their guilds for religious and social purposes, not to ameliorate their condition. Free labor had little power of bargaining, and skilled labor was not refined enough to bring pressure to bear: strikes are almost unheard of, and would probably have been repressed by the authorities. But in the second century the guilds did begin to make strict professional rules. Professional men came up in the world. A general "constitution" of Vespasian exempted from taxation and billeting schoolteachers, as protégés of Hermes and the Muses, and physicians and trainers, as protégés of Apollo and Aesculapius.

It is notorious that the inventiveness of the Alexandrian Greeks did not stimulate a technological revolution. The reasons appear to have been partly sociological. On the one hand industry and commerce were looked down on, and on the other there were slaves enough. Consideration for the interests of free workers could be a further factor, if Vespasian was not merely eccentric when he rewarded the inventor of a labor-saving device for moving columns but suppressed the invention with the words, "you must allow me to feed my poor."[2] Besides, transport was laborious, and fuel scarce. Water power tended to evaporate in summer. But the second century did bring some changes. Slaves became scarce, as Pliny complains. The Pax Romana had dried up the chief source, prisoners of war. Some of the ninety-seven thousand captured by Titus

---

[2] There was even "built-in obsolescence," if the story is true that Tiberius suppressed an inventor of unbreakable glass and his invention.

in Judaea went straight to the imperial mines in Egypt, the rest to the provincial arenas. The only other big haul was Trajan's fifty thousand from Dacia. Faced with this shortage and with the rules imposed by the guilds, landowners did intensify the exploitation of their estates. Thus one near Arles installed hydraulic flour mills with a chain of eight wheels, a new invention, and in eastern Gaul glass and textile factories arose.

At the same time free labor continued to be used, especially in building. Landowners short of slaves let outlying farms to free tenants, keeping only a nucleus with limited staff; and employers in general began to find that, even if they could get slaves, it paid to hire free workers especially for seasonal work, because they were more willing, having more to lose, while slaves had to be permanently guarded as well as fed and clothed, and their maintenance cost more now that they were better treated.

Such glimpses as we get of life on the land are not idyllic. The rural poor of Italy gained nothing, in the long run, from the movement started by the Gracchi. It was still hard for them to get to political centers and voice their grievances collectively. Columella about A.D. 60 refers to the great estates as being run by the bondage of citizens as well as slave gangs. Impoverished peasants sold their children into slavery. Galen, the great medical writer of the second century, refers to the frequency of local famines due to the draining of food from the countryside into towns, and of particular diseases to which rustics were prone through eating unwholesome shoots, bulbs, roots, and even grasses when their winter's store gave out.

The townsman at least could have his club: the chance of increasing his self-respect by attaining rank in the *respublica collegii;* the meetings in a temple; the processions with banners; the special dates to look forward to. In 1816 an inscription was found at Lanuvium, near Rome, giving the charter for a burial club founded there under Hadrian in honor of Diana and (tactfully) the recently dead Antinoüs, in which the Senate permits it to meet not more than once a month for the making of contributions. This was a momentous concession, the precedent for many other clubs whose activities were less restricted. The entrance fee amounted to four hundred *asses* (the *as* was the smallest monetary unit) and a flagon of good wine, the monthly subscription five *asses* (clearly these were very humble people). Each member had an appointed "heir" to finance his funeral, including a payment to all present, out of a grant of 12,000 *asses*; or if he was a slave, whose body belonged to his master, he had at least a funeral service, perhaps a cenotaph. Continuing care of one's tomb was all-important. But there were also parties, six a year. Before the ones for Diana's and Antinoüs' days the president (elected for five years) first distributed oil (for use as soap) to members at the public bath. Four members appointed annually arranged the parties, providing pillows, hot water, dishes, a loaf, and four sardines for each member, in addition to the wine contributed by new members and by slaves on manumission. Funds endowed by patrons and benefactors may have helped with the cost. There were fines too: sixteen *asses* for quarreling or leaving your seat, forty-eight for abusive language, eighty for insulting the president.

The poor man had another escape from the dreariness of his tenement room, the public baths. By 33 B.C., when Agrippa made a census, there were 170 in Rome, and the charge was so small that he marked his aedileship with the gesture of paying all fees for the year. The free baths he built himself shortly after were only the beginning of a movement that from the time of Nero onward revolutionized Roman life. Successive emperors built enormous establishments, which included playgrounds surrounded by colonnades, gymnasia (in which the Greek sports, including naked wrestling, finally became acclimatized), rest rooms, libraries, and exhibition halls. They were, in fact, true community centers, available to all, as well as masterpieces of the new vaulted architecture. Famous works of art, such as the *Laocoön,* have been found in such surroundings.

Most people apparently took exercise before entering the baths proper. Once inside, they went through a sequence—a dry sweat-room, a warm room for washing and scraping the body, a tepid room for cooling off, and finally a cold swimming bath. There was thus also available something to suit all seasons. Those who could afford it brought slaves to scrape and rub them down and to watch their clothes. Those who could not presumably applied the principle "you scrape my back and I'll scrape yours." Naturally there was a certain amount of dirt around, which offended Marcus Aurelius. Until the time of Hadrian there was apparently no formal prohibition of mixed bathing. ("Respectable" women would bathe at home or in special establishments.) He introduced the rule that women bathed in the earlier hours, men when they got out of work in the afternoon, when there began a period of deafening noise that continued until the establishment closed at sunset. There was a jingle that ran,

Baths, sex, and wine our bodies undermine;
Yet what is life but baths and sex and wine?

The baths at least, with their classless social amenities, must surely be reckoned as one of Rome's contributions to the civilization of the empire.

The same cannot be said of the spectacles, the other great pastime of the populace, to which people flocked before dawn (for only senators and Equites had reserved seats) to spend the whole day, bringing picnic lunches, which were supplemented sometimes by the emperor or the president, and protection against wind and rain. No one who does not object to automobile racing should be puritanical about the chariot races, in which freemen, freedmen, or slaves, selected by the severest competition and rewarded with prizes and glory, drove teams of two or four with admirable skill and courage, twelve times taking the hairpin turn around the end-posts as narrowly as wreckage or hardihood permitted. The excitement of the spectators in any competitive event is greatly enhanced by partisanship, and the random choice between four colors, though less explicable psychologically, was no worse than any other such fanaticism. Nor can we object to the trick riding and other turns familiar from our own circuses that were interspersed. It is the fights of gladiators and the slaughter of beasts that were the disease of Rome, to the infection of the empire. Inevitably these would pall without constant escalation in numbers and novelty. In the four months of his Dacian Triumph Trajan matched ten thousand gladiators, as many as Augustus had matched in the forty-four years of his reign. On the day in 80 when the Colosseum was opened by Titus nine thousand animals were killed.

Gladiators were mainly prisoners of war or condemned criminals, kept in schools or touring troupes by private individuals such as Atticus as well as by Caesar and the emperors. They lived, disarmed, guarded, and under rigorous discipline, in barracks that maintained expert armorers, trainers, masseurs, and surgeons. On the evening before a show they were given a banquet, watched by ghoulish spectators, at which some indulged while others bade tearful farewells to their families. On the day, gorgeously arrayed, they paraded around the arena, to halt before the emperor with the shout of "Hail, Caesar! In the hour of death we salute you." Actually by no means did all die. Even the defeated, provided they fought bravely, were spared if the majority of the spectators gave the "thumbs in" signal to the president.[3] If a gladiator survived for three years, he was offered the wooden sword of release, if for five, the cap of manumission.

There were also the rewards such as Spanish bullfighters enjoy: the finery for exhibitionists, the sense of being the focus of thousands of eyes, pride in prowess and satisfaction for blood lust, the adulation of fanatics, especially women, who might be, for instance, partisans of the Samnite or the Thracian style of arms, and the possibility of enjoying a glorious retirement. We hear of gladiators complaining that for lack of shows their prime was being wasted, and of others staying on when they could retire to become instructors. In all ages we hear of volunteers. There was even esprit de corps in the schools, with guilds and ranks. Among the few who rallied to Antony after Actium were the gladiators he had been training at Cyzicus for his Triumph.

As time went on novelty was demanded. From Caesar onward mimic naval battles were organized. Then barbarians captured on the frontiers appeared in their strange accouterments, fighting singly or in troupes or in scythed British chariots. Nero had Moors of both sexes fight all day as a spectacle for Tiridates, the king of Armenia. Domitian matched dwarfs with women and gave shows at night by torchlight. Boys were kept busy shoveling away the blood-sodden sand from which the arena took its name, while men masked as the Etruscan demon Charun prodded the prostrate with hot irons to see if they were shamming, and others dressed as Mercury, marshal of the dead, hurried the corpses to the mortuary.

---

[3] Thumbs out—not down as is popularly supposed—was the signal for death.

Animals provided the other great diversion, from 186 B.C. onward. Cicero as governor of Cilicia was pestered by the young aedile Caelius for panthers. Indeed in the years 58–46 B.C. Romans saw a succession of beasts for the first time, such as crocodiles, hippopotamuses, and giraffes. The elephants at Pompey's games, trumpeting in terror, even aroused the pity of the mob as seeming somehow human. Elephants were the torch-bearers who escorted the victorious Caesar home. Reserved for the emperors, they walked the tightrope for Galba and made possible Hadrian's stupendous task of moving the hundred-foot colossus of Nero. Animals were trained to perform more elaborately, it would seem, than those of our circuses. But too often they were simply adorned and killed, either by hunters with hounds, spears, and firebrands, or by being matched with one another after intolerable goading, bear against bull, rhinoceros against elephant. Criminals were exposed to them, either bound to stakes or sewn up in skins or inadequately armed. The story of the brigand Laureolus was reenacted for nearly two centuries; and Martial praised Domitian for having allowed his final torture to be performed on a condemned criminal. The ultimate horror was when mythology was dramatized, and to surpass in sensationalism the public castration of a new Atys and the burning of a new Hercules on an Oetaean pyre (witnessed by Tertullian), a criminal dressed as Orpheus ascended from the underworld, drew the animals to him, and was finally killed by a bear. The only thing on the credit side was that the assiduous hunts for supplies relieved the provinces from the menace of wild beasts.

The shows, religious ceremonies in origin, as was still betokened by the preliminary sacrifices and procession with gods, the wearing of the toga, and the reservation of front seats for the Vestal Virgins, were taken for granted. Children played at being gladiators, and men practiced their skills. They were the typical topics of casual conversation. Cicero, who could say on occasion in a letter, "What pleasure can a cultivated man take in seeing a huge animal tear a weak man to pieces or a splendid animal pierced by a spear?" and who realized how barbarous gladiatorial fights were, could yet produce the no doubt conventional defense that criminals fighting for their lives provided the most effective training for the eye in the endurance of pain and death; and Pliny says much the same. There was only occasional protest, as from Seneca, who spoke out for humanity: "man should be a sacred thing to man." Marcus Aurelius, a gradualist reformer, refused to watch fighting other than with blunted, harmless weapons and once conscripted all the gladiators for a campaign.

Wherever the Romans went they built arenas. We can see one at Rome or Verona, at Nîmes or Arles, or at Caerleon-upon-Usk on the remote Welsh border. One can well believe that the sadism latent even in cultivated human beings, thus indulged, led to habitual blood lust. Even the Greeks, introduced to such spectacles by Antiochus IV of Syria, after the first shock eventually succumbed, though Greece proper continued to prefer athletics. When Athens in the second century A.D. was tempted to follow her rival, cosmopolitan Corinth, the Cynic Demonax bitterly advised her first to demolish her revered Altar of Pity.

Imperial Law

It is a relief to turn from the spectacles to one of Rome's greatest contributions to civilization, her law. That it affected Europe and the world so profoundly is due not so much to its merits as to the purposes of the feudal monarchs of the Middle Ages and the early Renaissance. But merits it had—the combination to a high degree of the two primary desiderata of law, fixity and equity. Fixity is basic because people need something reliable by which to order their relations with one another; and in Rome this meant the derivation of legal relations and rules from a few simple and lasting principles—*potestas* (the power of the paterfamilias) in family law; *testamentum* in succession; *dominium* (absolute title) in the field of property; *stipulatio* (the oral contract) in the field of business; *formula* in the law of procedure. Equity is basic because people's affairs are never exactly alike or exactly reducible to legal rules. And that came, in Rome, through the *ius honorarium* of the praetors described earlier remedies and rights not provided by the civil law; protection of widows, wards, and minors; recognition of the slave as a person as well as a thing, capable himself of legal relationships of all sorts; protection of lawful possession as well as absolute legal title; power of the judge to assess the measure of damages according to good faith and as a reasonable man would set off one claim against another. And when, under the emperors, the old civil courts were gradually superseded by the emperor himself or his delegates, the courts of a bureaucracy, the principles of legal science by which they judged were already fully laid down and ruled them with a firm hand.

Roman law also exhibited great failings and deficiencies that are much canvassed nowadays. It perpetuated gulfs of status and class: the freeman as against the slave, with the freedman in between; the citizen as against the noncitizen, and, as that distinction faded with the grant of citizenship, the upper ranks (*honestiores*) as against the lower (*humiliores*). It enshrined the values of the upper class, and its most highly developed branches were those pertaining to their private affairs; though there is little evidence that the humble could not obtain justice at Rome. Roman law also clung tenaciously to outmoded forms and was slow to meet the changing needs of society.

The criminal law of Rome has been less well regarded. Nevertheless it had at its roots two very salutary principles. The first was the famous *provocatio,* the right of a citizen to demand a proper trial before the assembly of the people (or, by the time of Cicero, a large jury). The second was that criminal law was fundamentally "accusatorial": the state could not prosecute, and charges must come from individual citizens prepared to be penalized if these were proved to be false or malicious. Under the empire, in criminal as in civil law, the courts of the emperor and his delegates superseded the old juries; and since crime is often against the state, in offenses such as treason the empire gained a bad record for tyranny and arbitrariness. The criminal law also exacerbated the status divisions of society by developing a double scale of punishments, more severe for the *honestiores* than for the *humiliores.* And some of the punishments were of extreme cruelty, as the stories of Christian martyrdoms remind us.

What came through to later Europe, however, was the legal science, the writing about the law. Old Cato (as usual) was in at the beginnings, formulating the earliest legal generalizations; and by the time of Cicero the output of legal commentaries was already great. Antistius Labeo, in the time of Augustus, wrote the first substantial commentary on that main organ of legal progress, the praetor's edict; and from that time also, for more than a century, there existed two rival schools or traditions of legal interpretation. The specifically Roman character of the law largely survived the contact with Greek theory.[4] The Roman jurists did not seek deductive or inductive generalities: they looked from case to case, comparing and contrasting specific situations. "Here is a sale: suppose there was a mistake as to the object sold? Or suppose the price was merely nominal? Or suppose the object had been destroyed the night before?" "Here is a slave, acquiring automatically for his master: suppose he turns out to be a freeman—whose are the acquisitions?"

A large selection of such legal argumentation was preserved by the emperor Justinian in the sixth century, in the huge work called the *Digest* or *Pandects;* and that was the work that was "received" by the kingdoms of Europe between 1100 and 1600 and formed most of the law of most of the civilized world until very recent times.

Life in the Provinces

The empire was naturally not homogeneous. In North Africa there were large imperial domains partly let out under a procurator to tenants who paid with free labor for so many days a year. In the West particularly, but also in the East (e.g., at Beirut), there were Roman military colonies, ready to fight where necessary. These alone (until Caracalla) had the right to have their own Capitol with temples of the triad Jupiter, Juno, and Minerva. Some towns, such as Cologne, grew up around permanent legionary camps. The success of municipal life in the early empire was often due to the skill of the ex-slave combined

---

[4] The "earlier classical period" of Roman jurisprudence lasted from Trajan to Marcus Aurelius (98–180). This was the most creative. In it the jurists developed legal science and produced legal literature as never before. In the "later classical period," under the Severans, existing principles were worked out in the whole field of law. The great names were Julian in the second century, Papinian, Ulpian, and Paul in the early third.

with the discipline of the ex-soldier. Then there were other large towns that modeled themselves on Italian municipalities. Gaul, noted for agriculture and horsebreeding, metalwork and vehicle-building, was the province most receptive of Romanization. Emperor worship was introduced to the West in A.D. 12, when Drusus dedicated an imposing altar of Augustus and Roma at Lyon. A school for chiefs' sons was early established at Autun, and British chiefs, encouraged by Agricola, had their sons educated the Roman way (embracing their slavery, said Tacitus). The East was more varied, less Romanized, the pattern of the former Hellenistic kingdoms remaining. Mainland Greece declined, living on its memories, but the famous cities of Asia revived. Egypt, on the other hand, developed no big city outside Alexandria, the second city of the empire.

Roman policy was to refrain from interfering so long as tribute was paid and strife in or between cities suppressed. But in fact it supported everywhere an oligarchy of the rich, suspending popular assemblies sometimes and deporting agitators. The rich encouraged Greco-Roman to the detriment of local culture and aped Roman titles for their senators and magistrates. Even after Tiberius had deprived the Roman Popular Assembly of its electoral functions local politics flourished in Italian municipalities, as the graffiti on the walls of Pompeii show. But in the provinces at least democracy was liable to be a sham. Plutarch advised his fellow oligarchs at Chaeronea to stage a specious opposition and debate before putting their measures through.

Apart from the imperial tribute there was little direct taxation in the provinces. Revenue came from such things as water rates, bath charges, harbor dues, and rent of shops; but the cities really depended on a variety of the Roman system of patronage. In a society in which there was an immense, indeed scandalous, gap between the wealthy few and the great majority, the munificence of elected magistrates to some extent obviated the need for local taxation. The greatest of all benefactors was Herodes Atticus, son of the first Roman senator to come from mainland Greece, a Sophist impressive enough to be chosen by Hadrian as tutor to Marcus Aurelius. Having inherited a pile made by dubious means, he adorned many cities with buildings, notably Athens, where his Odeum, originally roofed in cedarwood, is still used for performances. But there were benefactors all over the empire. One, for instance, gave an aqueduct to Bordeaux. The givers were rewarded with Roman citizenship (if they had not acquired it already as local senators), and such things as wider seats at the games, free water, and a bigger share in largesses. They also managed to get hold of most of the land and to look after their own class. Above all, they valued the perpetuation of their name in inscriptions. Tombstones record all benefactions made, all offices held, sometimes even the income of the deceased. People calling themselves "Asiarchs" and "Bithyniarchs" felt themselves to be people of some consequence.

In Pliny's time private benefactions were apparently still given and received in the spirit of Hellenistic "philanthropy." But soon after that requests began to be peremptory. Magistrates were expected to pay thus for being elected, sometimes even to pay for the inscription of thanks for the benefactions extorted. The burden became too great, the honor too small; and both at Rome and elsewhere it became hard to find candidates. This took the heart out of local politics, with the bad result that in the third century the central government increasingly took over.

This trend was aggravated by what was one of the best features of the early empire, local patriotism. Paul of Tarsus, for instance, had been proud to be "a citizen of no mean city." But unfortunately this patriotism led to a mad competitiveness in building, which, while it produced many fine monuments, had two serious results. First, the burden of office became too great to be worthwhile, as we saw, since magistrates were expected to finance this competition by benefactions. Secondly, communities were impoverished by contributing their share. This led to the emperors' appointing in imperial provinces a special legate or procurator, a senator or an Eques, to act as governor, with jurisdiction over even the free cities in the area. It was in this capacity that the younger Pliny, who had proved himself in high financial offices, was sent by his friend Trajan to govern Bithynia on the southern side of the Black Sea, probably in 109–11. Their surviving correspondence so illuminates the life and problems of the provinces that even the briefest summary of some of the fussy procurator's questions and the sensible emperor's answers is worthwhile.[5]

To begin with finance and public works:

PLINY How shall public money be invested? There is no land available for purchase, and people prefer to borrow at the standard rate of 12 percent from private individuals rather than from the municipality.[6] Shall I lower the rate or make the city councillors borrow the money on security?

TRAJAN Lower the rate. To force people to borrow would be inconsistent with our modern standards of justice.

PLINY Nicomedia has begun, abandoned, and largely demolished, two aqueducts. Shall I authorize a third?

TRAJAN Yes, but please find out who was to blame and report to me.

PLINY Nicaea's expensive theater, financed by benefactors and not yet completed, is in danger of collapsing. So is the enlarged gymnasium. Please send out a qualified architect.

TRAJAN You're on the spot: you must decide. Greeklings are too fond of their gymnasia. Nicaea must be content with what it can afford. There are well-qualified architects in the provinces. It's no good applying to Rome: most of ours come from Greece anyway.

PLINY One of the former kings began a scheme for helping transport by connecting a large lake adjoining Nicomedia with the sea. Please send a surveyor to see if this work is worth resuming.

TRAJAN Get one from Calpurnius Macer. But be careful not to drain the lake dry.

[5] The complete correspondence may be found in the translation in the Penguin Series by B. Radice, *The Letters of the Younger Pliny* (1963).

[6] Presumably because no security would be required, and pressure for payment would be weaker.

Other letters have a political bearing:

PLINY   Since you have enjoined economies, I told the Byzantines to economize by not sending a yearly envoy to convey their complimentary address to you and to the Governor of Moesia. Do you approve?

TRAJAN   Certainly. You can transmit their address yourself.

PLINY   There's a custom here of entertaining the whole Senate with many others and giving each a denarius or two. This smacks of corruption to me.

TRAJAN   And to me: I chose you specially as a prudent man who would deal with such matters yourself.

PLINY   Nicomedia has suffered a disastrous fire. Should I organize a fire brigade, limiting the numbers to 150?

TRAJAN   No. Experience has shown that such associations always become political and subversive.[7]

Questions of discipline as to individuals crop up:

PLINY   A man exiled for life by Bassus is still around. His excuse is that the Senate rescinded Bassus' decrees and granted a fresh trial to anyone appealing against them within two years. He failed to do so.

TRAJAN   His contumacy deserves more than rebanishment. Send him here in chains for my Praetorians to guard.

PLINY   Should prisoners be guarded by public slaves (unreliable) or by soldiers (needed elsewhere) or by a mixture?

TRAJAN   By slaves, but it's your business to supervise them.

PLINY   What shall I do with two slaves found in the army?[8]

TRAJAN   Make sure first that they volunteered simply in order improve their status and were not conscripts or proxies.

PLINY   What shall I do with convicts condemned long ago to the mines or the arena who have actually been acting as (paid) public slaves?

TRAJAN   Send those convicted within the past ten years to the prescribed punishment. Put the rest to tasks resembling punishment—cleaning sewers and the like.

PLINY   What should I do about freeborn infants who, having been exposed, are picked up by strangers and reared as slaves? I can find nothing in the old royal files of the country.

TRAJAN   Nor can I find any precedent in the imperial files. Set them free without payment.

Then there are religious questions:

PLINY   Will you, as Supreme Pontiff, advise whether relatives can move their ancestors' ashes from tombs that have become unsuitable?

TRAJAN   Decide each case yourself on its merits.

---

[7] There is no more revealing piece of evidence than this of the realities of Roman domination, at any rate in the East.

[8] The official penalty was death.

PLINY   A house here was left to the emperor Claudius, a temple to him to be erected in the peristyle and the remainder let. It is now ruinous. Can public baths be built on the site?

TRAJAN   Yes; but if the temple was actually erected, that part must be reserved, as consecrated.

PLINY   I am worried because a statue of you has been put up in a building where there are graves.

TRAJAN   You shouldn't have worried, knowing well that I am determined not to surround my name with awe by accusations of treason.

PLINY   I am new to trials of Christians. Should one make any allowance for age, repentance, or merely being a Christian without committing the associated crimes? I have executed them, after solemnly warning them three times, only for inflexible obduracy. Any citizens among them I have remitted to Rome. I questioned those named by an anonymous informer and let off any who worshiped your statue and cursed Christ. The crimes they denied, and two slave deaconesses under torture revealed nothing.

TRAJAN   Quite right. There can be no fixed rule. Don't hunt them out, and pardon any who worship our gods or express repentance. Anonymous denunciations are a very bad practice unworthy of my reign. Ignore them.

Finally, a personal scruple:

PLINY   Was it all right for me to send my wife by imperial post chaise to look after her aunt, her grandfather having died?

TRAJAN   Yes, certainly.

The empire of the second century, the "Golden Age" of Hadrian and the Antonines, had the appearance of a union of self-governing states supervised by enlightened central control. The emperor was seen as a sort of universal patron bound to his subjects by *fides,* upholding the legal rights of the *humiliores,* the small proprietors, widows, orphans, and slaves. If there was a local disaster, an earthquake or a collapsed grandstand, it was the emperor who came to the rescue with comfort and relief. How much discontent there was in the provinces is very hard to assess. Hidden beneath the Latin and Greek crust known to us went on the life of those who spoke the vernacular languages, various dialects of Celtic from Scotland to the Danube, Punic in North Africa, Aramaic in Syria and Judaea, and on the outer fringes all the tongues of Pentecost. Moreover, there is discontent in all ages, and Roman governors did not become paragons overnight. Toward the end of Augustus' reign Messalla Volesus, Proconsul of Asia, executed three hundred people in a day. Tiberius, who tightened control, had to warn another that a shepherd should sheer his sheep, not skin them. Thrasea protested successfully against the expensive delegations of thanks the provinces felt obliged to send to Rome in the wake of any retiring governor however bad. It is true that from the time of Tiberius the annual meeting held in each province to celebrate the cult of Augustus and Roma provided an opportunity for appeals to the Senate against oppressive governors. When such an appeal was heard, the emperor might be present; and in any case he was increasingly well informed by his independent financial agents in the provinces. On the other hand the provincials could not fail to perceive that the tribute nominally required for defense purposes financed the blatant extravagances of the imperial court.

The freedman Ganymede in Petronius grumbles about famine and food prices in a South Italian town. the aediles are in league with the bakers, and the little people suffer, while the jaws of the bigwigs enjoy Saturnalia all year round; it's all this neglect of religion that's to blame; the town is going downhill like a calf's tail. Certainly we hear of riots because dealers are hoarding grain for profitable export amid a starving population. We hear of special rural police in Asia to deal with robbers and malcontents. The Egyptian papyri reveal grievances, and the non-Greek Egyptians under their priests hated Roman rule as much as did the Jews under theirs. We remember how Jesus, looking upon the multitude, had compassion upon them because they were hungry. We remember his parable of Dives and Lazarus.

The Edict of Caracalla extending citizenship to nearly all free inhabitants of the empire had various motives, and it has been suggested that one was to help pay for the armies that were by now fighting off the barbarians, by making as many people as possible liable for the 5 percent death duties. (Citizenship had already been cheapened by being given to whole communities.) But it was also expressly designed to increase the number of citizens sacrificing and praying to the immortal gods for the safety of the empire, to fortify the spirit of *Romanitas* against the onslaughts of the barbarians.

Intellectual Life and the Arts

"If a man were called to fix the period in the history of the world during which the condition of the human race was most happy and prosperous, he would, without hesitation, name that which elapsed from the death of Domitian to the accession of Commodus." The first reaction evoked by Gibbon's famous dictum should, in fact, be hesitation. "The human race" automatically excludes the millions outside what the Romano-Greeks complacently called "the inhabited world," that is, the empire. Within the empire a large proportion of the human race were slaves of widely differing condition. Of the condition of the greater part of the remainder, the ordinary freemen, whether in Rome, Italy, or the provinces, we do have fragmentary knowledge pieced together by historians and archeologists, but very fragmentary it is. The absence of war except on the frontiers was obviously a unique boon, though it must be remembered that before the advent of modern weapons and means of transport war was much more localized. Enlistment, billeting, and commandeering probably impinged as much as fighting and devastation. But what Gibbon probably had in mind was the upper classes affected by the court, and secondarily the Italian and provincial bourgeoisie, the people whose chief preoccupation was more than the struggle for existence; and what we have to consider is the quality of their life. The "affluent society" is not necessarily happy, and in the words of Tacitus, "It is only the ignorant who think that comforts and luxuries make up *humanitas.*"

What did the Romano-Greeks of this period lack that modern societies have, blessed as they were with freedom from strife? Primarily the idea of progress in this world. Many of the ancients had a conception of human progress up to their own time: it was magnificently imagined, for instance, in the Fifth Book of Lucretius' *De Rerum Natura.* Philosophers conceived Utopias like Plato's *Republic* and *Laws* and Zeno's *Republic,* and poets like Vergil dreamed of a return of the legendary Golden Age. But there was no general idea of future progress as the gradual achievement by human endeavor of various social and technological aims. The whole age was backward-looking.

The scientific curiosity of Aristotle and the Alexandrians was a spent force. Juvenal might gibe, "The Greekling is hungry to know everything: send him to the sky and he'll go"; but that was an anachronism. There was no longer any attempt to discover the laws of nature. Seneca's *Natural Inquiries,* based on Posidonius, inquire by a priori reasoning, not empirically, while Pliny's *Natural History* is an encyclopedia of sometimes garbled inheritances from Greek discoverers. He himself was puzzled that there had been so much scientific activity in the Hellenistic world at a time when it had been torn by strife and harassed by piracy, so little under imperial patronage amid universal peace. Our gratitude for what such writers preserved for us does not alter the case.[9]

Politically, there was a certain amount of wistful nostalgia for the republic. Even the emperor Marcus Aurelius admired Cato and Brutus, Helvidius and Thrasea. His practical alternative was freedom secured by monarchy; but that depended on the chance of who was monarch. In general the Romans became resigned to monarchy. Cerialis in Tacitus compares the passions and greed of bad rulers to a bad harvest or a flood: something to be endured, in the knowledge that there will be compensatory periods. The good emperors, in Gibbon's phrase, "delighted in the image of liberty." But it was only an image. No more than Augustus or Tiberius could they induce men who were not in fact free to behave as if they were. Local patriotism gave people something to live for in the early empire with the outburst of competitive building and adornment. Its incipient decline was noted and lamented by Plutarch. It was not only regular moralists but men like Galen who deplored a loss of ideals.

In Vespasian's time began the astonishing "second sophistic revival." Rhetoricians became the most prestigious people in the world, leaders of embas-

---

[9] An exception must be made of Galen, a Greek from Pergamum, physician to Marcus Aurelius. Though his medical encyclopedia was based largely on the Hippocratic corpus, several centuries old, he did correct it, and by observation and experiment he made considerable contributions to anatomy and physiology, especially neurology. Apuleius also claimed to have corrected and supplemented older authorities in his researches on rare fish. (He had been accused of buying them for purposes of magic.)

sies, presidents of the Olympic games, and so forth. Chairs were founded for them, and they drew disciples and devotees from all over the Roman world. Trajan had Dio Chrysostom ride with him in his state carriage, frequently exclaiming, "I don't know what you mean, but I love you as myself!" Hadrian extended to all the descendants of Polemo of Smyrna the right of free travel granted him by Trajan, made him a Fellow of the Alexandrian Museum, and appointed him to deliver the address at the inauguration of the Athenian Olympium. Hadrian of Tyre, professor at Rome under Marcus Aurelius, charmed even those who knew no Greek by his fluency, his exquisitely modulated voice, and his rhythms both in the spoken part of his orations and in the chanted peroration. News that he was performing drew senators in haste from meetings and plebeians from dancing displays to the Athenaeum. Powerless to influence current policies, such men invited their audiences to suggest themes from the classical age of Greece and proceeded to hold forth with an abundance of ingenious quotation from the poets—sometimes on both sides of a question, like Carneades of old. Their exemplars were the old Attic orators and Sophists. Of the themes mentioned by their biographer, Philostratus, none refers to any event later than the death of Demosthenes in 322 B.C.

The general stagnation of politics also affected literature. Tacitus makes a character in his *Dialogue of Orators* say, "The long ages of peace, the unbroken inactivity of the people, the static tranquility of the Senate, and above all the discipline of the emperor, has pacified oratory like everything else." The author of the famous treatise *On the Sublime,* probably of the first century, reports a conversation between a philosopher and himself. The philosopher expresses a widespread view that there is plenty of varied talent about, but no transcendent genius in literature; "slavery with justice" is the system on which men are reared; unstimulated by freedom, they are merely ingenious at flattery. The author protests that the passion for wealth and luxury is rather to blame, but he does not weaken the force of the indictment.

In these circumstances a good deal of literature was simply backward-looking, like sophistic rhetoric. Take Statius' epic *Thebaïd.* The theme, worn-out in Greek, is re-treated in a way that is Vergilian rather than new. Recent attempts to rehabilitate it evoke at most the response, "I would rather praise it than read it." Valerius Flaccus' *Argonautica* and Silius Italicus' *Punic War* are even more boring. The only literature that was alive was that of protest. It is possible that we should here include Seneca's tragedies. Being intended not for the stage but for reading, probably in private gatherings, they seek to compensate for visible action by heightened melodrama. Thus the classic rule against on-stage murder is violated: in defiance of Horace's precept Medea kills her sons in full view of the audience.[10] To us these plays may seem tasteless, strained, and rhetorical, and monotonous in rhythm though impressive as sound. But we must remem-

---

[10] The violence and horrors of the Renaissance stage are transferred from this Senecan drama intended for reading.

ber that they do reflect a horrific world such as Seneca knew from experience of the court of Nero. Romans were never slow to make topical applications. The last of the distinguished old Scaurus family had brought death on himself under Tiberius by a line from his *Atreus*.

The folly of monarchs must be patiently endured; and the existence among the manuscripts of Seneca of the maverick *Octavia*, probably by someone else, dealing with her persecution by her husband, Nero, that ended in death, a play in which Seneca himself is given a part, is sufficient to suggest what one like his *Thyestes* would convey.

His young nephew Lucan found another way of protest. His epic *The Civil War* deals with the death throes of the republic. His hero is Pompey ("Magnus"), though he is not so inept as to belittle Caesar. His saint is Cato. The choice of subject was admirable, and his exclusion of divine machinery cleared the air for sincerity: the personified Fortuna (indistinguishable from the Stoic Fate) suffices to impart a sense of universal drama. Seldom too was the astringent quality of the Latin language exploited to greater effort. Beginning with flatteries of Nero that by their very grossness may have been meant to combine self-cancellation with insurance, the work was driven underground after Book 3 by the emperor's jealousy and disapproval, becoming bitterly hostile to Caesar and, by implication, to Augustus and his successors. It developed into a monument of revolt for posterity, Book 7 containing outspoken advocacy of republicanism. We cannot judge it as a whole, since it was broken off in Book 10, when the poet was detected in Piso's conspiracy and committed suicide; but in any case it could never really succeed for us because of the same sort of rhetorical straining after effect as spoils Seneca's tragedies. But none of these poetical works could compare for telling denunciations with the somber tragedy of the history in which Tacitus vented the feelings he had had to repress under Domitian's terror. His pen freed by Trajan, he was able to put into the mouth of Cremutius Cordus, who under Tiberius had praised Brutus and Cassius, denigrated Augustus, and starved himself to death when arraigned for treason, a passionate defense of freedom of speech.

The spirit of protest expressed itself also in satire. Seneca's rather cheap lampoon *The Pumpkinification of Claudius* is a release of pent-up feelings about an emperor lately deified. The nature of satire is to exaggerate; but Juvenal's is so sweeping and all-embracing that it defeats its own end—that is, if the end was reform. But it surely was not. Juvenal was out to exploit for literary purposes the splendid epigrammatic resources of Latin as revealed by the rhetoricians. The fierce indignation may sometimes be as genuine as Swift's but it is the sheer audacity and memorability that exhilarates the reader. The Rabelaisian caricature of the freedman Trimalchio in Petronius is clearly more a joke than a criticism. So is most of the sometimes brilliant satire of Lucian, the only Greek writer of any consequence, apart from novelists, in the twenty-three-year reign of Antoninus Pius, a last reminder of the classical common sense of Horace.

For the rest, one might expect an imaginative literature with little political or social relevance to spring up in these circumstances, a literature of escape. In the early years of the principate a poem of this kind did appear, Ovid's *Metamorphoses,* a vast nexus of stories of transformation. Ovid, who in his *Amores* and *Ars Amatoria* had already produced poetry that, like comedy, sought simply to entertain, conceived the idea of treating the fancies of Greek mythology and legend with a straight face, as matter for a quasi-historical epic set in a coherent though magic world of the imagination.[11] This gave him opportunities for constant variety of treatment and tone—romance, burlesque, splendor, horror, pathos, macabre, rhetoric, debate, genre painting, landscape painting, antiquarian interest, patriotic pride. The poem is a baroque masterpiece, though marred both as a whole and in parts by his besetting fault of not knowing where to stop. But it could have no successor: it had worked out the vein once for all.

The other notable work of the imagination from the early empire that is known to us is Petronius' fragmentary *Satyricon.* This is not "satire" as we know it, but in the Lucilian tradition of social and personal criticism, yet in a separate tradition called Menippean, characterized by a mixture of prose and verse, though here and there we may gather that an Epicurean with an amoral theory of literature is poking fun at such Stoic moralists as Seneca and Lucan or laughing at such types as the *nouveau riche* or the legacy hunter. It is a picaresque novel with literary antecedents and allusions in which three low-life characters with abnormal sexual proclivities have a series of adventures, recounted by one of them. The attitude of the writer is ironical and detached. One recalls the rumors that Nero (for members of whose court we may take it to have been produced) used to wander by night through the lower quarters of Rome. The episodic rambling suggests Sterne's *Tristram Shandy,* while the fiction that the characters are being driven across the earth by the wrath of Priapus, as Odysseus was by Poseidon's in Homer, presages Joyce's *Ulysses.* But the spirit of Menippean medley confuses the consistency of purpose we expect of a novel; and it may be that we are beguiled by our gratitude for a rare glimpse of ancient low life and rare specimens of colloquial Latin to overrate this work, for all its verve and inventiveness.

There had long existed "Milesian tales," romances of Alexander and so forth, in Greek, but such middle-brow literature, easy and often charming entertainment, appears to have proliferated in the second century. These adventure stories with a love interest, sometimes with a quite complicated plot in the manner of New Comedy, seem to have had a special appeal to a rather bored, unintellectual age. Much more significant is the African Platonist Apuleius' *Golden Ass,* written in that century in a mannered but lively Latin, part colloquial, part poetic. It is as episodic as the *Satyricon,* between the changing of the hero, obsessed with sex and magic, into an ass and his final release through the

[11] "Shakespeare's *A Midsummer Night's Dream,* influenced by it, provides some analogy. The burlesque element recurs sometimes in Lucian.

mystic goddess Isis; but this climax is movingly impressive, and the famous story of Psyche and Cupid, an allegory of the soul, gives some color to the interpretation of the whole as an entertainment so modified from its partly extant Greek original as to be to some extent a fable of sin, suffering, and redemption. Archaism characterized the "new style" promoted by Marcus Aurelius' tutor Fronto and his like—a desperate attempt by literary men of no originality to get away from the classicism of "Silver Latin" (post-Augustan) that had reigned for over a century.

What the plethora of verse was like, which demanded those recitals heard and avenged by countless dilettantes such as Pliny, whose poetical works took two days to recite, we can only surmise. Perhaps the pleasant, largely occasional poems about people, places, and works of art that make up Statius' *Silvae* would be a favorable example. The great reputation enjoyed by Martial may sufficiently indicate the limitations of the rest.

Then did the Romans of this period enhance the quality of life by cultivating the other arts? Vitruvius includes a picture gallery in his specification for a gentleman's house, a public one is the scene of an episode in Petronius, and public places in general were adorned with Greek masterpieces; but Roman writers, by contrast with Greek, seldom mention the visual arts (though the elder Pliny naturally has a section about them in his encyclopedia). One has the impression that they were regarded as contributing to gracious living, but not as expressive of deeper values either for creator or beholder. Upper-class Romans were essentially passive as regards leisure occupations, spectators rather than doers.[12] Their attitude to artists, shared indeed by Greeks, was inhibiting. Seneca remarks casually, "we worship idols whose fashioners we despise." Plutarch assumes that no high-minded young man will ever want to become a Phidias or a Polyclitus from seeing the Zeus of Olympia or the Hera of Argos, while Lucian represents Rhetoric as a brilliant personality who looks down on these two as mere artisans, and Sculpture as a dirty, uneducated, uncouth old woman. Here again we meet that prejudice we encountered as to trades: those that deal with dirty things are disparaged, and sculpture involves rough manual labor. Painting is not so dirty, and from Fabius Pictor down to Hadrian there were aristocrats who painted for recreation. Varro wanted young girls to be taught this art; and in his *Hebdomades,* a biographical dictionary of seven hundred Greek and Roman worthies, which did include sculptors, painters, and architects, each was accompanied by a portrait.

This touches on what did interest the Romans, documentary art, from the murals depicting Marcellus' capture of Syracuse to the lively relief inside the Arch of Titus, where we see the sacred objects from the Temple of Jerusalem being carried in his triumph, and the successive scenes that coil vividly around

---

[12] Mention should be made of the Roman love of flowers, chiefly roses, lilies, and violets. There were roof gardens and window boxes, suburban nurseries to supply abundant cut flowers, and roses out of season from Paestum, Egypt, or local greenhouses.

the columns of Trajan and Marcus Aurelius. Similarly objets d'art were valued for their historical associations: "This belonged to Alexander." Portrait sculptors, creditably encouraged by Roman patrons to record "warts and all," reached their apogee in the third century, with flourishing schools all over the empire. Busts and coins made familiar everywhere the living features of the reigning emperor, with such revealing characterization in the third century that one wonders whether the subjects can have viewed them with complacency. After a flourishing period under Hadrian, art in general became more stereotyped as it became more widespread; but there is still considerable dignity as well as technical skill in the equestrian statue of Marcus Aurelius now on the Capitol, preserved for us because the Christians thought he was Constantine.[13]

As for music, it was part of an upper-class child's education. Choirs of boys and girls sang on solemn occasions hymns such as Horace's *Carmen Saeculare.* We learn that Britannicus and Titus were good musicians. Old-fashioned suspicion of music-making by adults lingered till the end of the republic. The elder Cato casually smeared an opponent with *praeterea cantat* ("besides, he sings"), and Cicero listed singing and dancing among the sinister characteristics of young Catilinarians. Under the empire such prejudice died down, but the moralists kept up their nagging. Seneca complains that at Naples a flute-playing competition drew more listeners than a debate on how to be good; and Tacitus, deploring Nero's musical competitions, comments inaptly, "Justice had nothing to gain from them." Nero himself outraged people not by playing music at all, but by aspiring to do so at professional level. Sensible people like Quintilian complained that the indecent and effeminate music of the stage had debauched the art, and so did Dio Chrysostom, Plutarch, and others. It is impossible for us to judge. (The same sort of thing was said when Wagner conducted *Tannhäuser* in London.) The attitude toward dancing was similar. Religious dances such as those to which Horace's Licymnia (Maecenas' wife Terentia) lent grace on Diana's day, and the Pyrrhic dance, a ballet for boys and girls, were approved; and even some private dancing was not disapproved, provided it was strictly amateur and also not like the sexy "Ionic movements" indulged in at disreputable parties.

All Roman music was Greek, Alexandria being the chief source. The main instruments were the tibia, a sort of oboe, whose range of stops was increased under Augustus (it was thought of as wild and passionate), and the cithara, a kind of lyre, whose strings were gradually increased to eighteen. The hydraulic organ came in under the empire. Horns and trumpets (military and funereal) later joined in, together with voices of all registers, so that sometimes not only the stage but all free space in the auditorium was crowded with performers.

The extent to which poetry at Rome was intoned to music has been exaggerated; like us, the Romans often used the anachronism "sing" of spoken poetry.

---

[13] Donatello drew inspiration from this work for his pioneering equestrian statue of Gattamelata at Padua, just as he derived from cupids on Roman sarcophagi the earliest Renaissance cherubs (*putti*).

But undoubtedly their music was originally accompaniment subordinated to words. Subtle effects were clearly also obtained by the use of the various Greek modes (ways of tuning the lyre)—Phrygian, Lydian, and so forth. We hear much of the ethical differences attributed to these, and of their profound effect. We should no more dismiss them as primitive, because simpler, than we should dismiss the analogous Oriental music of today. Yet such music had serious limitations. Its range was only two octaves; and although syncopation occurred, and the accompaniment could stray above the melody of the song, there was no part singing, no harmony in the modern sense, only unison of voices with instruments varying by octaves in pitch. Yet from Rome also there is evidence that pure music was appreciated. Quintilian speaks of the power of the organ alternatively to excite and calm; and Canus, a great virtuoso of the second century, boasted that his Phrygian flute could assuage sorrow, increase joy, fan the flame of love, and inspire the devout. The Odeum of Hadrian was built to hold more than ten thousand. But who made all this public music? Greek slaves, probably, for the most part, troupes of whom were maintained by great houses.

Philosophy

Philosophy came into its own again after Domitian's persecution, but it had ceased centuries ago to speculate. It now consisted in exposition of old systems and debate between them, while all preached contentment through upright self-sufficiency. It was part of culture, which had never been so widespread as in this highly literate, easy-traveling, cosmopolitan society, though Tacitus credits Agricola's mother with having wisely restrained him from studying it more deeply than was fitting for a Roman. Dialogues of Plato were sometimes performed at dinner parties in Trajan's time. Marcus Aurelius, himself a convert from rhetoric to Stoicism, had a Platonist and a Peripatetic among his teachers; and he broadmindedly included Epicureanism also among the four schools for which he founded chairs at Athens. Of course these schools were for an educated minority only. Trimalchio wished his epitaph to be "He left thirty million sesterces and never heard a philosopher lecture." But among the masses many listened, as they had done in Alexander's day, to the Cynics, who taught, as Jesus did, wherever a crowd would collect, and who did not mind using vulgarity as well as salty wit to put their message across. Naturally some of these were charlatans, distinguished by their bare feet, long, matted hair and beards, and knobbly sticks, who preferred to live on their "gift of gab" instead of working. These gave philosophy a bad name, and not merely with fastidious and discriminating observers like Lucian. But there were many also among them who were sincere preachers of moral regeneration; and Demetrius and Demonax were among the best men of their time.

In the Greco-Roman world philosophers, with their distinctive cloak, played part of the role later played by the clerical orders, the Cynics being the wandering friars. Some were like domestic chaplains and spiritual directors even to emperors, and they often figured in deathbed scenes. Demonax, the beloved peacemaker and conscience of second-century Athens, was given a public funeral. Epictetus, who catered to all classes, called the philosopher's lecture room a hospital for sick souls. The satirist Persius felt he had been "cured" by the Stoic Cornutus. In fact philosophers answered a need of the times.

But perhaps the most striking psychological feature of the age is a failure of nerve, the breakdown of the faith in reason that had been one of the great contributions of the Greek genius in its heyday. Belief in astrology, imported by Babylonians after Alexander had opened the door from the East, had captured millions.[14] The authoritative Posidonius, in accordance with the catholic spirit of Stoicism, which preferred to accommodate popular beliefs by refined interpretation rather than try to abolish them, had assimilated its ideas of "cosmic sympathy" to the Stoic ideas of a world soul and of the divinity of the heavenly bodies, which were the most impressive witnesses to order in the universe. All the early emperors, even the apparently rationalist Tiberius, were addicts. The Pantheon was dedicated to the sun and stars. If astrologers were occasionally banished, that was because they were politically dangerous. Astrology supervened on the old Roman customs of public divination: its horoscopes gave the excitement of hope as well as anxiety to simple individuals like Horace's Leuconoë. An art, obviously lucrative, grew up, teaching people how they might dodge their destiny. Another sign of the breakdown of reason was the prevalence of magic, more plausibly manipulable by individuals than astrology. Many Egyptian papyri testify to its prevalence in the second century A.D., and many curses scratched on metal, planted face downwards for the powers below to read, have been unearthed elsewhere. The romances of the period, such as the Golden Ass, are full of love spells and so forth.

Any description of secular life in any age is apt to make it sound futile, but this is particularly so of the early Roman Empire. The ideal of the Pax Romana expressed in visionary terms in Vergil's Fourth Eclogue and more specifically in his Aeneid had largely been realized by the second century—and found to be no more satisfying than any other mundane ideal: "to travel hopefully is better than to arrive." Epictetus had remarked on the contrast between its security and the insecurity of the human psyche. Augustus' Acts are full of pride, Aurelius' Meditations full of misgiving. The impression left by the "Golden" Antonine Age, when prosperity, as measured by exchange of goods, had reached a summit (which proved to be a plateau leading to a descent), is one of negativity. Not only were men chewing over the remote past. The whole burden of the two dominant ideologies, Stoicism and Cynicism, was to play for safety. Only get rid of needs and desires and you will be invulnerable. The right and freedom

---

[14] It is only proportionally less prevalent today, part amusement, part belief. Of the astrologers kept by British newspapers, none predicted the outbreak of the Second World War. Yet the event discredited them so little that Churchill's government had to ask editors to withdraw them, because whenever they prophesied that peace was around the corner, munitions workers eased off.

to commit suicide was reckoned among the god-given blessings of men (one that Seneca indeed had reason to appreciate). "Destroy the system" was the message of the Cynics; but they had nothing to put in its place.

Nowhere is this sense of negativity more oppressive than in those *Meditations* ("Self-Communings") jotted down in Greek, the language of philosophy, by Marcus Aurelius, when he was forced, against his kindly nature, to live a life of campaigning against barbarians on the Danube frontier. In them we can see into the mentality of an extraordinarily virtuous man who happened, through adoption, to be ruler of the world; and we can perceive the limitations that are characteristic of his age. Let us leave aside the fact that, insofar as he was conscious of the Christians at all, he regarded them (unless the passage is interpolated) as tiresome exhibitionists, and did not protect them from two terrible persecutions. Here was a man so clement that he burned the incriminating papers of Avidius Cassius and forgave his fellow rebels, and so expansive in his sympathy that he could think of the whole world as the "dear City of Zeus,"[15] yet he did not use his plenary powers to reform society, only to mitigate its cruelties. As a Roman, the heir to Antoninus Pius, he was dedicated to duty, "the task in hand." Yet the philosophies on which he was nurtured were all directed to securing the inward health of the individual, participation in politics being only a secondary duty. A Stoic emperor was almost a contradiction in terms. The perfect Stoic adapted to the moral sphere the old political concept of *dignitas*. He must be and appear irreproachable. Aurelius' meditations were self-examination. He confesses to himself that he has been tempted at times to retire to some remote seashore or mountain; and he rejected this course not because he had a duty to society but because a philosopher should always remember that he can retire into himself. "Live as on a mountain" was one of his maxims.

He even wondered whether he ought not to have committed suicide before being contaminated by the corruption of the world in which he had to live. Life is an unending circular treadmill. Everything is brief, banal, and petty by comparison with eternity: soon he himself will go the way of Hadrian and Augustus. It is all true in a sense, but so lacking in capacity for enjoyment. No doubt he was tired after his day of frontier duties; but his *Meditations* are characteristic of a listless age "in which it seemed always afternoon."

For serious people, indeed, it was more like twilight than afternoon. They had come to accept a cosmology, ultimately derived from Aristotle, in which earth at the center, insignificant in relative size, was compact of the sediment of the universe. Beneath the moon was the domain of chance, mutability, and death, beyond it that of unalterable law, with the fixed stars revolving in the outermost, fiery sphere. Everything earthly became more and more despised. Particularly despicable was man. He was like a puppet on a string, a play actor, in a

---

[15] Hence the title of Augustine's *City of God*, written after the city of Rome had been sacked by the Goths.

brief dream-life. The best that could be said of him was that without him creation would be incomplete. From the Pythagoreans, Orphics, and Plato the idea was familiar that man had a soul that was imprisoned or entombed in the body. He now revolted against the body. "It is hard for a man to endure himself," said Aurelius. His body was mere clay and corruption, his life like the public baths, all oil, sweat, dirt, and greasy water. The next step was to mortify the body. E. R. Dodds has diagnosed all this as "a disease endemic in the entire culture of the period ... an endogenous neurosis, an index of intense and widespread guilt-feelings."[16] As a result many began at this time more and more (as St. Paul had urged) to "set their affections on things above, not on things of the earth." And so we enter the world in which Christianity developed.

[16] On pp. 35–36 of his *Pagan and Christian in a World of Anxiety* (Cambridge, England. Cambridge University Press, 1965), a work to which I am particularly indebted.

Chapter Eight
THE SEEDGROUND OF CHRISTIANITY

It was during the reign of Marcus Aurelius that things began to go wrong for the empire. Troops sent to repel Parthian invasions brought back a pestilence that swept the Mediterranean world in 166, so much so that captives had to be imported to help repopulate Italy. In the same year German tribes crossed the Danube in force and had reached Italy before the emperor repulsed them. Plans to establish a defensive zone north of the river were abandoned because of an abortive revolt of his ablest general in the East. His son Commodus (180–192) brought peace by concessions and ruled through the Praetorian Guard. Power went to his head, he was murdered, and a war of succession followed. Emerging as victor, the African Septimius Severus (193–211) had to cope with threats from barbarians as far apart as Scotland and Mesopotamia as well as with those from rivals. His solution was to consolidate his power by promoting Equites to the command of legions, and above all by conciliating the army. Army officers were made provincial governors; the Praetorians were selected from frontier forces instead of from Italians; the soldiers were paid more, and at last allowed to marry and live outside barracks. The Edict of Caracalla, his son, not only made practically all inhabitants of the empire citizens but simultaneously made them liable for military service. Therein lay one part of its significance. After the murder in 235 of Alexander Severus anarchy broke out, the various armies backing their sometimes reluctant candidates. Of twenty-six emperors in fifty years only one died a natural death, while the barbarians took full advantage. Breakaway states emerged for a time in Gaul and the East. The hoards of contemporary coins we unearth betoken the panic of the times.

Marcus Aurelius had had to sell state property to pay for his wars. Septimius and the other Severan emperors dispossessed many of the rich and became the universal bankers. In the insecurity that followed, economic production declined, and the population of the empire may have fallen (although this is now disputed). Many of the remaining aristocrats retired for safety and quiet to their largely self-sufficient and now fortified country estates, and for lack of sufficient slaves let out parts to tenant farmers. With taxation rising sharply these landlords were charged with raising fixed sums. Widespread starvation and unwillingness to breed children were among the results. In 259, when the Sassanians, who had recently taken over the Parthian Empire, captured the emperor Valerian, there was a financial crash. A rush to turn money into goods led to an inflation that has been estimated at 1,000 percent in seventeen years. Meanwhile the currency was progressively debased. There was no decent silver left, and such gold as there was went to the soldiers, whom Septimius had already begun to pay partly in kind. When in 301 Diocletian issued an edict fixing the price of a thousand commodities, a large proportion of them simply disappeared into the black market. His further depreciation of the coinage was also only half accepted. There was another rush to turn money into goods, and prices soared again.

Meanwhile the barbarian incursions had become so dangerous that even the armies had to face the fact that their repulse must take priority over civil war. Gallienus (260–268) established a mobile cavalry reserve based in Milan, including heavily armored warhorses. A series of able emperors from the Balkans, ready to learn from their enemies, by incredible exertions and "Illyrian valor" restored the situation. The great twelve-mile wall that we see today around Rome is evidence both of the desperate situation and of the energy and efficiency of Aurelian (270–275). Still more able was Diocletian (284–305), who with his successor Constantine reestablished the empire so that Rome revived for another century, a breathing space during which a good deal of the Roman heritage was salvaged for posterity, literature being copied from fragile papyrus rolls into durable parchment books like ours in form. To the end of the fourth century belong the pagan poets Claudian, Ausonius, and Namatianus and the Christian poets Prudentius, Ambrose, and Paulinus; the distinguished historian Ammianus; the Vergilian commentator Servius; the littérateur Macrobius; and finally Jerome and Augustine. But the price was heavy. The state became totalitarian. Even the façade of partnership between princeps and Senate was broken down: "principate" became "dominate." The Eastern and Western Empires were separated, at first each under an "Augustus" with a "Caesar" as adjutant and heir. In this so-called "Tetrarchy" the chief Augustus was an exalted figure demanding amid royal pomp the obeisance paid to Eastern potentates. Advice was sought only from hand-kissing privy counselors, while administration was entrusted to a swollen bureaucracy and security to a ubiquitous secret police.

Naturally the decline was not uniform. Septimius built the spectacular ornamental façade called the Septizonium to meet the eye of the traveler entering Rome from the Appian Way, Caracalla the enormous baths whose vaulted halls presage the naves of Romanesque cathedrals. The rapid procession of emperors generated a profusion of fine coins and revealing portrait heads, as well as fine gold medallions for army officers. The deep-rooted idea of Rome as the Eternal City under divine protection was strengthened when in 248 Philip the Arab celebrated with great pomp the millennium of her foundation. Nevertheless there was a feeling abroad that, in terms of "the biological fallacy," the world was growing old. Cyprian, Bishop of Carthage (200–258), deplored the thinning of population and the lowering of all standards. The historian Dio Cassius, looking back over two generations to the death of Marcus Aurelius, wrote that then "the history of Rome fell headlong from a reign of gold to one of rust and iron." Yet to the Christian Eusebius, looking back from the time of Constantine, this seemed an age of awakening; and we must now consider what were the spiritual conditions preceding the triumph of Christianity, to what extent the latter was something new, and why it triumphed.

Morality

Morality may be taken first. The hard Roman virtues admired and cultivated in the early republic had been tempered by the soft Hellenistic virtues. What old-fashioned Roman would have remarked, as Pliny does, "The recent illness of a friend brought it home to me that we are at our best when weak"? The blend is conspicuous in Vergil, and also in Seneca, who, whatever his own shortcomings and inconsistencies, is an eclectic whose Stoicism is liable to melt with human warmth. Let us abstract the highest specimens (by Christian standards) of what pagans *said* about morality in the first two centuries A.D., what was familiar in precept, irrespective of practice.

Seneca, who did not always practice what he preached so high-mindedly, advocated living as though some saintly man, a Socrates or an Epicurus, were watching you, and examining the day's conduct every night, as the Pythagoreans did. "When a man is shut up in his room alone," said Epictetus, "God is with him and his attendant angel [*daemon*]." (Plato and Zeno had also recommended the examination of one's dreams, as revealing one's hidden tendencies.) Self-examination led to humility. Worried by those who accused him of not living up to his moralizing, Seneca confessed: "I am not perfect, nor ever will be. I am deep in all sorts of vices. I hope only to be better than the wicked, and to improve daily." His desire to put an end to his old faults is something like a sense of sin. Such humility is far from the old pride of the Stoic sage, or from the haughtiness of Aristotle's paragon, the "great-souled man." It is most remarkable in a lord of the world, Marcus Aurelius. "If I am still far from the goal, it is my own fault for not heeding the gods' admonitions." "The gods," he says to himself, "have repeatedly granted you further periods of grace, of which you have taken no advantage." In the spirit of the age already described, he belittled all human activities. His own satisfaction in his Sarmatian triumph he compares with a spider's in its web. Here is a Roman who thought that desire for an immortal name was a weakness to be fought against. And the final self-mortification: "Pride in humility is the worst form of pride." Things have changed indeed. As for prayer, it should not be for benefits to oneself. "Whatever parents pray for you to get, means depriving someone else," says Seneca. To him the very act of praying betokened a feeble lack of self-reliance: "*Make yourself* happy." Marcus Aurelius said one should pray, if at all, for deliverance from fears and desires. "Lord, give me my deserts," was the prayer of Apollonius of Tyana, the great first-century *guru*.

In personal relationships the Golden Rule was a commonplace: men were born to help each other, as Cicero had put it. "We must love one another from the heart," says Aurelius. Altruism appears in Seneca. Once (though not always) he transcends the deep-rooted Roman idea of reciprocity in favors: "a benefit is an act in which the doer gives pleasure and feels pleasure at the same time, the outcome of a natural and spontaneous inclination." Still further: "If you want to live for yourself, live for another." "I try to acquire a friend for whom I could die." In theory at least he extended such ideas to private property: it all really belonged to the human race. "Let us share things: we were born to." And as for enemies, "It is more wretched to harm than to be harmed"; and "Crime is its own punishment." Aurelius urged upon himself the Socratic doctrine that all wrongdoing was involuntary: if he constantly reminded himself of this, he would be more tolerant. One should love one's enemies: life is too short to do otherwise. Plutarch found that recalcitrant slaves responded better to forgiveness than to punishment, though friends criticized him for such laxity. Titus, with Caesarlike clemency, dealt with two conspirators by overwhelming them with favors.

Within the family the rule of the paterfamilias was mitigated, sometimes by official interference. Trajan compelled a father to release from his *potestas* a son he had maltreated. Hadrian banished one for killing, under cover of a hunt, a son who had lain with his stepmother. By his time marriage required the consent of the bridal pair. After Marcus Aurelius a paterfamilias could not break up a marriage without showing just cause. Indeed Pliny had already thought that perhaps fathers now indulged their sons. A third-century dictum in the *Digest* sums up the matter: "*Patria potestas* should be a matter of *pietas*, not *atrocitas*."

Quintilian spoke out against corporal punishment for children, which he said was generally accepted and was sanctioned by the old Stoic authority Chrysippus. It was an offense against the dignity of a free person. It only hardened the heart and made disciplining those too old for it the more difficult. The results could also be degrading—and he hints delicately at sadism. Lessons should be made enjoyable, with praise and prizes as incentives rather than censure. In a charming poem Martial put it to primary-school masters that in summer if children stay well they are learning enough. We have come far from Horace's master Orbilius "the Beater."

Seneca, who believed that love and fear were incompatible, sought to be revered rather than feared by his slaves. They had divine souls like anyone else, were in fact our fellow servants, our tent companions, humbler friends. It was shameful, if you had few slaves, to be so remiss as not to know them all, or to be so extravagant as to have more than you could know. We had seen already (p. 127) how the condition of town and house slaves improved during this period. There are signs too of greater kindness to animals. Pythagoreans had always urged this, because of their doctrine of the transmigration of souls. But Plutarch also shows good feeling in a delightful essay on animal sagacity; and it would be hard to read Apuleius' *Golden Ass* without sympathizing with the lot of asses. There were always a few who deplored the sufferings even of wild beasts in the arena.

The inequality of women with men before the law was criticized by the Stoic Musonius Rufus (see p. 118). He also advocated the same education and marital conduct for both sexes. But on matters of sexual intercourse he was severe. He not only condemned all extramarital sex; he condemned all intercourse not joylessly directed to procreation—unlike Plutarch, who emphasized spiritual and physical unity in wedlock. "Don't admire your wife's beauty," Musonius said: "then you will avoid being angry with any adulterer she may have." In his obsessive puritanism he anticipates such Christians as Augustine. Seneca too spoke of sex as "this secret bane planted in our very vitals," and insisted that it was given to man for procreation, not pleasure: erotic love was "friendship gone mad." Epictetus complained that women thought of nothing else from the age of fourteen, as Seneca had complained that they were as lustful as men though born to be passive. Like many people even to this day, the Romans found it hard to accept the fact of women's sexuality. Signs of a cult of virginity also appear at this time, in the Greek romances, of all places. There we find beautiful young people dramatically facing torture for their chastity, as the virgin martyrs of Christianity were to do. But the only person we know to have spoken out against prostitution is Dio Chrysostom.

In social morality we find the state increasingly taking a hand. Private endowments for poor children existed at least from Augustus' time; Nerva and his successors provided public ones. Aurelius and Septimius protected children's rights. In the third century abortion became illegal, and the suppression of infants, murder. Whether suicide was antisocial or not was a moot point. To Pythagoras and Plato it had been desertion of the post assigned one by God, to Aristotle an offense against the state. Few Greeks are known to have killed themselves, though they include the great Stoics Zeno and Cleanthes. The Roman world was doubtful. Seneca and Plotinus approved of euthanasia if you were losing your faculties. In times of imperial terror the younger Cato, allowed as an exception by Cicero, provided an example for many Thraseas, including Seneca himself, who had earlier considered suicide but been deterred by concern for his father. To Stoics and Cynics the option was the highest practical proof of ultimate human freedom, the supreme boon among the penalties of life. No Roman could fail to approve of the commander who, when captured by the Dacians, killed himself to prevent his life being used to blackmail Trajan; but

Hadrian decreed that in general the suicide of a soldier constituted desertion. Vergil, as often, anticipated Christianity in the dismal fate he assigned to suicides in the underworld of *Aeneid* 6.

Seneca (*Epistles* 1. 7) spoke out nobly against the horrors of the arena. Impressionable young minds, not yet sure of what was right and wrong, should be segregated from the brutal majority. Plutarch differed from Cicero and Pliny in considering the sight of bloodshed to be depraving. Dio Chrysostom, Lucian, and Apollonius were among others who agreed (*cf.* p. 160). Seneca also denounced torture (*Epistles* 1. 14) with his trenchant eloquence, and held the view that punishment was for deterrence, not retribution. He deplored class distinctions: all men are equally sprung from the gods, if you go back far enough; the only true nobility is a moral one. In gifts it was the spirit, not the status, of the giver that mattered. The man who blushed to be seen in a plain vehicle would be vain in an expensive one.

Old Roman ideas of warlike patriotism were gradually modified. Lucan looked forward to the day when the human race would abandon war and all nations love one another. "As an Antonine," says Aurelius, "I call Rome my country, as a man, the world." Trajan is represented on a frieze as trampling down barbarians, but Aurelius on his column as sparing anguished human beings.

One thing that emerges is that morality is becoming much more closely linked with religion. As early as about 100 B.C. a private shrine to Agdistis (Cybele) at Philadelphia, in Asia Minor obliged the enterer to abjure plotting against anyone, robbery, or murder; love charms, abortives, or contraceptives; adultery even with a slave, or intercourse with a boy or virgin. Mithraism also had a strict moral code. The philosophers had added perfect goodness to the two original characteristics of godhead, immortality and supernatural power. Plato's injunction "Follow God" becomes in Seneca "To imitate the gods is worship enough." "Live with men as though God were watching you, talk with God as though men were hearing you." Indeed "A holy spirit dwells in us as our watcher and guardian." The elder Pliny goes so far as to say that "God is one human being helping another." Plotinus, not primarily a moralist, recognizes that "Without true virtue all talk of God is mere verbiage."

It is apparent, if we abstract from all the ideas that were in the air, that there was little difference between the purest pagan and Christian thought on morality: the Christian Origen conceded as much to Celsus. "Seneca is often ours," said Tertullian. Indeed in some respects pagan morality was more exacting. Marcus Aurelius was supremely good with no thought of being rewarded in an afterlife; and he did not pray even for his daily bread. Where the Christians seem superior is in practice, comprehensiveness, degree, and spirit. They practiced what they preached, at least in the period when most were converts rather than hereditary members. Aurelius too believed in the brotherhood of man. He tried hard to like his fellow men, but it was an effort. The general standard of pagan social morality deteriorated in some respects, as in the hardening of class distinctions and discrimination against *humiliores*. But the Christians really did love one another. There is little evidence of charity in the pagan *collegia*, only of conviviality and attendance to the dead; whereas even the prejudiced Lucian could not repress his wonder at the kindness of the Christians to Peregrinus when he was in prison. Julian, the apostate emperor in the fourth century, had to confess that they helped the poor without distinction, whereas the pagans did not even help their own. Cyprian's flock at Carthage in the early third century stayed behind in a plague to do relief work and contributed a large sum to ransom children kidnapped by marauding Numidians. Not a few pagans deplored the increasing horrors of the arena; but it was not until the Christian monk Telemachus in 404 sacrificed his life in making a dramatic protest that gladiatorial contests were abolished.

The difference in spirit is seen most clearly in Stoicism. It was an ethic only for heroes, based on pride. Both the ex-minister Seneca and the ex-slave Epictetus believed that gods were superior to men by nature only in respect of their immortality. All gradations of vice were condemned: there was no concession to human weakness. Seneca distinguishes between clemency, which is a disposition to moderation in punishing, an exercise of judgment, and pity, which is an effeminate weakness, a flinching at the sight of suffering that takes no account of the cause. But the Christian's mercy was such as "droppeth as the gentle rain from heaven." The Stoic ideal of controlling emotion by reason might too easily freeze the wellsprings of philanthropy.

Pagan Religions

The religious scene in the second and third centuries is particularly confused, and the evidence for what the masses believed may conflict with the testimony of literature. There had never been many professed atheists. Even so rational a person as Galen, though perplexed about the relationship of soul to body, believed in a spiritual power and in providence. But now, it seems, the thoughts of most serious people were moving toward preoccupation with the divine and looking beyond this world, even to the detriment of the empire. Let us try to survey the scene and then see how Christianity fits into it.

To begin with, the old polytheistic religion was far from dead, as innumerable inscriptions testify. There was a return in the second century, as Pausanias' guidebook shows, both to the Olympians and to local cults. The Capitoline triad retained their prestige with ordinary people, as well as Venus Genetrix the foundress and vaguer deities of venerable antiquity such as Semo Sancus and Dea Dia. In the country, where belief was to survive longest (hence the name "pagan," from *paganus,* "villager"), Silvanus was particularly present, and the Nymphs. The Lares and Penates were deeply rooted, and the cults of *numina* and local *genii* revived. The deified Hercules was everywhere, the laborious hero of the Stoics and Cynics. Asclepius retained his hold because of the doubtless genuine relief given to many sufferers whose psychosomatic symptoms were removed by faith in the dreams they experienced in his shrines. Situated in beautiful and salubrious surroundings, these shrines had a sanatorium attached, with chaplains, physicians, and sympathetic nurses, male and female.

The official attitude remained the same. Each emperor, as Chief Pontiff, carried out the traditional rituals. The Capitol, burned by Vitellian soldiers, was carefully restored by Vespasian, whose son Domitian was particularly orthodox. Antoninus Pius took an antiquarian interest in religion reminiscent of that of Augustus; while Marcus Aurelius, a Salian priest from the age of eight, knew by heart the almost unintelligible old rigmaroles. Inscriptions found in their sacred grove reveal how meticulously the Arval Brothers still performed their rituals.

Among the educated there were varied shades of opinion. Seneca in the first century may stand for the old Polybian attitude. After a devastatingly satirical account of the ceremonies on the Capitol and the credulity of the congregation (which Augustine cited with relish) he concludes, "The wise man will observe all these rites as being enjoined by the law, not as being pleasing to the gods." Pliny at the turn of the century may stand for a more relaxed, aristocratic conformism. He restored a temple of Ceres on his estates; and he was delighted to be elected an augur for purely sentimental and snobbish reasons—he had been nominated by Trajan, he was succeeding an eminent man, Cicero had been one, and the appointment was for life. But there were others who felt more sincerely that in some way the safety of the empire did depend on the maintenance of the "peace of the gods." Such is the supporter of paganism against Christianity in Minucius Felix's Ciceronian dialogue *Octavius,* composed about a century later; and Celsus wrote his *True Account* (ca. 178) because he believed that Christianity was harming the state by causing deviations from traditional piety. Paganism meant patriotism and classical culture. In the dark days of the third century the emperor Decius sought to rally the empire under the auspices of the old religion, demanding certificates of sacrifice, which led to his short-lived but terrible persecution of Christians who refused to comply. The overwhelming majority of citizens were still nominally pagan when the empire became officially Christian. The Altar of Victory, erected by Augustus in the Senate House, had become the great symbol for a few passionately pagan aristocrats such as Symmachus, rival to St. Ambrose as leading orator in the later fourth century. The Sacred Way still echoed more loudly in times of crisis to the lowing of oxen bound for sacrifice on the Capitol. Half Augustine's *City of God* had to be devoted to attacking the idea that the greatness of Rome had been due to her observance of the old religion; and it was not until 494 that the festival of the Lupercalia was converted into that of the Purification of the Virgin Mary. By then some people had begun to experience conversion *to* paganism, as in the case of the emperor Julian, and even sometimes to be persecuted in turn.

The emperors, though not officially deified in their lifetime, continued to deify their predecessor in some cases. Marcus Aurelius, in particular, was given a place among the Penates in many a family for generations after his death. They could be identified with some god (as Horace in the time of hopeful relief after Actium had suggested that Octavian might be Mercury). Hadrian was Zeus Olympios and Zeus Panhellenikos to the Greeks. At least the emperors were assumed to reign *Dei gratia*. Quintilian defended earthly subjection to a monarch as an image of the government of God. Indeed an absurd web of taboo was woven around emperors. A man was reported for touching a chamber pot, when drunk, with a ring on which Tiberius' head was engraved, and a woman was condemned to death for stripping before a statue of Domitian. We have seen how Trajan had to chide Pliny for his scruples. In practice the tendency to worship the emperor even in his lifetime became more marked under the Severans.

Ever since Hellenistic thought began to influence Rome there had been a marked trend toward monotheism. (In Seneca and Plutarch, as in Plato, divinity is indifferently spoken of in the plural or singular.) The trend showed itself in various ways. Jupiter remained chief god of the Roman state. On the one hand primitive people prefixed his name to that of their chief god. On the other a philosopher could say, as Seneca did, that he was "the creative mind and breath of the Universe—call him Fate, the Prime Cause, Providence, Nature, or the Universe." In the words of Lucan, "Jupiter is whatever you see, whatever you feel." We find him identified with Serapis, the highly successful god who had been more or less created by Ptolemy I five centuries before to draw Alexandrian Egyptians and Greeks together; also with the primarily Persian sun god, associated with Mithraism. The sun god was gradually popularized at Rome as Eastern influences increased, his devotees including Apollonius of Tyana and Septimius' wife Julia Domna, daughter of his high priest at Emesa in Syria. Indeed it looked as if he was becoming the official chief god of the empire when Aurelian built a great temple for him on the Campus Martius in 274 and established a college of pontiffs. With his distinguishing title "Unconquered" he appealed especially to soldiers, and his *roi soleil* image suited monarchs, easing the transition from principate to dominate. His birthday on December 25, merged with the Saturnalia, we still celebrate under new auspices, and *Sunday* remains the Lord's day. Another magnet for monotheism was Isis, worshiped by Apuleius' Lucius as "Panthea of the myriad names," embracing all other divinities.

Isis here is an example of syncretism, the idea that all human notions of godhead are perceptions, dimmer or clearer, of one god. Toleration had always been a Roman characteristic. A statue of Jesus stood with ones of Orpheus, Abraham, and Apollonius of Tyana in the private chapel of Alexander Severus. Only the animal deities of Egypt proved hard to stomach: the dog-headed "barking Anubis" was an object of special scorn. And there were other ways of salvaging polytheism. Barbarous gods were assimilated, as Moloch to Saturn in North Africa. Their cults were taken over, as they were later to be by the Church. Euhemerism still enabled some, such as Asclepius, to be seen as men posthumously deified for their benefits to mankind. Conversely men might be seen as gods in disguise, as Paul and Barnabas were at Lystra. Some gods could be taken as symbols of natural forces, as Neptune of the sea, or of human faculties, as Minerva of intelligence. The reputation of Homer as all-wise had long been salvaged by allegorical interpretation, and this process was now applied wholesale to polytheism by such experts as Dio Chrysostom and Maximus of Tyre.

One of the commonest means of harmonization was to invoke the idea of daemons, lesser divinities in the great chain of being, inhabiting upper regions this side of the moon, which goes back to Hesiod and Pythagoras but whose vogue at this period was derived from some mythical passages in Plato. Most people now believed in their reality. In the tradition of the daemonic sign that guided Socrates they were assimilated to the old Roman idea of an individual's *genius*. [1] They were the inspirers of prophecy. But chiefly they were the executives of the will of God (now felt to be more remote the less anthropomorphic he became, enthroned above the starry firmament), and conveyors to him of prayers from men. The astonishing question put to Apollo of Claros, "Are you God, or is another god?" received the equally astonishing answer, "*Aion* (Eternity) is God: Apollo is one of his messengers." Many pious pagans believed the gods of Greek mythology to be daemons, preferring this explanation to farfetched allegorization. Plato's daemons were only good ones, and only such were recognized by Maximus of Tyre. But Plutarch followed Plato's pupil Xenocrates in believing that there were bad ones too, and so accounted for all the immoral tales in Greek mythology that had long caused offense. Such dualism was to become crucial in the debate on the problem of evil. As "devils" daemons took possession of people and even animals: any abnormal condition was so explained. Jews had long claimed to be able to exorcise them, as Jesus was said to have done at Gadara, and this was an art to which Christians (who had yet to forswear magic and astrology) were to lay special claim. Indeed to Tertullian it was to redeem the world from daemons that Christ had come.

Conversely, magic papyri, which are found in abundance, give instructions for entrancing mediums, usually boys, for the purpose of making them receptive to a daemon of prophecy, another obsession of the age. The Phrygian Christian Montanus, claiming to be the mouthpiece of God, announced the imminence of the Second Coming. (Its failure to happen did not prevent his having followers who were prepared to immolate themselves for Montanism nearly three centuries later.) We are here in the semantic no man's land that divides religion from superstition. It was an age in which miracles were widely reported and easily accepted. The skeptical Vespasian is stated by both Tacitus and Sueton-

---

[1] There was a "pecking order" among *genii*. As Macbeth said of Banquo, (act 3, sc. 1, lines 56–58):
    under him
My genius is rebuked, as it is said
Mark Antony's was by Caesar's.

ius, when at Alexandria, to have essayed successfully to cure a blind man (by the application of spittle) and a cripple (by touch). The reality of magic was taken for granted. Apuleius had to defend himself against prosecution for it, and even the eminent philosopher Plotinus believed himself a victim of it.

As for oracles, they had declined in the first century. Plutarch, as a pious priest of Delphi, was concerned about this: the daemons that previously inspired them must have migrated or died. But he was too pessimistic. Though Nero had suppressed the oracle because the Pythian priestess had branded the mother-killer as another Orestes, there was in fact some revival of Delphi in the second century, despite a regrettable deterioration in the verse of the responses, resulting in a prudent change to prose. Apollo of Claros also flourished: in remote Britain, at Borcovicus on Hadrian's wall, Tungrian soldiers from the Ardennes made dedications at his behest. It was, in fact, increased competition that had reduced some oracles to dumbness.[2]

In such an age there was every opportunity for fraud. Sophisticated miracle machines and conjuring devices were exploited. Lucian has made famous the case of Alexander of Abonutichus. Senators hastened from Rome to his new oracle in remote Paphlagonia, on the Black Sea. Claiming that, like Endymion, he had slept with the Moon, he ascribed to this the origin of his daughter, whom a sexagenarian governor of Asia was pleased to marry. The new Mysteries he founded had the paradoxical distinction of uniting Epicureans and Christians in opposition.

Dreams are in a different category. They were assumed to be significant, as indeed we now know them to be, though the symbolic interpretation they were subjected to differed from that of Freud.[3] They were also assumed to be some-times prophetic. And further, gods appeared in them. To people unaware that a person's preconceived ideas condition the content of his dreams, these appear-ances naturally seemed irrefutable evidence of the god's existence. Marcus Aurelius believed himself helped by them with medical advice. The *Sacred Account* of Aelius Aristides is a remarkable record of the dreams he had over a long period beginning in 140 in the sanctuary of Asclepius at Pergamum, in the course of which the god prescribed him drastic remedies for his many maladies, which he convinced himself were effective. He came to believe him-self uniquely chosen by his "savior," who guided him in all his doings, and to whom he henceforth joyfully dedicated his life, almost indeed to the extent of self-identification.

[2] It was not until 1696 that the validity of pagan oracles was questioned.

[3] Sir Samuel Dill, in 1904, just before Freud, characterized Artemidorus' *Interpretation of Dreams* thus: "A subtlety and formalism of system . . . are employed to give order and meaning to the wildest vagaries of vulgar fancy. . . . It is difficult to conceive what was the ordinary state of mind and the habits of people whose sleep was haunted by visions so lawless." (*Roman Society from Nero to Marcus Aurelius,* pp. 469–471.)

So far we have been dealing with matters of piety, cult, and speculative or superstitious beliefs. But what a bewildered generation, bereft of self-reliance based on reason, was craving for was a savior, like Aristides' Asclepius but for the next world as well as this. Once indeed Aristides did receive a vision of the underworld, but it did not come from the earthly healer Asclepius. It came from Serapis; and in the so-called mystery religions we find scope for a more developed personal religion.

Traditionally the Roman authorities had drawn the line at admitting foreign deities into the *pomerium,* the precinct that was the heart of the old city. The great exception had been Cybele, with her attendant Atys (see p. 22). But pressure from the masses was insistent for recognition, and under the empire the barriers fell one by one, partly because the upper classes became less rational, partly because the citizenship became more and more foreign in origin. Claudius reformed and reestablished the cult of Cybele, whose chief priest was henceforward an uncastrated Roman. Antoninus Pius and his wife Faustina were devotees, and her cult spread especially throughout North Africa and Gaul. Enthroned beside Father Jupiter she was the Great Mother of all. The cognate "Syrian Goddess," Atargatis, half woman, half fish, with her wandering, begging, flagellant eunuch priests, had a particular attraction for Nero. She acquired a temple beyond the Tiber in the second century. Bacchus continued to have his devotees, his Mysteries being alluded to on many sarcophagi from the second century A.D. onward. The Egyptian deities, Serapis and the triad Isis, Osiris, and Horus or Harpocrates, banished by Tiberius, were welcomed back by Caligula. Domitian, who had escaped in the disguise of a devotee of Isis in the troubles of 69, during which her temple was burned, rebuilt it sumptuously in 92. A friend of Hadrian's became her chief priest, and Commodus actually took her tonsure. These religions, somewhat effeminate in spirit, flourished around the Mediterranean. By contrast that of Mithras, which was thoroughly masculine, though long established—largely by slaves—in the seaports, the capital, and North Italy, was most popular along the northern frontiers and in the third and fourth centuries. Akin to that of the "Unconquered Sun," with a myth of heroic endeavor, a hierarchy among initiates, and an elaborate discipline, it appealed, as we have said, to soldiers, especially officers. Brought back directly from the East by the Fifteenth Legion, it became centered in Carnuntum (near modern Bratislava) and spread from there through the armies up the Danube, down the Rhone and the Rhine, and as far as Britain.

It is clear that during the first three centuries A.D. the tide of the mystery religions was rising. They maintained priesthoods and cults financed not solely by alms. Their initiations, sometimes graded, were not cheap, as Apuleius' Lucius found. Not everyone could afford a bull for a *taurobolium* (see below), or even a ram for the alternative *criobolium;* and to that extent they excluded the poorest class. Their organization was local, not ecumenical, though their spread was greatly helped by the excellence of imperial communications. They were aggregates of individual pieties rather than churches, and were thus no real threat to the state religion. Indeed in a Western sample their inscriptions comprised only some 15 percent of the total.

They might claim to be exclusive. Thus Isis tells Apuleius' Lucius, "The remainder of your life till your last breath is made over to me, and in the Elysian Fields thereafter you will continually adore me. I and I alone have power to prolong your life beyond the bounds of Fate." But the fact that people were initiated into several Mysteries, as Apuleius himself was, suggests reinsurance rather than absolute faith. (He kept their sacred objects wrapped up in cloths in the cupboard of his Penates.) There was indeed much interchange between them. Statius closes the first book of his *Thebaïd* with a hymn to Apollo who is also Titan, Osiris, and Mithras the bull-slayer. The *taurobolium* of Cybele was borrowed by Atargatis and Mithras. Plutarch's friend Clea, leader of the Dionysiac Thyiades at Delphi, recognized (he said) that Dionysus was the same as Osiris, into whose mysteries she had been initiated by her parents. The chief priest of Isis in Apuleius was called Mithras, and a high priest of Mithras was the last hierophant of Eleusis.

What these religions had to offer was escape for their initiates, without distinction as regards race or status, from an unsatisfying existence. In this world it was a sense of enhancement for the individual, of belonging to an elect body, together with the appeal of colorful vestments, exotic music, hymn-singing, and taking part in processions and impressive rituals such as the launching on March 5 of the ship of Isis that inaugurated the navigational season—for one of her titles was Stella Maris. Another striking ritual was the *taurobolium* of Cybele already referred to. The candidate stood in a pit under a grid over which a bull was sacrificed, so that the blood ran down onto his (or her) tongue and all over him, after which he was "reborn," originally for a period, in later times "forever," and adored by the congregation. Most of the religions also involved myths connected with the annual death and rebirth of vegetation symbolized by the death and resurrection of a symbolic figure, Osiris or Atys or Adonis; and these held out to their initiates the promise for the purified of eternal happiness in the hereafter.[4] In some there was a ritual of sudden change from darkness to bright light, as in the Eleusinian Mysteries, revealing symbolic emblems or a sacred drama. One result of the spread of belief in an afterlife was a move from cremation toward burial of the dead; for this was an afterlife for the person, not a mere Stoic remerging of the borrowed spark of soul into a world soul. Sarcophagi, at least for the wealthy, begin to multiply in the second century.

The nature and extent of belief in survival is hard to assess. "Farewell forever" continues to be the sentiment of many tombs; "I was not, I was; I am not, I care not." But the great majority ostensibly attest belief. The Roman's tomb

---

[4] In the Dionysiac religion Ariadne, deserted by Theseus, wakes to marriage with Bacchus. An interesting example in literature is Daphnis, hero of the shepherds in Vergil's *Fifth Eclogue:* in Mopsus' song he dies and the countryside is desolate, in Menalcas' he is raised to the stars and it revives.

was an everlasting home, protected by law. Objects were left in it for the use of the dead, and the coin in the mouth for Charon was ubiquitous. Importance was attached to tending to it, and there were flowers on birthdays. There were regular festivals of the dead—the cheerful Parentalia, which ended with the family communion of *cara cognatio* (dear relationship), and the grim Lemuria, when those who had died a violent death were appeased. Continued connection with the living was desired, wayside tombs soliciting a greeting from the passer-by. What cannot be assessed is how much was pure convention, how much hope that went beyond mere sentiment.

Educated people differed, as ever. The elder Pliny dismissed survival with Lucretian contempt, and there were always Epicureans committed to this view. The Socratic alternative of either a happy afterlife or painless nothingness is often mentioned—in Seneca's phrase, *aut beatus aut nullus* (either happy or non-existent); nevertheless, his remark that fear of going nowhere is as bad as fear of the underworld was and is no doubt true for many people. Epictetus was agnostic on the subject, and so was Marcus Aurelius. To Quintilian it was a stock debate. Tacitus' farewell to Agricola is "If there is any place in the shades for the righteous—if, as the philosophers hold, great souls are not extinguished with the body—may you rest in peace." Here we have the idea of Elysian survival for an elite, which we meet with in Anchises' exposition to Aeneas in the Vergilian underworld. Vergil also has the idea of purgatory for all. We cannot use the extensive literature of *Consolations* as evidence for belief: these were concerned to adduce all possible optimistic considerations, even incompatible ones. Pythagoreans were committed to the doctrine of transmigration of souls, and Platonists believed with Plato that survival was a demonstrable fact, while Stoics were divided as between no survival, survival for all or for an elite until the next great conflagration, and reabsorption into the world soul.

The relaxation of the hold of reason had created by the second century a climate favorable to mysticism, a feeling of direct union of the human spirit with the fundamental principle of being, "a mode of experience and of knowledge different from and superior to the normal," (Lalande, as quoted by Dodds). So much emerges from all attempts to describe it by those who have experienced it. Mystical experience seems to occur in any age or culture; forms of it can be invited or induced, in people aware of its possibility, by ritual, by yoga, by drugs, or by contemplation. Apuleius' Lucius (here, surely, himself) achieved something like it by adoring contemplation of the image of Isis. In the same century Albinus, starting from Plato's *Symposium,* and Numenius, a Pythagorean acquainted with Jewish thought, were interested in achieving it by a more philosophical path. These are among the forerunners of the reviver of Neoplatonism, Plotinus (205–270), who from the age of forty taught in Rome, a major figure and the last pagan to attempt a grand philosophic synthesis. "Dig within," said Marcus Aurelius. "Within is the fountain of good which is always ready to bubble up." This is halfway to Plotinus' "All things are within."

Plotinus was certainly an introvertive mystic, indeed the archetypal mystic for Gregory of Nyssa and other such Christians.[5] In one passage he describes mystical experience, which he achieved four times in the six years in which his Syrian editor and biographer Porphyry was with him, as "the union with God which earthly lovers imitate when they seek to be one flesh." But the interpretation put by mystics on their experience (it would seem) depends on their cultural ambience. Plotinus, a contemplative who meditated founding a monastic "Platonopolis," a sort of *ashram,* or retreat, in Campania, shared the contempt of his age for this earth and the human body. (Porphyry reports that he could not bear to talk of his parentage or his upbringing in his native Egypt.) He presented in more organized form some of the ideas to be found in the confused writings of the Gnostics and Hermetists. But the foundation of his philosophy, which is too elaborate to be outlined here, is his own experience of the ineffable One and Good, and its distinctive feature is his Greek insistence that the approach should be intellectual. His object was to bring his own soul, and those of others, by the way of the intellect to union with the One.

Rise of Christianity

In such a spiritual climate Christianity grew up, and, as in the sphere of morality, we observe that many of its elements have parallels elsewhere. Mithraism, for instance, had its myth of a miraculous birth, the babe in a hallowed cave, with neighboring shepherds adoring and offering their firstlings; it had its sacramental meal of bread and water (or wine), baptism, and promise of resurrection. (The early Christian Fathers took it to be a parody inspired by the devil.) But Christianity was really unlike other religions, though it owed much to Judaism. It was urban, but had no local ties. Its exclusive God was lovable as well as loving; his consubstantial Son, voluntarily incarnate, suffered a criminal's death ("to the Jews a stumbling block, to the Greeks foolishness"); he did so to atone for the sins of the whole world; he was also the Word made Flesh. It was a revealed religion and an organized entity, ultimately with canonical scriptures and a formulated creed. Its adherents could participate, not merely acquiesce like Stoics, in a universal plan.

The "Galileans," first called also Christians at Antioch, infiltrated Rome under Claudius, who expelled them on suspicion of provoking riots (as we know from the Acts of the Apostles they were likely to do)—ineffectually, it would seem, for Paul, remitted to Burrus by Festus, procurator of Judaea, addressed "the brethren that are of the house of Caesar." They first came to general attention at Rome when Nero made them scapegoats for the great fire of 64. But they are never mentioned by Seneca, nor even by Plutarch in the second century or Dio Cassius in the third. Indeed they only occur a dozen times in extant pagan

[5] It is odd that he is not mentioned in William James' classic, *The Varieties of Religious Experience.*

literature before Constantine, though we know that Fronto wrote against them and Celsus' well-informed *True Account* can be reconstructed from Origen. Being generally taken at first to be a sect of Judaism, they shared its privileges as well as its unpopularity.

Why did they prosper nevertheless? Apparently because they brought to ordinary people of both sexes, often slaves, a simple and joyful message of love and hope that was not so novel as to be unacceptable or incomprehensible: love of a Savior who had quite recently lived man's life, and through him of one another; hope of an eternity of bliss for believers as a compensation for the trials of this life. Their community was a haven for the lonely, far more than the pagan *collegia*. Their initiation of baptism was not a means of raising money; rather they had, at least originally, all material goods in common. Their idea of the fatherhood of God, warmer and more personal than that of the Stoics, diminished earthly distinctions. Paul told slaves not to mind their earthly position, but to work heartily as for the Lord, being "the Lord's freemen"; and indeed the word "slave" has not been found on the walls of Christian burial catacombs. The Christians were unique in transfiguring the sufferings of the poor. Few of them were rich in the first two centuries.

In attempting to account for the success of Christianity, too much stress must not be laid on the attractiveness of the human personality of Jesus. In early Christian literature the emphasis is on his teaching, his fulfillment of prophecies, and his miracles culminating in his resurrection (though no Christian contested the validity of pagan miracles.) But the Gospels of Matthew, Mark, and Luke were there to be read, and men cannot have failed to be attracted by a man-god who was a historical, not a mythological, character and who, though he died as man, was living still and ready to have a direct personal relationship with living men in all ages.

The Christians' exclusiveness also preserved them. Unlike the Gnostics, they refused to compromise and be swallowed up, or indeed to see any value in any other religion. They demanded of their converts a new start and continued repentence for past sins for the sake of One who had suffered to give men a chance of sinlessness. And whereas Celsus in 178 referred to their doctrinal squabbles, by the end of the second century they had at least isolated a canonical New Testament to which appeal could be made. This, despite some interpolation, narrowed the scope for heresy and schism, giving an enormous advantage for survival over the Hermetics of Egypt, for instance, whose multifarious literature claimed to hand down the ancient wisdom of Thoth. Finally, they prospered just because they were persecuted: "The blood of the martyrs was the seed of the Church." Galen was impressed, and Tertullian converted, by their courage in the arena; and their sufferings drew them together for comfort and in loyalty. Besides, as Lucretius observed, in bitter times men turn with much more alacrity to religion. The anxieties of the third century, and the appalling economic conditions of the years 250–284 in particular, may well have benefited the Church.

But why were they persecuted? Why did Tacitus call them "enemies of the human race"? First of all, they were censorious. They derided the gods on whom many of their neighbors believed the safety of the state to depend, and carried devaluation of the old martial and patriotic virtues sometimes even to the point of pacifism. They also denounced their neighbors' pleasure not only in the cruel arena but in chariot racing, gambling, and the baths. Conversion, often by domestic slaves, could divide married couples and set children against their parents and teachers, since Christianity was, like Judaism but unlike the other contemporary religions, exclusive. Besides, they met for secret rites, and that was enough to generate talk of incest and cannibalism, which even Fronto believed and second-century apologists felt obliged seriously to rebut. Those signs of the cross they made were probably some kind of magic. Along the Rhone they also incurred the unpopularity of the successful business immigrant. Altogether they were ideal scapegoats for disasters such as earthquakes: as Tertullian said, whenever anything went wrong, the cry was "Christians to the lion." So much for popular clamor. There were governors who took the easy way out by sacrificing them to it, as Pilate had sacrificed Jesus himself. Hadrian had to warn, and the Antonines punish, ones who did this. Other governors however made things easy for them: all that they really required was an oath of allegiance.

More serious people might object that they were bringing back the fear of death, which generations of philosophers had striven to banish, threatening hell, or at least purgatory, to backsliders and heretics as well as outsiders in general. The alternative of immediate torture here and eternal torture elsewhere was unbearable to the less steadfast among the persecuted. Above all, the authorities were deeply suspicious of them. Secret societies were forbidden, and especially dangerous when they included slaves. The Christians' talk of "the Kingdom of God" was ominously reminiscent of Bar Kochba (see p. 147); and some were believed to be eager for an apocalyptic "great and terrible day" that would destroy even Eternal Rome. But in truth Christians did not object to the empire. It provided a suitably peaceful milieu for their existence and preaching until the Second Coming, which was at first believed to be imminent. Paul and other New Testament writers enjoined civil disobedience: the author of the Revelation was exceptional in denouncing Rome and its upper classes. But, as some scholars at least believe, Nero laid it down that Christianity was a crime simply because of the enormities associated with the name, and none of his immediate successors reversed this decree. The conscientious Pliny, after imposing a special test, did execute the obdurate. Trajan however told him to turn a blind eye when possible; but Trajan's pardon for recanters was unique. It was regretfully understood that Jews would not worship an emperor: their national religion forbade it, and Romans respected any devotion to *mos maiorum,* a people's traditional way of life. But Christianity was no longer a national religion, and it proselytized more aggressively. In vain Christians pleaded willingness to regard the emperor as second only to their God, and to pray *for* him.

Why should they then refuse to burn a few purely symbolic grains of incense *to* him?

Persecution was intermittent and haphazard from Nero onward. Under Domitian it affected Christians less than others until his last year. Under Marcus Aurelius frontier disasters may have been the cause of a fresh outbreak. It is noteworthy that the Bishop of Sardis, complaining to him, described the persecution at Smyrna as a new phenomenon. Aurelius, perhaps influenced by Fronto, permitted the governor of Lyon to behead Christians if they were Roman citizens, otherwise to throw them to the beasts: it is possible that slaves under torture had been driven to confirm the enormities with which they were popularly credited. But Tertullian a generation later did not mention him among the persecutors, and Aurelius' son Commodus, influenced by his mistress Marcia, was lenient. Though Septimius in 201 forbade Jews and Christians alike to proselytize anywhere, he gave his son Caracalla a Christian nurse, and Alexander Severus protected them. These were the years of awakening to which Eusebius looked back. Origen thought there had been few martyrs before his time (248).

Serious trouble then began. By now the Christians had become what Celsus had feared, a state within a state. The emperor Decius, panic-stricken by Gothic invasions and seeking to rally the empire under the banner of the old religion, tried systematically to extirpate their leaders; and if he had not died after only two years he might have succeeded. As it was, some persecution was continued by Valerian, perhaps because he had no money and there were now rich men among the Christians. The years between 249 and his capture by the Persians in 259 were the worst they ever endured. There followed a breathing space, granted by Plotinus' patron, the admirable Gallienus, that lasted for forty years, until the great persecution under Diocletian, chargeable rather to his "Caesar" and successor Galerius. This raged for six years—though Britain and Gaul were unaffected, and Spain, Africa, and Italy only in the first year—till on his death-bed in 311 Galerius suddenly issued an edict of partial toleration.

Martyrdom had a psychological aspect. In this age of sick souls in an affluent but disillusioned society the death wish, that *libido moriendi* which Seneca had diagnosed and Epictetus confirmed, found fulfillment for some in martyrdom. But there were many whose motives were nearer the surface: the desire to imitate Christ and to please him by faithfulness even to death, the prospect of glory in this world, with a tomb that might become a shrine, and the assurance of everlasting bliss.

Despite Tertullian's boast, "we now fill the world," the Christians in his day (ca. 200) were still only a comparatively small minority. Their numbers in Rome have been estimated at about twenty thousand. During the third century the Church became more organized, bureaucratic, and hierarchical, perhaps also more worldly and comfortable, settling down as the prospect of the Second Coming receded. From the time of Alexander Severus church buildings begin to appear, taking over worship from private houses. The majority of Christians may by now have been hereditary rather than converted. More people joined who had a financial stake in this world, while the poorer may have been attracted by hope of shared possessions and a hierarchy open to talent. It is not surprising that in Galerius' persecution there were many renegations, while on the other hand there were more pagans who, better informed now about Christianity, were reluctant to persecute. The anxiety of better-educated members to accommodate classical culture, deplored by Tertullian ("What has Athens to do with Jerusalem?"), led to a variety of heresies, but at synods a central core cohered.

The number of Christians in Rome, after Constantine emerged victorious at the Battle of the Milvian Bridge, has been estimated at about eighty thousand. They were thus still very much a minority, but like Lenin's Bolsheviks they were a minority that knew its own mind. They had a steadfast code of morality, and their communities held together. The rest were either lukewarm or else bewildered, piling one religious insurance on another from the variety bred by tolerance, and still not feeling safe. Stoicism, a creed for the few, declined after Marcus Aurelius. Tatian was able to contrast the senseless and hopeless doctrine of recurrent cycles held by some Stoics with the Christian doctrine of resurrection on the Last Day. Cynicism, its poor relation that survived it, had much in common with Christianity, but had no organization or common life, no myth or cult, no basis of revelation from outside, no compensatory promise of an afterlife. Nevertheless the decision to give Christianity a privileged position, following the Milan Edict of Toleration of 313, was personal to Constantine, as personal as the decision made by Henry VIII and infinitely more momentous. While his own deepest loyalty may have been to *Romanitas,* which he saw would be best served by Christianity, he does seem also to have had a mystical streak that affected his choice.

Christianity and Its Pagan Heritage

Paul had preached that the wisdom of God was the foolishness of men. The second century, the Age of Unreason, led up to Tertullian's *certum est quia absurdum* (its absurdity proves its truth). Exclusive salvation as a reward simply for faith appealed to the multitude, and especially to women. Lucian, Galen, and Celsus were astonished that people could hold so fanatically beliefs based on unproved assertion. Celsus compared them with those who preferred quacks to doctors. He also objected to Christians for preferring the uncultured to the cultured. But by the end of that century, when Christianity was more sure of itself, it faced up to presenting a reasoned case. Clement of Alexandria undertook the work of harmonizing the classical heritage with the Christian. He saw philosophy as the *paedagogus* as the Greek world, as the Law was of the Jewish, to bring the heathen to Christ, and declared roundly that Plato had been inspired by God; and Origen after him, who considered reliance on faith alone as a weakness, though inevitable for the masses, made far-reaching concessions in an attempt to synthesize Christianity and Platonism.

By the third century the Western Church, whose language had originally been Greek, had been Latinized and separated from the Eastern. Hippolytus at Rome, as Clement and Origen at Alexandria, dressed and behaved as a philosopher. With Irenaeus' *Against Heresies* (185) the age of theology had begun. One great topic was the problem of evil: how could a God who was both almighty and good have created all the evil in the world? Seneca had given an explanation on Stoic lines as far as individuals' suffering is concerned: God, being a loving father, is exercising them for virtue, as the trainer prescribes exercises for an athlete that involve pain. Tertullian accepted plague, famine, and war as a providential "pruning of the overweening human race." Platonists and Stoics insisted that we saw only a minute fraction of an inscrutable master plan. But in the third century a commoner explanation was that there is a fundamental dualism in the world. Paganism did not develop the concept of an organized celestial opposition of daemons, as Judaism and Christianity did. But the Roman world was influenced by Manichaeism, the teachings of the Persian prophet, Mani, which held Augustine himself for thirteen years, of a perpetual struggle between the powers of darkness and light. Another topic was the divinity of Christ. If Christ was not divine, how could his superiority be maintained against rival teachers and miracle workers put up against him by pagans, men such as Apollonius of Tyana? Study of theology inevitably bred heresies. Augustine reckoned that by his time there were eighty-eight. It also bred *odium theologicum* (hatred between theologians). Constantine himself summoned in 325 the Council of Nicaea, at which Athanasius, who believed the Father and Son to be consubstantial, prevailed over Arius, who believed the Son to be subordinate —a controversy that continued however to arouse the deepest passions.

In their attitude to pagan literature Christians varied. Unlike the Jews, they did not set up schools of their own: they simply added their own religious education in church and family. Children had to be taught there how much of what they learned in school was to be regarded as incompatible with their faith. The author whom all Western Christians read as a model of style was Cicero. He was also so like a Christian in his views on morality, his deism was so respectable, and he contained so many arguments that could be used against paganism, that the Church, in its period of uphill struggle, was content to have him as an ally and ask no awkward questions. But when, after the final catastrophe of Rome, the sack of the city by Alaric the Goth in 410, the British monk Pelagius wandered over the Mediterranean world preaching a humanist Christianity with its roots in Stoicism and Ciceronianism, he came up against Augustine. Pelagius was primarily a puritanical reformer, crusading against moral laxity and materialism in the Church and the world around. His theology was that of a moralist. He asserted that nature, including human nature, was fundamentally good. It was inconceivable that God should condemn souls of infants who died unbaptized to eternal hell-fire. God had given man free will so that by his own unaided effort he might become even perfect. Augustine swiftly grasped that this was incompatible with Christianity as he conceived it, with the doctrines of original sin, divine grace, and the atonement of the Cross. He marshaled his forces and secured Pelagius' condemnation as a heretic. So ended the last significant Christian compromise with pagan thought, and the course of the Church was set for the Middle Ages.

The Empire of the East was to live on for more than a thousand years. Creative genius sometimes evokes organizing genius. So Plato evoked Aristotle, and Jesus Paul; and so the genius of Greece evoked that of Rome. The Greek world, whose culture, bred in the city-state, had captivated its Roman conquerors, had by now derived from the Roman character the administrative ability to hold together a wide empire, ruled from Constantinople. There, in the sixth century, the emperor Justinian gathered up the threads by codifying the law, which was to be Rome's greatest tangible legacy to posterity. He also finally closed the philosophic schools, a symbolic act: the classical world they had educated had passed away, and the future lay with Christianity. But Christianity itself owed not a little to Roman *humanitas*.

Bibliography

This brief bibliography covers only less technical works written in or translated into English. Translations of ancient works may be found in the Loeb Library, or in paperback series such as Mentor and Penguin. For general reference see the *Oxford Classical Dictionary*, 2nd ed. (edited by N. G. L. Hammond and H. H. Scullard), Oxford, 1970.

Classic histories such as Mommsen's *History of Rome* (for the Republic) and Gibbon's *Decline and Fall of the Roman Empire* can, in a sense, never be superseded. The former is available in the translation of W. P. Dickson (1862–1875). The latter has been abridged in paperback form in the Pelican Library, and as *The Portable Gibbon* (Viking P60, Washington Square Press WSP 1108). A full but compartmentalized history of Rome is given in *The Cambridge Ancient History*, Vols. 7–12 (1926–1939). The major source for the social history of the Empire is L. Friedländer, *Roman Life and Manners under the Early Empire* (1863–1901), 7th ed., translated by L. A. Magnus and J. H. Freese, 1909–1928. M. Rostovtzeff's *Social and Economic History of the Roman Empire* (1926), revised by P. M. Fraser in 1957, is another major work.

General History

BOAK, A. E. R., and SINNIGEN, W. G. *A History of Rome to A.D. 565*. 5th ed. New York: Macmillan, 1965.

CHARLESWORTH, M. P. *The Roman Empire*. London: Oxford, Home Univ. Lib., 1951.

COWELL, F. R. *Cicero and the Roman Republic*. London: Putnam, Pelican, 1948.

GRANT, M. *The Climax of Rome, A.D. 161–337*. London: Weidenfeld and Nicolson, 1968.

GRIMAL, P. *Hellenism and the Rise of Rome*. Translated by A. M. S. Smith and C. Wartenburg. London: Weidenfeld and Nicolson, 1968.

ROSTOVTZEFF, M. *Social and Economic History of the Roman Empire*. Revised by P. M. Fraser. Oxford: Oxford University Press, 1957.

SCULLARD, H. H. *From the Gracchi to Nero.* 3rd ed. London: Methuen, 1970.

SYME, R. *The Roman Revolution.* Oxford: Oxford University Press, 1939.

TOYNBEE, A. J. *Hannibal's Legacy.* 2 vols. Oxford: Oxford University Press, 1965.

Source Books (in translation)

JONES, A. H. M. *A History of Rome through the Fifth Century.* 2 vols. London: Macmillan, 1968–1970.

LEWIS, N., and REINHOLD, M. *Roman Civilization.* 2 vols. New York: Columbia University Press, Harper Torchbooks, 1951–1955.

TURNER, P. *A History of the World.* (Selection from Philemon Holland's translation of Pliny's *Natural History.*) New York: McGraw-Hill, 1964.

WILKINSON, L. P. *Letters of Cicero.* London: Hutchinson's Univ. Lib., 1949.

Short General Accounts

ARNOTT, P. D. *An Introduction to the Roman World.* London: Macmillan, 1970.

BALSDON, J. P. V. D. *Rome, the Story of an Empire.* London: Weidenfeld and Nicolson, 1970.

———, ed. *The Romans.* London: Watts, 1965.

BARROW, R. H. *The Romans.* Harmondsworth: Pelican, 1949.

DUDLEY, D. R. *The Romans.* London: Hutchinson, 1970.

RAND, E. K. *The Building of Eternal Rome.* Cambridge, Mass.: Harvard University Press, 1943.

ROSTOVTZEFF, M. *Rome.* Translated by J. D. Duff. New York: Galaxy, 1928.

STARR, C. G. *The Ancient Romans.* Oxford: Oxford University Press, 1971.

Social and Cultural History

BALSDON, J. P. V. D. *Life and Leisure in Ancient Rome.* New York: McGraw-Hill, 1969.

———. *Roman Women: Their History and Habits.* New York: John Day, 1962.

BARROW, R. H. *Slavery in the Roman Empire.* London: Macmillan, 1928.

BRUNT, P. A. *Social Conflicts in the Roman Republic.* London: Chatto and Windus, 1971.

CLARKE, M. L. *The Roman Mind.* London: Cohen and West, 1956.

DILL, S. *Roman Society in the Last Century of the Western Empire.* 2nd ed. London: Macmillan, 1899.

———. *Roman Society from Nero to Marcus Aurelius.* London: Macmillan, 1904.

DUFF, A. M. *Freedmen in the Early Roman Empire.* Oxford: Oxford University Press, 1928.

FOWLER, W. WARDE. *Social Life at Rome in the Age of Cicero.* London: Macmillan, 1908.

FRANK, T. *Life and Literature in the Roman Republic.* Berkeley: University of California Press, 1930.

GRANT, M. *The World of Rome.* London: Weidenfeld and Nicolson, 1960.

KIEFER, O. *Sexual Life in Ancient Rome.* Translated by G. and H. Highet. London: Routledge, 1934.

MARROU, H. I. *A History of Education in Antiquity.* 3rd ed. Translated by G. Lamb. London: Sheed and Ward, 1956.

MATTINGLY, H. *The Man in the Roman Street.* New York: Numismatic Review, 1947.

————. *Roman Imperial Civilization.* London: Arnold, 1957.

SCARBOROUGH, J. *Roman Medicine.* London: Thames and Hudson, 1969.

STARR, C. G. *Civilization and the Caesars.* New York: Cornell, 1954.

TREGGIARI, S. *Roman Freedmen during the Late Republic.* Oxford: Oxford University Press, 1969.

Politics, Law, and Army

ADCOCK, F. E. *Roman Political Ideas and Practice.* Ann Arbor: University of Michigan Press, 1959.

CROOK, J. A. *Law and Life of Rome.* London: Thames and Hudson, 1967.

HOLMES, T. RICE. *The Architect of the Roman Empire.* 2 vols. Oxford: Oxford University Press, 1928–1931.

HOMO, L. *Roman Political Institutions.* 2nd ed. New York: Alfred A. Knopf, 1962.

JOLOWICZ, H. F. *Historical Introduction to the Study of Roman Law.* 2nd ed. Revised by B. Nicholas. Cambridge: Cambridge University Press, 1952.

JONES, A. H. M. *Augustus.* London: Chatto and Windus, 1970.

NICHOLAS, B. *An Introduction to Roman Law.* Oxford: Oxford University Press, 1962.

TAYLOR, L. R. *Party Politics in the Age of Caesar.* Berkeley: University of California Press, 1949.

WATSON, G. R. *The Roman Soldier.* London: Thames and Hudson, 1969.

WEBSTER, G. *The Roman Imperial Army.* London: Black, 1969.

Religion and Philosophy

ARNOLD, E. V. *Roman Stoicism.* Cambridge: Cambridge University Press, 1911.

COCHRANE, C. N. *Christianity and Classical Culture.* Oxford: Oxford University Press, 1944.

CUMONT, F. *Afterlife in Roman Religion.* New Haven: Yale University Press, 1922.

_____. *Oriental Religions in Roman Paganism.* Chicago: Kegan Paul, 1906.

DODDS, E. R. *Pagan and Christian in an Age of Anxiety.* Cambridge: Cambridge University Press, 1965.

FESTUGIÈRE, A. J. *Personal Religion Among the Greeks.* Translated by M. and B. Barry. Berkeley: University of California Press, 1954.

FOWLER, W. WARDE. *The Religious Experience of the Roman People.* London: Macmillan, 1911.

GLOVER, T. R. *The Conflict of Religions in the Early Roman Empire.* London: Methuen, 1909.

NOCK, A. D. *Conversion.* Oxford: Oxford University Press, 1933.

OGILVIE, R. M. *The Romans and their Gods.* London: Chatto and Windus, 1969.

ROSE, H. J. *Ancient Roman Religion.* London: Hutchinson's Univ. Lib., 1949.

TAYLOR, L. R. *The Divinity of the Roman Emperor.* Middletown: A. P. A., 1931.

WALLIS, R. T. *Neoplatonism.* London: Duckworth, 1972.

Literature

DUFF, J. W. *A Literary History of Rome in the Silver Age.* 3rd ed. Revised by A. M. Duff. London: Unwin, 1964.

_____. *A Literary History of Rome to the Close of the Golden Age.* 3rd ed. Revised by A. M. Duff. London: Unwin, 1953.

GRANT, M. *Roman Literature.* Revised ed. Cambridge: Cambridge University Press, 1958.

Some Verse Translations

CATULLUS J. MICHIE. *The Poems of Catullus.* London: Hart-Davies, 1969.

HORACE S. P. BOVIE. *Satires and Epistles.* Chicago: Chicago University Press, 1959.
   E. MARSH. *The Odes of Horace.* London: Macmillan, 1941.
   J. MICHIE. *The Odes of Horace.* London: Hart-Davies, 1964.

JUVENAL P. GREEN. *The Sixteen Satires.* Harmondsworth: Penguin, 1967.

LUCRETIUS R. HUMPHRIES. *The Way Things Are.* Bloomington, Ind.: Indiana University Press, 1968.
   A. D. WINSPEAR. *The Roman Poet of Science.* New York: Russell, 1956.

OVID E. P. BARKER. *Ars Amatoria.* Oxford: Blackwell, 1931.
   G. LEE. *Amores.* London: Murray, 1968.
   A. E. WATTS. *Metamorphoses.* Berkeley: University of California Press, 1954.

PROPERTIUS A. E. WATTS. *The Poems of Propertius.* London: Centaur, 1961.
R. MUSKER. *The Poems of Propertius.* London: Dent, 1972.

VIRGIL C. DAY LEWIS. *The Eclogues, Georgics, and Aeneid of Virgil.* Oxford: Oxford University Press, 1966.

Daily Life

CARCOPINO, J. *Daily Life in Ancient Rome.* Translated by E. O. Lorimer. London: Routledge, 1941.

COWELL, F. R. *Everyday Life in Ancient Rome.* New York: Putnam, 1961.

PAOLI, U. E. *Rome, its People, Life and Customs.* Translated by R. D. Macnaghten. London: Longmans, 1963.

Art and Architecture

ROBERTSON, D. S. *Greek and Roman Architecture.* 2nd ed. Cambridge: Cambridge University Press, 1943.

STRONG, E. *Art in Ancient Rome.* 2 vols. New York: Scribners, 1928.

TOYNBEE, J. M. C. *The Art of the Romans.* London: Thames and Hudson, 1965.

WHEELER, M. *Roman Art and Architecture.* London: Thames and Hudson, 1964.

Entertainment

BEARE, W. *The Roman Stage.* London: Methuen, 1950.

FLOWER, B., and ROSENBAUM, E. *The Roman Cookery Book.* London: Harrap, 1958.

GRANT, M. *Gladiators.* London: Weidenfeld and Nicolson, 1967.

JENNISON, G. *Animals for Show and Pleasure in Ancient Rome.* Manchester: Manchester University Press, 1937.

Index

ABOUT THE AUTHOR

L. P. WILKINSON is Brereton Reader in Classics in the University of Cambridge. Specializing in Latin literature, he received an M.A. degree from the University of Cambridge in 1933, and has been a Fellow of King's College since 1932. Books he has written include *Horace and His Lyric Poetry* (1945), *Letters of Cicero* (1949), *Ovid Recalled* (1955), *Golden Latin Artistry* (1963), and *The Georgics of Virgil* (1969). He has also contributed articles to *Classical Review, Classical Quarterly,* and *Hermes.* He was president of the Classical Association 1971–1972.

A NOTE ON THE TYPE

The text typeface used in this book is COMPANO, the Videocomp counterpart of PALATINO, which was designed by Hermann Zapf and is characterized by breadth and the inclined serif.

Manufactured in the United States of America.
Composed by Datagraphics Press, Inc., Phoenix, Arizona.
Printed and bound by Halliday Lithograph, West Hanover, Mass.